DAYS OF GRACE IN INDIA

DAYS OF GRACE IN INDIA;

A RECORD OF

VISITS TO INDIAN MISSIONS.

HENRY STANLEY NEWMAN

GYAN

Published by

Gyan Publishing House
5, Ansari Road
Daryaganj, New Delhi-110002
Phone: 011-47034999, 9811692060
E-mail: books@gyanbooks.com

Distribution Network
gyanbooks.com
India, USA, Canada, UK, Australia, France

ISBN: 978-81-212-9340-2 (PB)
First Published, 1882

2nd Impression 2023

Printed at: Gyan Press, Delhi.

DAYS OF GRACE IN INDIA

AUTHOR: HENRY STANLEY NEWMAN

H. R. H. THE PRINCE OF WALES,

WHOSE EASTERN TOUR IN 1875 DID SO MUCH TO PROMOTE THE GOOD WILL OF HER MAJESTY'S SUBJECTS IN INDIA, AND TO AWAKEN INTEREST IN OUR INDIAN EMPIRE AT HOME.

DAYS OF GRACE IN INDIA;

A RECORD OF

VISITS TO INDIAN MISSIONS.

BY

HENRY STANLEY NEWMAN,

LEOMINSTER.

"The present condition of India seems very similar to that of the Roman Empire before the coming of Christ. A complete disintegration of ancient faiths is in progress in the upper strata of society."

Monier Williams.

Publishers:

London:	S. W. PARTRIDGE & Co., Paternoster Row.
United States:	J. B. LIPPINCOTT & Co., Philadelphia.
India:	SAMUEL BAKER, Hoshangabad.
Leominster:	ORPHANS' PRINTING PRESS, Broad Street.

PREFACE.

In recording a visit to some of the Mission Stations of India, my aim has not been to compile a Missionary Directory, but to afford an insight into some of the various phases of the work. I have endeavoured to suggest some of the lines of thought and of national habit, which the missionary has to deal with in India, in order that the churches at home may be able to sympathize more fully with the workers abroad, and be able to realize the progress that has been made, and how much remains to be accomplished. While apologizing for any errors that may inadvertently have occurred, I would gratefully acknowledge my obligations to the writings of Max Müller and Monier Williams, the Church Missionary Atlas, Badley's Indian Missionary Directory, and other works that deal with Hindu thought and with missionary enterprise, and I must also express my gratitude for the uniform kindness and welcome I received from missionaries of all Societies in India, and for the courteous assistance rendered by the Secretaries of committees at home.

If the following narrative of the Lord's work in India contributes to deepen interest in the work of Christian Missions, and serve as a witness to the power of the Gospel, my object will be accomplished.

H. S. N.

CONTENTS.

Chap.		Page
	Map of Languages of India	
	Preface	v.
I.	Bombay	1
II.	Bombay *(continued)*	19
III.	Hoshangabad	35
IV.	Hoshangabad *(continued)*	53
V.	Sohagpur, with Map	65
VI.	Central Provinces	79
VII.	Among the Marathas	97
VIII.	Among the Telugus	119
IX.	Among the Kanarese	129
X.	Malabar	139
XI.	Madras	149
XII.	Madura	163
XIII.	The Tamils of Tinnevelly	179
XIV.	Travancore	189
XV.	Benares	203
XVI.	Among the Santals	215
XVII.	Calcutta	225
XVIII.	The Brahmos of Bengal	241
XIX.	North-West Provinces, Allahabad and Lucknow	261
XX.	North-West Provinces, Agra	273
XXI.	The Punjab, Delhi and Loodiana	287
XXII.	The Punjab, Amritsar and Lahore	299
XXIII.	Summing up	315
	Index	321

DAYS OF GRACE IN INDIA;

A RECORD OF

VISITS TO INDIAN MISSIONS.

"The clear eye of the wise beholdeth in every leaf on the green trees a book of the wisdom of God."—*Sâdi of Shirâz.*

CHAPTER I.—BOMBAY.

As the 'Cathay' anchored off Bombay in the early morning of the 1st December, 1880, the beautiful harbour lay placid as a mirror, studded with the vessels of many nations. Our cabins were overflowing with passengers proceeding to the East, who now crowded the deck, after a successful run of fourteen days from Port Said, through the canal, down the Red Sea, and across the ocean. Lord Ripon, the Viceroy, was among the first to welcome our arrival. The Marchioness of Ripon being on board our vessel, he came, like several other Indian officers, to claim his wife. As the state launch hove alongside, the 'Cathay' was decked with flags, the Lascars manned the rigging, standing in their clean white dresses in rows in mid-air with military precision, and the brass band struck up a welcome, as, with the ringing cheer that only Englishmen can give, the passengers saluted Lord Ripon. Other vessels in the harbour had an abundance of streamers flying, their yards manned with long rows of brave sailors; the docks were decorated; and with the unfailingly bright Eastern sky, our welcome to India was one not likely to be soon forgotten.

Elephanta, Mazagon, Colaba, and other spots of interest, lay around us; and in a few minutes I had settled affairs on board, had obtained some hieroglyphic chalk-marks on my baggage from the Custom-house officials, and found myself clambering from one little boat to another amid the unintelligible shoutings of nearly naked native boatmen. Hindi, Tamil, Gujerâti, Marâthi, and any other medley of tongues and peoples mattered little just then, as one passenger after another made for *terra firma.* My old friend John H. Williams, piloted me through, and I was soon sitting down to breakfast at the hotel. Amid all the apparent confusion and hubbub of nationalities, order rules. The strong arm of the English Government is felt and respected even where it is not seen. Not only does the traveller learn to admire the English governing faculty, with its quiet power, but the intelligent native merchant and scholar also recognises and respects it. As Sir Richard Temple well observes, 'The people accept British rule without any appeal to arms, because we keep the peace and do justice, because we have done and are doing much material good to the country and the people, and because there is not inside or outside India any power that can adequately occupy our place. To the minds, at least, of the educated among the people of India—and the number is rapidly increasing—any idea of the subversion of British power is abhorrent, from the consciousness that it must result in the wildest anarchy and confusion."

The English set foot in India for purposes of commerce, and not for the acquisition of territory, with all its attendant responsibilities and cares. But such a dense mass of diverse populations without the elements of mutual cohesion must be governed by some one, if they are to enjoy prosperity.

I had not been in Bombay more than two hours, before a special edition of the morning papers was thrust into my hand, with a list of the latest arrivals from Europe; and I soon discovered that the Hindus are wide-awake, shrewd business men, quick to learn, and understanding their own interests and purposes, and withal possessing a suavity and courteous gentlemanliness of bearing that is often lacking in the insular Englishman.

Bombay, like so many other Eastern cities, is a motley mixture of some magnificent European buildings and streets, with very many more crowded narrow native thoroughfares. It is only in these old native streets that we really can get any clear understanding of native life.

And first of all, let us disabuse our minds of any thought of the Hindus being a downtrodden people. Remember that the hot climate that oppresses an Englishman, suits the native admirably. He enjoys the heat, and eschews any approach of cold. The people do not look wretched. They thrive on a little, look healthy, and have no appearance of destitution or distress. They are under the best Government they have ever known, and are probably better off than they have ever been before.

The native population increases at a ratio unrealized till British rule. The English have the happy faculty of establishing their Government, and settling among the people without grinding down the immense native population. The Bombay citizen walks the street with a contented swinging gait, and a bright intelligent countenance, and takes stock of you pretty accurately as you pass. He patronizes the railway abundantly, crowds into the street tram-cars, chatters away at business, makes money easily, dresses simply, spends his wealth in jewelry for his own person and for his wife and children, and looks you in the face as though he thought he was quite your equal, and in some respects decidedly your superior. He also acquires that city air of minding his own business and expecting you to mind yours, which contrasts strongly with the communicative Hindu of the mofussil, or up-country districts.

The Parsis are conspicuous in Bombay, though their numbers are comparatively small, and here and there one of the Jains passes us in the streets. These Jains have much in common with the Buddhists; they lay great stress on the transmigration of souls, and one of their chief characteristics is an intense regard for the sacredness of life. What man cannot create, what right has man wantonly to destroy? They are so morbidly conscientious on this point that they scrupulously strain all water they drink, lest they should take the life of some animalcule. As they walk the streets of Bombay they hang a little cloth over their mouths, lest by any accident they should swallow an insect.

The Hindus in Bombay greatly exceed the Muhammadans in numbers. The population exceeds Glasgow or Liverpool, and there are 154 males to 100 females. Seeing that 'in the multitude of people is the king's honour,' our wealth in India is as much in the people as in territory.

The city is singularly well adapted for a large commercial centre. The Island of Bombay, with its dependencies, covering an area of twenty-two miles, originally formed part of the dowry which Charles II., in 1662, received on the occasion of his marriage with Princess Catherine of Portugal. In 1668, Charles II. handed it over to the East India

Company, and it has been growing, and continues to grow in importance ever since.

The English were in Bombay for fifty years before they had either church or chaplain; and it was a hundred-and-fifty years before they put forth an effort for the evangelization of the inhabitants. When at last, in 1813, the Christian duty incumbent on England of sending the Gospel to Bombay was undertaken by two American missionaries, Hall and Nott, their arrival was at once the signal for a peremptory order from the supreme Government at Calcutta for them immediately to leave the country. Fortunately, Sir Evan Nepean was then Governor of Bombay, and he was slow in carrying out the injunction. Meanwhile, our Parliament compelled the Court of Directors to change their policy, and these pioneers of Christian enterprise were allowed to remain. Seven years later, the Church Missionary Society planted its first Mission in Bombay; and many other Societies have since entered energetically into the work.

One of my principal objects in visiting India was to become personally acquainted with the working of the various Missionary Societies; and my first call was at the "Money Schools" which are under the care of the Rev. Thomas Carss, of the Church Missionary Society. Their origin is peculiar. They were founded, in 1840, as a memorial to a successful merchant of that name who had done much for the city. Robert Money did not endow the Schools in any way; and, as there was no fund for their permanent support, they were handed over to the Church Missionary Society, who have long sustained them in vigour, with such assistance as they could locally obtain from subscriptions and grants. The scholars, of whom there are about two hundred, are mostly Hindus, and pay something like sixpence a week for their tuition.

As I passed from one class-room to another I was struck with the bright faces of the boys and young men. The Scriptures are regularly taught. The aim is not so much to fill their heads with theological doctrine as to make them thoroughly acquainted with the history of our Saviour's life, and with the historical parts of the Bible. Many children of good caste attend these schools, and are often successful in getting introduced into the Post Office, and other such-like Government departments, when they have passed through their standards. The object of parents in sending their children to such a Mission school is certainly not to put them under Christian teaching, but it is to win for them, at a moderate cost, an education that will enable their boys to take a superior position in life.

I asked Mr. Carss whether they had many converts from among the boys. He answered, 'No.' The utter desolation of all social and family ties that results from any open confession of Christianity keeps back converts. "I was talking," he said, "to one of the young men on this very subject—as I knew he was under deep religious convictions,—and he answered, 'How could I bear to hear my mother say, I *had* a son ?' "—that is, his mother would regard her son as dead if he confessed Christ.

Another instance mentioned to me was of a dying father whose son had made an open confession of Christianity long before, and had therefore become an outcast. As the young Christian approached his father to bid a last farewell, the old man exclaimed, "Oh, do not let that one come near me to pollute me with his presence."

Mr. Carss says that the Hindus of Bombay declare that there never has been a Hindu who became a Christian; and when a missionary replies, "But here is a Hindu standing before you at my side who has become a Christian," the heathen replies, "Oh, no; God saw that he was not fit to be trusted with a soul, and so God took his soul from him." Most of the converts to Christianity in Bombay have been from the lower castes. These men have little to lose and much to gain in social position. Their former caste, or absence of caste, is hidden when they have become Christians. They dress differently, and pass better in the world than before, when they are known to belong to the Christian caste.

Some of the converts have also been spoiled by receiving too much attention from the English. The European missionary comes to England, speaks at missionary meetings, gives a plain unvarnished statement of facts, and by his very candour perhaps kindles but little enthusiasm. But an English-speaking native convert comes over to England, attends crowded meetings, is greeted on all hands with a cordial welcome, is received and entertained at the mansions of the wealthy, ladies press forward to have the privilege of shaking hands with their swarthy Christian brother, and the man's head is turned with so much attention. He returns to his own country full of conceit, does not care to associate on an equality with people of his own position in society, expects great consideration from the missionary, and finally proves a hindrance to the work rather than a help. I asked Mr. Carss as to the usual effect of bringing native youths to England for education. He replied, "It is a plan which is abandoned now by the more experienced Missionary Societies." The general result is a failure. A young man gets his head full of European ideas. He returns to India as little of a native as he can; and his own sympathies have changed by his acquaintance with English life. When he is needed as a catechist, or teacher, he requires and expects so much consideration from all around him, that his influence for good is lost, and his service to the church forfeited.

In passing through the streets, hardly a single European was to be seen in the dense crowd of thousands of jabbering Hindus swaying to and fro. Here and there was a man standing conspicuously on the causeway saying his prayers, seen of men as he clasped his hands. The people are in a multitude of different costumes, buying and selling, chattering and singing wild songs, in groups, or lying with bare legs and arms and breasts in the arrack shops, or with keen eyes squatting cross-legged in all attitudes in their ugly dens of shops selling all manner of unnameables. Here is a jolly round copper-coloured baby rollicking on a shop counter, utterly naked, but loaded with jewelry, ankle rings, necklaces, and arm rings. The strong bronze limbs of the people show their health and vigour. Numbers of them are Brahmans and Rajputs, with their caste marks painted conspicuously on their foreheads. Just above the nose and between the two eyes are their tokens of idolatry. Some have a pure white dot, others a red trident, some with yellow marks painted on, while others have quite little sketches typifying the gods they worship. The Vaishnavas, or disciples of Vishnu, are distinguished by a talak or frontal mark, consisting of three perpendicular lines, while the Saivas, or the worshippers of Siva, are distinguished by three horizontal lines. Whatever else is covered or uncovered, these idolatrous marks on the forehead are intentionally left uncovered and conspicuous. They would seem to represent thousands of gradations of honour to themselves, or to their gods, or their caste. There is evidently no feeling of shame respecting these marks in their foreheads. And yet the gross degradation and abyss of heathenism forces itself upon attention the more closely we come in contact with it. Men at home may talk about "points of contact" between Christianity and other religions, and gems of truth may be picked out of heaps of rubbish if men will search Eastern literature. Sanscrit is, without doubt, an incomparable language. Many of the Vedas, the Ramayan, and other early works, contain much that is exceedingly beautiful, yet the plain testimony of Macaulay respecting Hinduism, after his practical experience of India, is mournfully true: "In no part of the world has a religion ever existed more unfavourable to the moral and intellectual health of our race. The Brahmanical mythology is so absurd that it debases every mind which receives it as truth. And with this absurd mythology is bound up an absurd system of physics, an absurd geography, an absurd astronomy. Nor is this form of Paganism more favourable to art than to religion. Through the whole of the Hindu Pantheon you will look in vain for anything resembling those beautiful and majestic forms which stood in the shrines of ancient Greece. All is hideous and grotesque and ignoble. As this superstition is of all superstitions the most inelegant, so is it of all superstitions the most immoral. Crimes against life, crimes against property, are not only permitted but enjoined by this odious theology. But for our interference, human victims would still be offered to the Ganges, and the widow would still be laid on the pile by the corpse of her husband and be burned alive by her own children."

It is well that there are active witnesses for Christ in Bombay to combat this giant error. Standing at the foot of a monument, I saw Mr. Mody, a converted Parsi, preaching the gospel in Gujerâti, to an attentive group of listeners, and as evening came on, I visited the Mission compound of the Presbyterian Free Church. Our driver cracked his whip and vociferated, and the mass of foot passengers had to clear aside to let us pass, and we in turn had to stand aside as the tram-cars with their tinkling bells and their freight of coloured passengers swept by in the narrow streets. I soon found myself in the comfortable bungalow of the Rev. Alexander C. Grieve. This Mission was the one to which Dr. Wilson gave so much of his valuable life; and memories of that good and great man could not but come to the front as we chatted together. If any man knew how to reach a Hindu audience, it was Wilson. Approaching a large number of people carrying a heavy tree, he would say to them, "I see a heavier burden on your back than that tree." "What is it?" they exclaim. "It is the wife and children," cried one. "No, it is the Government taxes," said another. "No," answered Dr. Wilson, "the Government spends the taxes on the improvement of the country, and in obtaining justice for you. It is *the burden of sin* I mean."

Another time, when surrounded by a group of beggars, he said, "I see a great many lepers here to-day." The people looked around and said, "Sahib, there are only fourteen." "Count again," he replied, "I think there are more." One of the company then said, "I think you must be speaking figuratively." "Yes," answered the Doctor, "the leprosy of sin cleaves to you, and if you are not washed in the Fountain which has been opened for sin and uncleanness, it will destroy you."

Being at a loss for a congregation at a certain village, Dr. Wilson went up to a goldsmith and said, "What is better than gold?" The goldsmith replied, "Nothing is better than gold." A young man then suggested, "A diamond is better than gold." Another bystander said, "I think the Sahib means something besides gold or diamonds." "Yes," replied Wilson, "wisdom is better than gold;" and thus he secured an audience for his Gospel message.

"What is your employment?" Dr. Wilson enquired one day of a man sitting by the roadside. "My employment," replied the man, "is that of going forwards and backwards." The postman then retorted, "And pray, sir, what is your employment?" "It is that of going forward," answered Dr. Wilson. "Where are you going forward to?" the man asked, "to Surat?" "Further." "To Baroda?" "Further." "To Persia?" "Further." "To another world?" "Yes, you have found out." And by that time a concourse was collected to listen to the Sahib's discourse on the Christian's pilgrimage. This freedom of question and answer is a striking peculiarity of Hindu character. An Englishman is asked what his business is, where he is going, where he came from, and what his income is, in a way that is rather startling on first arrival, but we soon learn to be communicative, and lose some of our prejudices.

The Scotch missionaries are great educationalists, and Mr. Grieve devotes himself to college work. The students are systematically taught Holy Scripture. "Is the result their conversion?" I asked. "Not exactly so," replied Mr. Grieve. "They give up their idolatry. They lose faith in the religion of their fathers. They are, many of them, believers in the truth of Christ in their hearts, but they do not choose to openly confess Him." "Do you think," I enquired, "that the time is coming when they will come over in a mass, as they have done in the islands of the Pacific and in Madagascar?" "That is just what a great many people do think," replied Mr. Grieve, "and there is no doubt that a great work of preparation is going on; but this college work, with its examination of scholars' papers, and so forth, presents very little romance, and cannot produce the graphic reports of striking conversions that some are so fond of." "It is, nevertheless, a very important and essential part of the great missionary enterprise," I replied. "I quite agree with you," answered Mr. Grieve, "but, from its nature, can never present those features of striking encouragement that subscribers at home like to see."

The next morning we called on the Rev. George Bowen, the American Episcopal Methodist Patriarch. He lives in great simplicity, and is altogether a unique old man. He said at once, "I do not call *myself* a Patriarch." His establishment is some twelve feet long, by eight feet broad, and furnished with well-fingered Bibles and concordances, and manuscripts; but though the man lives in a small place, he has a large heart, and at once commands respect. Mr. Bowen oversees the native workers in connection with the Methodist chapel on the opposite side of the road, and he often preaches in the open air at their street meetings. Only one of the native exhorters receives any pecuniary help from the Mission. All the rest, to their honour be it spoken, earn their own living at their own trades. Their ministry is mostly in Marâthi. Mr. Bowen remarked, "I do not find, generally, that we have direct conversions from the preaching in the streets, but it is *one link in the chain.* There are many influences, before and after, that bring a man to the point of decision, but it is nevertheless the Gospel that is still the power of God unto salvation, whether it comes to a man in one way or in another." The Methodist Episcopal Mission is not supported by contributions from either England or America, but by the people who are blessed by the work, whether English or natives. I found that Mr. Bowen had been at work here for thirty-three years, and was, probably, the oldest Christian missionary in Bombay. "Then you mean to die in harness?" I queried. "I have never made any fixed determination in my own mind on the subject. I leave it with the Lord."

We drove on to Surgeon Major Partridge's, on the Camballa Hill. His grounds abound in palm trees, towering up one above another, and, with the blue sea lying placidly in front, it forms a "Bella Vista," in truth. Mr. Partridge has had more than thirty years' experience of India, and is thoroughly baptized with the missionary spirit. "I do not trouble myself about sects," he began, "it is Christ and Christianity that is to be our aim. I can see a *marked change* for the better in the attitude of the people towards Christianity during the last thirty years. They will now listen, and learn, and treat us with respect, although they may not be convinced. I have seen many brought under the power of the Word as they listened to the catechist, and in the gaols, but they need to be kept under that power. It is in Bible classes, and in the simple exposition of Scripture, that the best work is often done. In the long sermon you may drift right away from Christ, and from the Book, into outside arguments, but in the Bible class your own soul is blessed in the careful preparation of the lesson, and you have often more real power over the hearts of the people, because you commonly keep closer to the Word."

"The Hindus place unbounded confidence in a doctor. They will travel long distances to meet him, throw themselves at his feet, and expect that he can cure them of anything and everything. Perhaps the doctor replies, 'I really can do nothing in your case, it is absolutely incurable.' The Hindu simply considers he has not sufficiently used his powers of persuasion, and at once proceeds to entreat you all the more earnestly. Thus, a medical missionary can obtain a powerful hold on the people in opening the hearts of his patients to hear and to receive the Gospel." Dr. Partridge told us of a Muhammadan who was so much interested in the New Testament, that he took it to one of the mosques in Bombay, and read it aloud, and, though some one objected, saying, 'you ought not to read that here,' the people were so much interested, that he was allowed to proceed. Such an unusual incident shows an extraordinary amount of indifference among the Muhammadans in certain directions, although they are such hot and bitter disputants in other ways. They appear to have considerable respect for the history of Christ, but are quickly roused if their own faith is expressly attacked.

We next called on Dr. Macdonald, of the Free Church of Scotland Mission, at Mr. Conder's bungalow. "When I was a missionary," observed Dr. Macdonald, "and I hope in one sense I may still rank myself as such, I was greatly interested in the work in the villages. I used to travel as a medical man with the missionary. In the Nizam's territory, I came across the Mângs, a wild native tribe. By some means, in one of these villages, a Mâng had got hold of two tracts and a

New Testament. No missionary had been there before us, but the tracts and this New Testament so wrought upon the man that he made up his mind to become a Christian, and read them diligently to his relatives and fellow-villagers of the same caste. This village of Wat-wud became a little centre of Christian light. The Rev. Chas. W. Park, of the American Board, took cognizance of it, and the work spread from one to another among the Mângs, until it resulted in many conversions, and much permanent good still remains there." "But," added Dr. Macdonald, "what I want you to notice is this, that it did *not* spread among the Brahmans or any high caste people, neither did it spread in any lower caste people than these Mângs of Wat-wud. It permeated *one stratum* of society only. It spread wider and wider among them, but no other caste or tribe appeared to be affected." Dr. Macdonald continued, "I do not think it is generally desirable to establish separate Christian villages, or to isolate the Christians in any way. It tends to narrow up the work. It is better for the converts to mingle with the surrounding population."

We also met with Mrs. Amanda Smith, who has been working for some time in several of the leading Indian cities. Her principal effort has been among professing Christians. "My aim," she says, "has been to bring them out thoroughly into the joy of the Lord, instead of stopping short in a half-hearted dwarfish state."

In the evening we attended the street preaching of the American Board. We were the only Europeans present, and the whole service was conducted by the natives. The meeting was held under the porch or verandah in front of the Mission chapel, with gas-lights above us, and quite open to the crowded street. A few forms stood round on three sides, and we were at once offered seats. A native catechist—a Brahman convert of the name of Shahurao—was preaching earnestly, with a Marâthi New Testament in his hand. He was dressed in a large white turban and white dress from head to foot, with a tall full figure, bushy black whiskers, dark eyes, and Turkish shoes on his feet. Young and old were clustering so close around him, that, time after time, the policeman had to hold them back. As one sentence of Marâthi after another rolled from the tall man's lips, there were frequent ejaculations from the people of assent and dissent. They looked as though they would search him through and through; and then suddenly, after various murmurs from the back part of the crowd, and swaying to and fro, and sundry imprecations, a fine young Muslim stepped forward and commenced arguing eagerly with the catechist, pleading with his whole soul for Muhammad. Shahurao kept on responding, the crowd pressed closer and grew denser, and the Muslim, with his fine forehead, had abundant answers ready. Sometimes there was a laugh, then a dozen ejaculations from the crowd, almost of anger. Such an audience intensely enjoys repartee and the clever reply, whether from catechist or Muslim; but the crowd sided with the Muhammadan. After a while some cleanly-dressed youths from Ahmadnagar struck up a Christian hymn; the crowd was quiet, and a six-foot Rajput, named Totanath, with his splendid red turban, stood up and quietly commenced in Hindustani, "My friends." He left the previous controversy alone, and the people listened attentively as he led them straight on to Jesus, the man of Nazareth, the man of the East. His speech waxed warmer and more fervid as he proceeded. A multitude of bright dark eyes were fixed upon him. The old men listened earnestly, and the young men gave a half puzzled thoughtful look as though they queried, "What is truth?" One or two stones were thrown from the back part of the crowd; but I admired the self-control and good temper with which these men stood unflinchingly in the midst of opposition. When we remember the wild freebooting life the Marâthas led for centuries, and the terror they were, in the days of their power, to all the surrounding country, and see what men of stature and physical force they are to-day, we may rejoice that from among them some are found courageously witnessing for Christ.

We dined with the editor of the *Bombay Review* at the Marine Lines; and early next morning drove to Major Oldham's in the suburb of Girgaum. His residence is surrounded with palm trees and bananas. In large letters over the entrance-hall are the words, "Behold I stand at the door and knock."

On the compound there is a girls' school belonging to the Church Missionary Society, partly composed of Christian children, who are boarders, and partly of day scholars from heathen families.

More than 500 girls receive Christian instruction in Bombay, about 100 of whom are in the Church Mission schools. The Christian girls under the care of Miss Morris stood up and sang to us in Marâthi, the native hymn, "Longing for Peace," with the chorus, "O God, give me Thy true Peace." They also sang, "Christ the best Friend." The Hindu girls who did not sing had idolatrous caste marks painted in colours on their foreheads; the Christian girls have no caste marks.

GOING TO SCHOOL.

CHAPTER II.—BOMBAY *(continued.)*

"My life has been passed in a vain thirst for happiness,
For a single moment I have never made a right effort for liberation,
I am exhausted by my wanderings to and fro,
My soul is covered with the veil of delusion."

Confession of Tukerâma, the favourite poet of the Marâthâs.

THE Bombay Education Society was incorporated in 1815, for the education of the poor of Bombay. It is a purely local philanthropic effort, and represents the thoughtfulness of the European residents for the welfare of those around them. The Society's press and schools are in Byculla, which is a densely populated part of the city. They cast their own type, and print "in all the vernaculars," as well as in English. We saw tons of type, and the compositors at their work in Persian, Sanskrit, Marâthi, Gujerâti, Hebrew, and other languages. Compositors' wages in India are very low compared to England. The profit realized last year for the support of the schools was £2,250. But, as the superintendent pointed out, the business does not realize sufficient profit in proportion to the large capital invested in it. I found that there was £35,786 value in type, litho-stones, and machinery. Printing in such a large number of languages necessitates a large amount of comparatively "dead stock."

Mr. R. E. Walters, the head master, kindly took me through the schools. There are 300 boarders, 197 of whom are on what is termed "the Free List," consisting of orphans and destitute children. Thus about two-thirds of the whole number are orphans. The schoolrooms are lofty, and the classes in good order, and the children receive a good English education. There is a large boys' bedroom, where 150 sleep every night. This room is cleverly ventilated. The beds are taken down daily, and we saw them laid out on the grass in rows in the sunshine. The children get half-a-pound of meat, one pound of bread, and half-a-pound of vegetables, daily, for dinner. They dine in a large play-hall, capable of containing a thousand people. This huge playroom is finely vaulted, and is built of solid teak wood, the long sides entirely open to the fresh air, the grass and gymnastic poles being to the right and left. This hall was built through the generosity of Sir James Outram after the capture of Scinde. Sir James conscientiously objected to the Scinde war. His share of the prize money was 30,000 rupees, and he devoted the whole of it to charitable purposes, giving 15,000 rupees for the erection of this playroom.

Mr. Walters says the boys easily get situations under Government in the Post-office or telegraph department, or in merchants' offices. Bible-classes are held every day with the children ; and the teachers are all Christians.

One interesting feature in the undertaking is the Apprentices' Home. The proposed accommodation is for forty young men, but there are not so many at the present time. The Home is for the boys in situations in the city, whether at the Byculla Press or elsewhere. Boys earning from fifteen to twenty-seven rupees per month pay two-thirds of their wages for their board and lodging. Boys earning less than fifteen rupees a-month pay the difference between their own earnings and five rupees, that is, each apprentice-boy is allowed five rupees a-month for his own personal expenses or savings.

Almost the whole of the children in the Byculla Schools appear to be Europeans or Eurasians. There are two hospitals in connection with the institution, one for the boys and the other for girls.

The origin of some of these practical undertakings is suggestive. It was the Bombay Bible Society that initiated this work in the Byculla when it had only been two years in existence. Thus one good work helps another: and one right step taken by the citizens led to another of a different character, yet of a kindred spirit. Those whose hearts were stirred to promote Bible circulation were also stirred for the destitute "children of Protestant Christians in the Black Town of Bombay."

Passing the Jewish Synagogue, we found ourselves, in a few minutes, in the compound of the American Board of Foreign Missions, and were introduced to Mr. and Mrs. Hume. Both belong to old-established missionary families. Mrs. Hume is the daughter of a missionary of the name of Chandler, and several of her relatives are still earnestly labouring in the Madras Presidency. Mr. Hume introduced himself saying, "My father came out here forty-two years ago; and I was born in the house I live in." It is one of the beautiful features of Indian missionary life that the missionary zeal kindled in one member of a family spreads to brothers and sisters, and descends as an heirloom from father to son, and from mother to daughter, even to the third and fourth generations. Mr. and Mrs. Hume, in speaking of some of their relatives in America, said: "It is only because of the delicate state of their health that they are not out as missionaries. They consider it one of the greatest trials of their life that they are not allowed the privilege of personally taking part in the work."

Of such workers as these can truly be said, "The joy of the Lord is their strength;" and the motto hanging up in their parlour, "Simply to Thy cross I cling," would seem to be the motto of their life. They can realize what it is to tread in the footsteps of Him who said, "My meat and my drink is to do the will of Him that sent me." It is often evident that such people are working up to the utmost limit of their physical strength, and their spiritual energy may seem to outrun their bodily vigour. May the Lord be with such workers, and sustain them!

One inscription on their walls ran thus: "Do IT NOW.—A worthy Quaker thus wrote: 'I expect to pass through this world but once; if, therefore, there be any kindness I can show, or any good thing I can do to any fellow human being, let me do it NOW; let me not defer or neglect it, for *I shall not pass this way again.*'"

"How do you get on with your open-air work?" was one of my first questions. "As long as we speak to the people in Marâthi we get on," Mrs. Hume replied, "but if we speak in Hindustani we are continually stopped by the Muslims for the sake of controversy. We avoid abusing any of the Hindu gods or the Ko-ran, but we can freely speak against idolatry." Mrs. Hume added, "We have had a number of converts recently from among the Jews. One conversion in the family has resulted in others, and although the opposition is often very strong, and the persecution of a Jewish convert very bitter, we are making way among them."

The schools for boys and girls here are in the house the missionaries dwell in; in fact the best rooms are freely surrendered to the exigencies of the work. Several of the older scholars are converts, and these Christian scholars sang most beautifully to a native tune one of the ancient hymns of India, in Sanskrit, called "The praise of the faithful." The exquisite harmony and rhythym of the Sanskrit conveys some idea of the power of the language.

After a short call on the Rev. Charles W. Park, of the American Mission, at his bungalow, we proceeded to the Free Church High Schools, under the superintendence of Mr. Macdonald, of the Bombay Scottish Education Society. In these schools are Jews and Jewesses, Europeans, Armenians, and Eurasians. There are forty boarders, and one hundred-and-eighty day scholars. Boys and girls are taught in the same schools with excellent results. They are carefully instructed in Scripture, and the teachers are Christians. The teaching is thoroughly undenominational. The parents and friends of the children pay about £1,000 a-year, and this is supplemented by a Government grant and by subscriptions. The Schools are under Government inspection. The high tone and manly bearing that pervades the whole, speaks well for Scotch influence.

Through the kindness of our friends in Bombay, a steam launch lay alongside the Quay one evening, to take us to Elephanta. Mr. Carss, Mr. Mody, and several ladies accompanied us. We were fully two hours under steam from Bombay, ere we reached the island, which lies north-east of the city in the Bay. The water was too rough for us to land from the steamer, and a native boat took us on shore.

The island of Elephanta is covered with tropical woods, and palm trees grow almost to the water's edge. We ascend the hill some distance ere we reach the caves. They are cut out of the solid rock on the side of the hill, and many of the elaborately decorated pillars are still in excellent preservation. In this cave the Prince of Wales had a banquet, on the occasion of his visit to India. At the extremity of the cave is an enormous bust with three faces, representing Brahma in the centre, with Vishnu the Preserver, and Siva the Destroyer, on either hand. While there are evidences of its having been a genuine Buddhist Temple, it would appear as though Hindu worship had succeeded the Buddhist ritual. At the same time, the Buddhists evidently incorporated into their own worship many of the forms of other religions with which they came in contact; and though Brahmanism has survived Buddhism in India, and with the exception of Ceylon and the borders of Thibet, scarcely any Buddhism remains in our Indian Empire, yet we must remember that it was in India that Buddhism arose, and the Caves of Elephanta and Ellora, and the ancient inscriptions of Asoka, still bear witness to the power it exerted.*

Gautama, or Sakya Muni, the original Buddha, is supposed to have been born about the sixth century, B.C., at Kapula Vastu, at the foot of the Nepâl Mountains. Gautama stood forth as the deliverer of a priest-ridden, caste-enslaved nation, the courageous reformer who dared to break down the great ecclesiastical monopoly of the Brahmans. The mother of Gautama died seven days after his birth; and the child grew up fond of meditation, never so happy as when alone, and his father, the King, to prevent the young Prince becoming a dreamer, determined to have him married. He requested seven days for reflection, and then assented. The princess chosen for him was Gopâ, and the marriage proved a happy one, but he continued to be absorbed in the problems of life.

* The religions of the human race at the present time are, in the main, divided somewhat as follows: Buddhists, 31·2 per cent.; Christians, 30·7; Muhammadans, 15·7; Brahmanists, 13·4; Heathen, 8·7; Jews, 0·3.

"Nothing is stable on earth," he was wont to say, "nothing is real. It is lighted and extinguished. We know not whence it cometh, or whither it goeth. It is like the sound of a lyre."

Tradition informs us that one day the Prince with his retinue drove to one of the parks, through the east gate of his city, and met on the road a broken and decrepid old man. "Who is that man?" enquired the Prince of his coachman. "He is sinking with old age," was the reply, "and he is forsaken of his friends, and left like a dead tree in the forest." "Alas!" answered the Prince, "and are we so weak and foolish as to be proud of our youth when old age awaits us? Turn my chariot home again."

Again the Prince drove through the south gate of the city, and perceived on the road a man parched with fever, and he exclaimed, "Alas! health is but the sport of a dream. Where is the wise man, who can any longer think of joy and pleasure?" and he turned his chariot home.

A third time he drove through the west gate, and saw a dead body lying on a bier, with friends weeping round it, and exclaimed, "Woe to youth, which must be destroyed by age! Woe to health which must be destroyed by disease! Woe to life, where man remains so short a time! Let us turn back, I must think how deliverance is to be accomplished."

Once more he drove through the north gate of the city, on the way to his pleasure gardens, and saw a mendicant. "Who is this man?" enquired the Prince. "He is a mendicant," replied the coachman. "He has renounced all pleasure, all desire, and leads a life of austerity. He tries to conquer himself. Without passion, without envy, he asks alms." "This is good and well said," observed the Prince, "The life of a devotee has always been praised by the wise. It will be my refuge, it will lead to immortality." And he returned again to the city.

Having declared his intention to his father and to his wife, he escaped one night from the palace, and retired to become the disciple of a famous Brahman. But after learning all the Brahman could teach him, he went away disappointed. He then sought another Brahman, enquiring the way to deliverance, but was again disappointed; and finally retired with five other fellow-students, and for six years lived in solitude and ascetism. At the end of six years he came to the conclusion that all this austerity was a snare and a stumbling-block, and no true way of salvation. He gave up his religious exercises, and was at once deserted as an apostate by his five fellow-disciples. He then imagined he had received the true knowledge, and took the name of the Buddha, or the Enlightened. Shall he keep this knowledge to himself or shall he communicate it to the world? Compassion for the sufferings of man prevailed, and the young Prince became the founder of a religion which, after 2400 years, is professed by 455,000,000 human beings.

The history of the Buddha places us in a better position to comprehend the plan of the Elephanta Caves. As we enter the smaller rooms, we find no emblems of idolatry, but four square rock-walls, and an absence of everything that can delight the eye. Here the devout Buddhist might surely attain Nirvana, or a state of nothingness, if anywhere in the universe,—all passion, all desire, all wandering thoughts, may they not be subdued here? In the blank recesses of an inner cave, in a room without furniture, on a solitary island, is there no hope of Nirvana?

The aspiration of the recluse two thousand years

ago in India has found many an echo among mystics ever since; but the true enlightenment is not in Nirvana. The "four verities" of Buddha are, (1st), there is nothing but sorrow in life; (2nd), sorrow is produced by the affections; (3rd), our affections and desires must be destroyed to destroy sorrow; therefore, (4th), all desire is to be rooted out of the soul. This doctrine of spiritual Nihilism, or "none of self," is a bewildering stopping-point for man; but there have been many who assert that "in nothingness is fulness." The revelation of God manifest in the flesh can alone fill the void. To stop short at the doctrine of the emptiness of the world is misery, but it is at any rate a "call" to the Church of Christ to make known to such weary millions the true Gospel of Salvation.

The Buddhists were the dissenters of India. They were the protestants against caste and priest-craft. They aimed at destroying so much that we may well ask, what remained? There remained the spirit of charity, kindness, and pity. The Brahmans were, and are, intensely exclusive. The Buddhist was a missionary seeking to gather converts, to impart truth as he understood it, denying himself for the good of others. It was a religion for the people. The Buddhists, therefore, soon numbered millions. But no creed can ever live by dissent or by negation; and although Asoka did his best as King to make it a State religion, it could not hold its own in India, even against Brahmanism.

In China and Ceylon other elements were introduced; but every effort of man to be good without God, *to empty the soul without filling it*, must, like Buddhism, crumble to dust.

The rock-hewn temples of Elephanta, with their huge sculpture and antique pillars, are in strange contrast to the busy stream of all nations that crowd the streets of Bombay. It may be appropriate that Buddhism should find refuge under the earth while the busy wheels of commerce course on in the sunshine. As we sat under the shade of the mangoes on the hillside, and looked across on the wide and beautiful bay, the exuberant life of nature seemed infinitely more glorious than the "vanity of vanities" of the Buddhist philosopher.

Before finally leaving Bombay I was conducted by Mr. Mody to the Park on Malabar Hill, where the Parsis have erected their Towers of Silence. The Parsis occupy such a prominent position among the merchants of this great eastern city, that they necessarily claim attention, presenting as they do phases of thought that command respect. The Jains lay stress on the fact that all life is sacred. The Parsi maintains with equal emphasis that mother-earth is sacred and is never to be defiled by the dead. A special "permit" is requisite to pass the gates to the Towers of Silence, but this being once obtained every courtesy and assistance is rendered to visitors. To the right-hand of the entrance are the three Sagrīs, or Houses of Prayer. The principal of these contains the sacred fire, which having been once kindled and consecrated, is fed day and night with incense and sandalwood, and never extinguished. The view is magnificent. In the foreground the Park is adorned with flowering shrubs, and cypresses, and palms; and down the slopes of the hill are dense cocoanut groves, with here and there the mansion of some princely merchant peering through the trees, and then beyond is the fine stretch of sea to the horizon as the water glitters in the sunlight. There are five round towers in front, standing about twenty-five feet high and fifty feet broad. They are built of solid granite, and covered with white chunam. The oldest of these towers was constructed 200 years ago, and is only used by the Mody family, whose forefathers built it when the Parsis first settled in Bombay, and here the bones of many generations of the Modys lie commingled. Mr. Mody is a member of this family, though in becoming a Christian he is now treated as an outcast.

There had been a funeral a few hours before my visit, and round one of the largest of the towers in weird silence was a circle of hugh black vultures. They sat on the coping for the most part like statues, as if they might have been the mourners, and then ever and anon one or two of them make a swoop into the centre, and round in the air, returning to exactly the same position he had previously occupied.

The Parsi who kindly showed me round, and who had charge of the grounds, exhibited a model of the interior of the towers, which illustrates the whole. The roof of each tower is rather lower than the outer walls, and consists of seventy-two concentric apartments, radiating like the spokes of a wheel from the central well, in which charcoal and sand are mingled with the bones. There are three large circles of open stone coffins, the circles of coffins being divided from one another by a pathway for the bearers as they convey the body to its resting place. The innermost of the three circles is for the children, and represents "good thoughts." The second circle is for women, and represents "good words." The third circle is for men, and represents "good deeds." The bones of convicted criminals are never allowed to mingle with the rest of the community, but are placed in a sixth tower, which stands apart from the rest. The bearers are supplied with perfectly new garments for each funeral, and not a thread of the funeral garments is allowed to leave the park lest it should carry defilement to the city. When a body is placed in one of the stone coffins, it is so arranged that a ray of sunlight shall fall upon it, and a ray of light from the sacred fire in the house of prayer on the summit of the hill. In a few minutes the vultures have done their work, and nothing but the skeleton remains. In two or three weeks' time the bearers return, and with their hands gloved they remove the bones with tongs to the central well to mingle with the ashes of their forefathers.

Zoroaster, the founder of the Parsi faith, is supposed to have lived in the reign of Darius Hystaspes. The earliest of the Zend writings, known as the Gathas, or Hymns, are supposed to have been written about 1200 B.C.; while the Vesparad, or Prayers, are ascribed to the seventh or eighth century B.C. The morality of Zoroaster was simple and practical, and the Parsis believe in the resurrection of the dead, and a state of future retribution. They worship one god, Ormuzd, and regard earth, air, fire, and water as sacred symbols of the deity. They also believe in the spirit of evil and of destruction as opposed to the spirit of good, and this evil spirit they call Ahriman. The Zend Avesta, or Parsi scriptures, contain many foolish fables and absurd assertions which a modern Parsi quietly ignores though he does not contradict. The entire absence of the worship of idols among the Parsis is a great relief after the gross degradation of surrounding Hinduism. "We believe," they say, "in only one God, and do not believe in any besides Him. That one God created the heavens, the earth, and the four elements. Our God has neither face nor form, colour nor shape. There is no other like Him. God has commanded us, through His prophet, to believe in the goodness of God; to avoid bad deeds; to exert good deeds; to pray five times a-day; to believe in the reckoning and justice on the fourth morning after death; to hope for heaven, and to fear hell; to remember always that God has done what He willed, and shall do what He wills; and He commands us to face some luminous object while worshipping God." "In the other world you shall receive the return according to your actions. If you repent of your sins, and reform, and the Great Judge consider you worthy of pardon, or would be merciful to you, He alone can and will save you."

The creed of the Parsi with his white shirt and white girdle practically consists in "pure thoughts, pure words, and pure deeds." The shirt has a little empty bag in the front of it to show that the wearer holds the faith of Zoroaster, which is supposed to be entirely spiritual and to have nothing material or visible about it. The kusti or girdle is made of seventy-two interwoven threads to denote the seventy-two chapters of the Yasna, and is wound round the body in three coils. Very many of the Parsis speak English as fluently as if they resided in Great Britain. They maintain a large college of their own, and have a thousand pupils in their girls' schools, and are, in fact, one of the most flourishing communities in the Indian Empire.

The wise men of the East, who came to worship the infant Saviour, are supposed to have been of the same race from which the Parsis are descended, yet very few of the modern Parsis have as yet forsaken the religion of their forefathers and become Christians. Three were baptized by the late Dr. John Wilson, and others were converted by the American evangelist, the Rev. William Taylor of California.

Mr. M. H. Mody was educated at a school composed of Europeans and natives. Here he received some tracts from his fellow scholars, and became much impressed in favour of Christianity. He attended St. Andrew's Kirk and St. Thomas' Cathedral, but grew up without making an open confession. In 1868 his wife died, and this produced a great effect upon him. He turned to Zoroastrianism again with all his heart. He says, "I began to rise at three a.m., and after a bath commenced praying according to the Parsi religion and very strictly performed all the outward ceremonies. I never took my breakfast or dinner before my prayers, which generally lasted two hours. When I drank water or tea it was with covered hands. I gave money for religious rites for the dead, and in charity to the priests and the fire-temples. I was led to go early every morning to the Towers of Silence, where I had my prayers offered for eighteen months nearly continually. I used to offer every day a piece of sandal wood to the fire in the Sagrī."

Mr. Mody was then informed of the preaching of Mr. Taylor, and concluded to hear him. Deep conviction for sin was the result. "Though my former life was moral it was unsafe; my heart was unchanged and desperately wicked. All my strictness in religious observances was of no avail. I had no strength or power to resist temptations or evil desires, and I found myself entirely condemned. I knew not what to do. To be baptized openly was a thing seldom done among Parsis, and I knew very well what the consequences would be. So I delayed a long time to come out boldly and confess the Lord Jesus Christ as my Saviour. At last, on the 21st of September, 1873, I was constrained to stand up for Jesus, and confess Him openly. I was baptized the same evening by the Rev. W. E. Robbins, in the presence of several witnesses. Now the days of my crosses and trials began to dawn. There was a great commotion among the Parsis. False reports were sent to the Gujerâti newspapers, and editors published them willingly. In my own family there was nothing but fury and lamentation. My relations and friends have no regard for me now. But amid all these trials I am rejoicing in Jesus. It is He only who has washed me from my sins in His precious blood. He has made me a free man. Though I have been a great loser in a pecuniary way, I am very rich in Jesus."

Mr. Mody came to England and studied some time at Harley House, under Mr. H. Grattan Guinness. He married an English Lady, Miss Isette Teresa Torr, and now boldly preaches Christ in Bombay night after night. He has meetings regularly throughout the week. The Parsis are very bitter against him for becoming a Christian, and a Parsi spy is appointed to attend his meetings and watch him. This spy offered to start a Bible class to study the Bible and prove that it was false. Mr. Mody says, "Many of the educated heathen natives know more of the Bible than many Christians." He was not allowed to visit his mother in her last illness, was not even informed when she died, and had all the property willed away from him, and is treated as an outcast by his own family. His wife is an excellent linguist, and industriously engaged in Zenana work, as far as her strength permits. She teaches sewing to the Zenana ladies, reads them some Bible story, sings a Christian hymn, explaining everything as she goes on, and concludes by giving them some text of Scripture to learn, seeking to win them for Christ.

In leaving Bombay for the mofussil I could not but rejoice that amid this dense mass of heathenism there are many voices lifted up for the truth. This "fair haven," as its name implies, with its splendid harbour of forty square miles, is emphatically the gate of India. Its population of 700,000 souls of many races, and its rapidly extending commerce, make it a centre of great importance to the missionary. The magnificent buildings that are rising one after another, the new Secretariat, the Government Post-office, the High Courts, and the University, are all tokens of progress, and it is well that in a great variety of ways the Gospel message should be brought before such a city. We found that Inskip, Wood, and Macdonald, the American evangelists, were there with their large tent on the greensward, on their errand of "Round the world for Christ." A valuable series of lectures to English-speaking natives was being delivered in connection with the Free Church Mission. Father O'Neill, of the Cowley Fathers, was holding special mission services. Each in his own fashion, and according to his own light, was seeking to impregnate the popular mind with divine truth ; and every agency for the exaltation of Christ, and the welfare of humanity, will surely, in the great measuring-line of futurity, receive its own meed of success.

Chapter III.—Hoshangabad.

> "When men imagine they do ought by stealth, He knows it—
> No one can stand, or walk, or softly glide along,
> Or hide in dark recess, or lurk in secret cell,
> But God detects him, and his movement spies.
> Two persons may devise some plot together, sitting
> In private and alone, but He, the King, is there
> A third, and sees it all. The boundless earth is His,
> His the vast sky, whose depth no mortal e'er can fathom."
>
> *From the Atharva Véda.*

At the Bombay Railway Station we found ourselves amid a plentiful vociferation respecting our luggage. Railway tickets for passengers are easily obtained, but the continual delay and annoyance of having luggage weighed and booked by lethargic officials, as a crowd of passengers wait amid a still greater crowd of porters and baggage, is something in which the experiences of Indian railway travelling exceed all other. Five packages commonly require five coolies to carry them on their five heads. These coolies run off at tangents with your luggage wherever they think best. When you have succeeded at last in getting your luggage weighed, a slow native writer sits at a desk and charges you so many rupees per maund, and the European pays it with a sort of presentiment that the Eastern mind must be very defective in its powers of calculation to make so light a weight equivalent to so heavy a charge. But an attack of fever may be the result if you do not keep your temper, and wherever all the coolies may have disappeared to when they seized your baggage on arrival, they are all sure to congregate again at the door of the railway carriage at your departure, and each several coolie will stand waiting for his gratuity of annas or pice if he has touched a package.

We found ourselves seated in a large railway compartment, with double roof to protect the passengers from the heat ; and outside shades at the side to prevent the sun shining in at the windows, with upper storey accommodation for lying full length all night, and a lavatory in the carriage. As each passenger is supposed to carry his bed with him, and a provision basket, it is not much marvel that the *impedimenta* take up more room than the passenger himself. It was politely suggested that I should give up my roosting place for the night in favour of a heap of somebody's luggage, and I climbed to the upper storey and lay down for a long journey on the Great Indian Peninsular Railway. This afforded me the opportunity of taking stock of my fellow-passengers. The natives and Europeans usually ride in separate compartments, so that my companions were mostly Europeans. One was a wounded soldier just returned from the Afghan campaign, and a number of other soldiers were in the train. They had come down the coast from Karâchi, and were moving inland. The miserable experiences of the wretched conflict in Afghanistan, its huge expenditure and wastefulness, were impressed indelibly on their minds. Not one word about the glory of war escaped their lips. The reality was too bitter to rouse any enthusiasm as they wearily returned home.

Another group of our fellow-travellers were sportsmen making for the hills, rough, hardy men, who could eat and drink, and talk loud. Igatpuri was their destination, and about midnight they decamped.

Another group consisted of two Swedish missionaries, who had come down to the coast to welcome their brides from Europe. Both had been married that day in Bombay. One of them had never seen his lady before. The brides, with their bridecakes added much to the interest of our journey. One of the brides was from Finland, and both had the fair complexion and flaxen hair that belongs to the North-land. The bridecakes were bestowed bountifully upon us, and were of good quality. The merry smile of the ladies as they caught each other's eyes showed that they realised the novelty of their position. Their husbands made the best of it, each took care of his bride, and we all made ourselves comfortable for the night. The ascent of the Thul Ghât is one of the marvels of railway engineering. Here we leave the Konkan and ascend to the Deccan, amid magnificent scenery. The mountains are precipitate, and the railway wends its way in zigzags, rising at an angle of one in thirty-two. Bombay is very hot, but ere we reached the reversing station we found the chill night air blowing in upon us. The gradients here are so steep that the engine changes ends and the whole train is reversed to strike up-hill again at a fresh angle. There are twelve tunnels and six viaducts in about nine miles, and at Igatpuri we are 1900 feet above the sea.

The railways of India are not only a powerful civilizing agency, and by the opening up of intercourse a great additional wealth to the country, but beyond all social advantages, they are, in the hands of Providence, a great help to missionary enterprise. The great centres of missionary activity in India are now knit together by railway communication, greatly to the economy of time, strength, and money, as well as provocative of mutual help and intercourse. There are 8545 miles of railway already open in India, for the most part guaranteed by the Government. These railways convey annually at least 43 millions of passengers, and 131 millions of letters pass to and fro in the year. Norman MacLeod justly remarks that "the indomitable power of England, with the extension of its government and the justice of its administration, has, in spite of every drawback that may be brought against it, largely contributed to the destruction of Hinduism. So also, in their own way, have railroads and telegraphs, helping as they do to unite the people and the several parts of India to each other, and all to Europe."

The next day we travelled for hours through the jungle, and as the train shot along, we started bucks, stags, antelopes, monkeys, foxes, and parrots, and in due course found ourselves in the great valley of the Nerbudda. The jungles abound in beautiful flowering trees. Here and there the foliage is hid amid masses of crimson blossom, and very many of the trees have leaves on them the whole year round, a succession of young leaves clothing them with verdure long before the old leaves fall, and thus a grateful shade is always secured both for man and beast.

This valley presents two notable characteristics: firstly, the immense fertility of the ground under cultivation; and, secondly, the great jungles entirely uncultivated.

Sir Richard Temple estimates that nearly one half of the whole of India is still uncultivated. "In the suburbs of the cities, throughout the empire," he remarks, "the ever-flowing stream of trade, great and small, imparts to an observer the impression of national vitality bursting forth in every quarter from the humblest to the highest." And yet, with all the dense population of India, "no symptoms have appeared of any dangerous preponderance of population over production." After the recent famine, the recuperative power of the country was extraordinary. In 1879, £7,000,000 worth of silver was absorbed by India. In 1880, gold to the value of £3,664,300 was imported. Within seven years, the value of the export trade of India has risen from fifty-six millions to sixty-nine millions, exclusive of treasure. "It is vain," says Sir Richard Temple, "to estimate that the people must ere long be famished for lack of agriculture, when vast culturable areas within India itself are seen inviting the plough. It is futile to offer statistical proof that the food-supply must be insufficient, when large quantities of edible grain are being stored at home and exported abroad." It is true that the Hindu has a strong prejudice against emigration, but the Government may easily offer inducements to the natives to break up the vast fertile jungles of Central India, and bring them into cultivation.

Some steps were made a few years ago to encourage farmers to settle on uncultivated land, but when the Government found that they had, in some cases, to pay heavily for land that was needed for railway purposes that they had sold cheaply a few years before, they suddenly reversed their policy, concluding not to sell land, but to let it out on short leases. These short leases, with no security of tenure, at once check the introduction of capital and debar colonists from erecting permanent buildings, and it is to be regretted that a restrictive policy of this kind should be re-inaugurated when the advantages of bringing more land into cultivation are so self-evident, and at a time when the Indian Government, in so many directions, is showing such an enlightened policy.*

As the railway bore us along, magnificent grain crops were waving in the fields, and later on there were the plentiful heaps of wheat lying by the roadside at the country stations waiting an opportunity of transit to the coast.

We alighted at Etarsi, and found Mr. Samuel Baker and a group of native Christians awaiting our arrival. Carriages were in readiness, and a run of eleven miles, on an excellent *puckka* road, took us to Hoshangabad. Two roads run alongside the whole distance, the one with good bridges for the English, guarded with police, the other, the native road for bullock carts, with deep ruts and ill-tended gullies and *nullahs*.

Rich cotton soil, to the depth of fifteen feet, runs along this broad Nerbudda valley. The open fields need no manure and receive but little culture, yet produce magnificent wheat crops. We go for miles without hedges. Each village is surrounded with groups of trees, and usually possesses its own mango grove, under which travellers encamp and gossipers promenade.

Familiar faces that I had known in England greeted me as I caught sight of the Mission

---

* The following is the present form of Lease for Government Land, in the Central Provinces :—

I son of resident of in the district of do hereby agree to take lease of the plot of Nazul land measuring and bearing No. in the Nazul Register, and do hereby bind myself to comply with the following conditions :

1. The lease will run from to or a period of twenty years.
2. That the rent of the said land, viz., Rupees, will be paid by me on or before each year.
3. That the arrears of rent will be recovered from me under the rules applicable to the realization of arrears of Land Revenue.
4. That I will submit a plan of the building to be erected on the said land, for the approval of the Local Committee.

bungalow at Hoshangabad, and many old home associations had to be discussed. As I entered the bungalow that was for awhile to be my Indian home, my heart overflowed with thankfulness to the Giver of all good.

European bungalows in the civil stations have their share of English comforts. The lofty rooms, the abundance of fresh air, the daily bath, the obsequious attendants, the clearness of the atmosphere, and the perpetual sunshine day after day, all combine to make five months of the year enjoyable.

These European bungalows have no upper storey. The glass doors form the windows, and usually open on the spacious verandahs, where lounge chairs invite the weary Englishman in the evening. There is a good reception-room in the centre of the house, with bedrooms and bathrooms on either side. There are no apartments for servants in the bungalow. Caste prejudices, and the peculiarities of Eastern life, make a considerable number of servants absolutely requisite, and they are almost entirely men-servants. The upper class of servants, such as the *bearer*, who is your personal attendant, are generally Muhammadans. The others are some

---

5. That the land, building, and its compound, will be kept clean by me to the satisfaction of the Municipal Committee.
6. That I shall not be at liberty to sell, convey, or transfer the said land, or any part thereof, without the written permission of the Local Fund Committee.
7. That after expiration of the term of this lease, it will be incumbent on me, my successor, or my representative, to renew this lease, subject to any rent which the Local Committee may then think fit to assess.
8. That in case of doubt and dispute arising in respect of any of the above conditions, such dispute will be decided by the Chief Commissioner, *whose order will be final.*
9. If, after five years from the date of this lease, the Local Committee revise the rent assessed, on some valid and satisfactory grounds, *I will submit to such revision.*
10. That if at any time the said land will be required by the Committee for some public purposes, I will give it up, *without demanding any compensation.*

of them Muslims and some Hindus. There is the *chaprasi* or messenger, carrying his master's name and address on a brass plate when sent on an errand. There is the *chowkedar* or watchman, who perambulates the compound during the night, the *syce* or groom, who minds the horse, the *bhisti* or water carrier, who brings water from the well on the buffaloes, in large and uncomely skins, the *dhobi* or washerman, who pounds the clothes severely on large stones by the river side, the *durzi* who sits cross-legged in the verandah, and sews on buttons and mends the clothes, and lastly the *sweeper*.

In these country districts one European willingly helps another. Far from home the English clan together. Information on every possible subject is readily accorded, carriages are lent, and kindnesses reciprocated.

To the Englishman who leaves the London fogs early in November, and arrives in India just after the heavy autumn rains have drenched the earth, and the young wheat is springing, and all nature rejoicing in having received the copious showers of heaven, India is a pleasant land. As soon as the earth is sufficiently dry in November, the agriculturist scratches the soil with his primeval plough, sows the seed broadcast, expects no rain whatever, and takes no further trouble, till he reaps the harvest in February and March.

On the Mission compound was a crop of cotton waiting to be gathered. Week after week the women threaded their way among the tangled plants and brought in the white produce. They then turned a very simple machine for separating the seeds from the cotton, and it was ready for use. The *rezai*, stuffed with this short cotton, is the common accompaniment of the traveller everywhere. The native wraps it round him when he thinks he is cold, he lies down on it contentedly at night in the verandah, or under the shade of a tree, or in the omnipresent bullock cart.

The handsome foliage of the bananas, or plantains as they are called in India, is another common accessory in each European compound. The broad, bright green leaf is an excellent non-conductor of heat; and the leaves are wrapped round bread and other eatables to keep them cool and moist. One side of the leaf is used for healing wounds, and the other side keeps a wound open when there is danger of it healing too quickly. If the coolie is diligent with his watering pot, the flower garden in front of the verandah abounds in brilliant blossoms and handsome creepers. At the back of the bungalow is a row of little out-houses where the servants sleep. Here little round-headed native children play in close proximity with chickens, goats, bullocks, and buffaloes. The cook-house stands by itself, where the cook produces well-served meals with the merest modicum of fire. Kitchen ranges have not penetrated here, and there is an open field for the patent ironmongers of England. Another group of cottages is allotted to two or three families of native Christians. The squirrels are quite at home in all these departments. They run into our bedrooms, and with lizards in the *almirah,* and bats flying about the room overhead, animal life in India is self-assertive, and exists on good terms with mankind. The Hindu scrupulously avoids shedding blood or taking life. His religion teaches him that life is sacred, though he may often violate this law where it suits him. Kindness to animals is national. Beyond this, he believes in the transmigration of souls,—who can tell whether the spirit of his uncle or his forefathers may not be in the bullock or the bird at his side? Nothing, perhaps, in a European's habits so disgusts and shocks him as eating beef. "The bullock is our best friend," he exclaims, "and you kill the bullock and eat him! When you have eaten up our bullocks you will eat our children next!" After *chota-hazri*, my first stroll in the morning was down to the Nerbudda. A glance at the map will show how wealthy India is in rivers. Not only is the country studded with rich coal measures and mines of the precious metals, but on the very surface her rivers spread fertility. The rivers are the objects of worship as the wealth-bringers to the districts through which they pass. During the festivals at Hoshangabad the people bring out lamps, consisting of castor-oil in a small earthenware saucer with a wick in the centre. These they light in the evening and push out from shore, and thousands of them float down the river as an offering to "Mother Nerbudda."

The first time I walked along the banks it was my lot to see a different sight. During the night the jackals were howling vigorously round the bungalow, and in the morning we found that it was on account of a Hindu funeral. The patient bullocks were standing in the country cart that had brought the deceased from some neighbouring village. A pile of wood had been erected on the shore, and one of the near relatives, stripped nearly naked, was burning the body. It is usually a brother or the nearest male relative that performs this mark of respect to the dead. An East wind was blowing, and three or four of the relations were holding up a brown sheet to protect the fire from the force of the wind. When the body is partially burnt the remains are cast into the river and feed the turtles.

There is a fine view of the Vindhya Hills from the Mission compound. These hills lie immediately to the north of the city on the Bhopal side of the river. To the south the valley is skirted by the Satpuras ; and to the south-east, among these hills lies the beautiful sanitarium of Pachmari, 4,000 feet high.

Hoshangabad consists of two parts, the European and the native. The European station is laid out with well-metalled roads, and contains a number of bungalows standing in their own grounds and surrounded with the necessary accessories for English residence. In the station is part of a native Palamcottah regiment with the inevitable accompaniment of Madrasee servants and attendants. The military are stationed here under an arrangement with the *begum* or queen of the native Muhammadan State of Bhopal which lies to the north of the river. The population, including the suburbs, is 13,070. It is principally in the native part of the city that the Mission work of the Society of Friends is carried on.

The city is supposed to have been founded by Hoshang Shah, the second of the Ghari kings of Malwa, who reigned about A.D. 1405. The fort, which is a massive stone building with its base on the river, is now in ruins. It was much enlarged about 1720, when Dost Muhammad, the founder of the Bhopal family, took Hoshangabad and annexed the surrounding district to Bhopal. The Gônd rajahs in the eastern part of the district were not dispossessed, and this Tahsil still contains a considerable mixture of Gônd population, and descendants of Gônd rajahs. The fort was attacked in 1795 by Beni Singh Subadar, an officer of the Rajah of Nagpur, and after a two months' seige was evacuated by the Bhopal troops. It was afterwards held by a Marâtha Brahman, but his fears were so easily worked upon that he again gave it up to the Bhopal troops without a blow, about 1802, and it was immediately reoccupied by Wazir Muhammad the virtual ruler of Bhopal. Wazir Muhammad called in the Pindharis to his help, and for several years the country was laid waste and the fertile plains of the Nerbudda given up to rapine and plunder. In 1809 the fort was again beseiged by a Nagpur force, and after a three months' seige retaken. In 1817 General Adams occupied the town ; and it became the residence of the chief British official in charge of the district. The present resident Deputy Commissioner is Major Brooke, who has recently been transferred from Nagpur.

Early in the morning on my first Sabbath in India I found myself in the covered *tonga* with a lively Hindu sitting in front who used his legs as well as his arms in driving, and urged on the bullocks by catching hold of their tails and twisting them round and round, as though there was some arrangement of wheels in the interior of the bullock to promote locomotion. The Hindu bullock is a decidedly "steady" beast, but appears to act up to the light it has received in honestly plodding on at a given pace that finally brings us to our destination.

The Meeting-house in the city is capable of holding some 300 souls, and is a substantial well-built structure, with a strong verandah in front. As the time approached for the morning gathering, a man on the roof rang a sonorous gong which assured the inhabitants of the approaching hour of prayer. The native Christian women are on the front seats with clean dresses, and a veil thrown over their heads. Behind them sit the men who are in membership, and in the rear those who have not yet united themselves with the church.

The language of the Central Provinces is Hindi. With it is mixed a good deal of Urdu or Hindustani. Urdu is the camp language, a compound of Hindi and Persian, written in the Arabic character, and spoken by Muhammadans throughout India.

A scene still more oriental in its character was the family gathering for Bible reading and worship at the Mission bungalow in the afternoon. Fifteen natives were present, all of them men. They formed a semi-circle on the parlour floor, each sitting crosslegged. Their Hindi New Testaments lay open on the floor in front of them. They read round verse by verse, the missionaries explaining the meaning. Of the fifteen natives present four were Christians. These four were distinguished by having their heads uncovered, while the remaining eleven sat with turbans on. When the reading was concluded each man was questioned, from one end of the class to the other. The Lord's Prayer was solemnly repeated, and the gathering dispersed.

One young man, who had been working in Hoshangabad some months, loitered behind to speak to Sahib, desiring to bring home his wife. She was still under the care of her parents. It was doubtful whether he would be allowed to have her now that he professed to be a Christian. One of the first questions Sahib put to the young man was, "Have you ever been legally married?" The answer was, "Yes."

One of the most important parts of the Hindu wedding ceremony in the eye of the law is that the bride and bridegroom have their clothes tied together in a knot, and walk ten or fifteen times round a pole. They then sit down upon a yoke and feed each other with rice and milk. The bride has a little broom erected on her head decorated with flowers to shew her humility and to typify that she is to mind house and keep it tidy and clean for her husband. These ceremonies take place very early in life, perhaps when the children are seven or eight years old. They are thus legally bound to one another; and the husband takes his wife home a few years later. Parents are considered very negligent if they suffer many years to run on without providing for the marriage of their children. When I showed a photograph of one of my own children to a native lady, the first question she asked was, "Is she married?" that is, "have you as a parent made proper provision for her?" It is considered a great misfortune for any one to remain unmarried. The marriage is, for the most part, a purely family arrangement of the parents, without any choice on the part of the children.

The young couple accept the decision of their parents as right; and it is only surprising that so many happy relationships are thus formed. By complacently accepting the inevitable, much of the asperity of life is toned down and hard things become smooth. The Hindu has a greater faculty of contentedness than the Englishman. He bows obsequiously to circumstance where the European galls himself by resistance.

The missionary is expected to act very much as a Patriarch. For instance, another young man comes to the missionary and says, "I want to get married. Will you find me a wife?" As a Christian it is hard for the young man to obtain one locally. The missionary writes to an orphanage and finds two or three likely girls ready for the occasion. The young man is satisfied and is established as a family man. A man does not always prove, even in England, to be the best judge as to what is good for himself. There is something to be said for the Hindu view that the father and mother know better than the children what matrimonial alliances will tend most to their welfare. It is the very early age at which the marriage takes place that is the greatest injury.

At the Mission Book-store in the bazaar the native brethren have religious conversations with enquirers. As evening approaches, the missionaries with two or three native Christians take their stand in the bazaar on a week-day and commence an open-air service by reading a portion from the Christian Shastras. This is followed by a translation in Hindi of that well-known hymn, "God loved the world of sinners lost," with the chorus,

> "Oh, 'twas love, 'twas wondrous love, the love of God to me,
> It brought my Saviour from above to die on Calvary."

The brilliant costume of the people, their picturesque attitudes, the keen attention of the copper-coloured faces, and the throngs passing to and fro, form a vivid picture. Out of a hundred men standing round, no two are dressed exactly alike. A young Brahman convert stepped forward and gave an earnest argumentative address. Sahib Baker followed. There was not one word of reproach, good order prevailed from first to last. The Hindus have a great capacity for listening, and open-air preaching is a power for good in Indian Mission work. In the large cities comparatively few of the higher classes stay to listen, but in country districts it is otherwise, and native gentlemen of position listen attentively in the open air.

Close to the book-store is an opium-den. Here a group of dingy men are reclining, some chatting, others smoking, while the opium vendor every now and then as a customer arrives takes out his keys and opens the strongly-locked box in which he keeps the pernicious drug.

The Mission school for Boys is in the Balagunj, the *chamars* or leather-workers quarter of the city. The Mission provides a *chaprusi*, or school-attendance officer, who sees to the attendance of the children.

After a satisfactory school examination, the boys played at the Hindu game of *kho* on their play-ground. The inimitable way in which Devi Dyal, the master, threaded his way in and out among the children at this game showed that he knew how to sympathize with boys, and that his Christianity was of that practical turn which is contagious.

The Mission school for Girls is in another part of the city, just opposite the public hospital, at the approach to one of the finest of the river ghâts. The house is after the pattern of so many native interiors, four square. There is a high wall outside, a courtyard and garden in the centre, with all the rooms on the ground floor opening on to the central court. On the flat roof the pigeons have their head-quarters, and there is a good look-out on the city. But a bevy of Indian wasps, who had their nest in the roof, soon let me know I was a trespasser. Their body and wings are held together by thin and frail ligaments, but they are free in attack, and I found it best policy to take refuge again among the musquitoes below.

The school is under the superintendence of Rachel Metcalfe, who has been in India since 1866. She landed in Calcutta, having worked her way out as a nurse to an European family, with some assistance from her friends in England. The natives call her the *mem sahib*, and although now an invalid, the native Christian women come and sit on the floor at her feet and look up to her for counsel.

There was considerable commotion because one of the school children had been suddenly married. The whole tenor of Hindu society tells against girls' schools, they are subject to many fluctuations, and it is difficult to keep the scholars long enough to give them an efficient education.

A *dhai*, or nurse, is kept to escort the children to and fro, and while it is essential to educate the girls as well as the boys, it is a department freighted with a heavy ballast of adverse social customs.

In the evening we often met groups of women going to the temple-worship singing through the streets, or rather chanting some chorus of praise to the gods.

The mid-week meetings of the Mission are quite as large as on the Sabbath, every member considering it his duty to be present. The Sabbath is no day of rest to the Hindu. He recognises no difference until he becomes a Christian. The grindstone of life's mill runs heavily the whole week; the compensating balance-wheel consisting in the superabundance of idolatrous festivals. Scarcely a month passes without some great national feast or fast. The waste of time and vital energy at these prolific festivals is enormous.

PARSI CHILDREN.

CHAPTER IV.—HOSHANGABAD.

"O, Creator of the world, show me Thy favour,
And deliver me from evil.
Maker of all that has been, and will be,
Of all that moves and is immovable,
Worthy of praise, I come to Thee, my Refuge."

From the Vishnu Purāna.

THE ghâts of the Nerbudda are specially frequented at the festivals, and consist of huge flights of steps for the people to go down to the river to bathe. They form a public promenade. The English Government has spent a large sum on them, and they are the most imposing object in the whole city. At the top of the ghât are several Hindu temples, and these temples are almost always open for the people to go in and out to worship the hideous idols. The Brahman priest solemnly descends the ghât and bathes in the sacred river. He takes his polished brass *lota* with him, and fills it with water for his own exclusive use, for he is an exclusive man. He lives in a sort of dreamy abstraction and supreme indifference as to any sympathy for other men. He is above the world, in the world yet not of it, a twice-born man, whose prerogative it is to hold communion with the divine. To our eyes he appears a perfect ritualist and formalist, but the well-formed outline, the sleek clean limbs, the fine thoughtful brow, and the quick intelligent eye, bespeak him to be a man of strong capacity.

When the annual floods sweep the valley the ghâts are a lively scene. The river is then 700 yards wide from bank to bank, and many a loose piece of property belonging to the farmers is carried away with the huge stream. In one of the recent floods a man had been sitting hour after hour on his little wickerwork *moirá* in the midst of his field keeping watch over his crops, and trusting to the four posts on which his resting-place stood to keep him safe. But on and on across the country came the inundation, and bore the man on his raft into the full current of the Nerbudda. Night came on as he drifted further and further down the river. In the darkness some animal approached his raft and clambered on to the far end of it. The man was nursing a little pet kid in his arms, but dare not move lest he should topple over into the water. As the morning dawned he saw it was a tiger that was his companion balancing the other end of the raft. They looked each other in the face, but neither moved; both realized their uncertain tenure on the raft. Presently they came to the curve of the river at Hoshangabad. Crowds of people were standing at the ghât watching the spectacle. The tiger, as he approached the land at the angle, gave one bound and was in the midst of the crowd. He was so startled at the novelty of his experience that he attacked no one, but rushed straight through the street off to the jungle.

On another occasion, a man-eating tiger, as the dangerous kind is called, was rambling about among the villages to the south of this district. One person after another had been carried off until the people dare not live in their villages. One thousand rupees was offered to any one who would kill him, but without success. The villages were deserted; and the reward was raised to fifteen hundred rupees.

A native on Government business went one day to a village, but found the doors closed. The people were shut up in their houses, and he called them. "No," they replied, "we cannot come out, our destroying god is at the well." He knew what they meant. He walked through the village with his rifle heavily loaded. He saw the tiger lying in state by the well, and with his curious superstition began talking: "Salaams to you, tiger; how are your father and mother? Are you quite well?" drawing nearer and nearer to the animal. When within fifteen or twenty yards he levelled the rifle at him, and the great beast rolled over dead. The Gônds came out of their villages by hundreds and escorted the tiger-killer, with the body of the "destroying god," back to town amid great shoutings. The man received the fifteen hundred rupees, and a village was given him for his bravery.

The Gônds are scattered among the recesses of the hills to the south of Hoshangabad and Jabalpur. The Rev. Elias Champion of the Church Missionary Society is now actively at work among them at Mundlha, fulfilling the desire of many years. The Gônds, like other hill tribes belonging to the Non-Aryan races, have been driven to the hills by Aryan invaders as our own Welsh and Gaelic neighbours. Nine-tenths of all the Christian converts of India belong to the Non-Aryan races, including the Dravidians of South India. These highlanders of India among the Satpuras are a simple-hearted race and much less sophisticated than the mixed populations of the plains. Many Gôndee families are now found in the Nerbudda valley and along the Tawa, and have acquired the habits of ordinary Hindus. Akin to them is another Hill tribe dwelling among the Satpuras known as the Bhîls. The Bhîls are like the fossil remains of a past age, and have little intercourse with the outer world. But the word of a Bhîl is to be trusted, and there is little drunkenness among them. Sir James Outram induced a number to enrol themselves as policemen, and the Bhîl Police Corps bears the character of being a brave, well-disciplined, trustworthy body of men."

The District Jail at Hoshangabad contains 159 prisoners. I found some of them working a small lithographic press; another group were grinding *mukka*, or Indian corn; others were making flat brown cakes, which form their principal diet. There is a Factory, where the men with fetters on their legs make *chánti* for their clothing and blankets. The prison has taken contracts to supply 1000 blankets and 2000 yards of cloth to Jabalpur, and 100 coats for Narsingpur. The prisoners sit at their looms making ten yards of blanket a day. At the oil mills groups of three and four prisoners toil round and round amid the clanging of their fetters, grinding *tilly*, a common seed of the district, from which oil is extracted. The mills consist of little hard wooden vessels; the *tilly* is cast in at the top, and the oil drops into a bowl, as the men slowly walk round turning the mill. A man came up to us with his hands in the attitude of prayer, saying, "I don't get enough to eat." We passed on to a long row of men on the ground knitting "treasury bags." One of these men moaned out to us, "I cannot do so much in a day." They make one bag in two days. The jailer explained that they have no fear of additional imprisonment; that many of them come into the jail over and over again, and if they get extra imprisonment for insubordination or discontent, they do not trouble about it. "They call the jail their father-in-law's house, that is, where they get fed and cared for, for nothing."

Mr. Norman de Lange gave me some interesting figures respecting the diminution of crime in the Hoshangabad district. In 1877 there were 3950 cases brought before the magistrates. In 1878, there were 3588 cases. In 1879, there were 3023, and in 1880, there were only 1906. The police are as vigilant as heretofore, but habitual offenders have been steadily brought to justice, and cases of robbery have very much decreased. The excellent harvests, and the prosperity of the people at the present time, are probably important factors in this encouraging result.

But the jailer bows to us, and we again breathe fresh air. Our quick-footed pony takes us across the hills to the junction of the river Tawa with the Nerbudda. These Indian rivers monopolize an immense amount of land. On both sides there is usually a wide reach of sand and shingle and rough ground. Just now hay harvest is commencing, for it is December.

The term "haymaking," is a misnomer in India. The hay makes itself, or the sun makes it, and the grass is ready to carry as soon as it is cut. The people cut it and carry it home on their heads, just as they have done since the days of father Abraham. The oxen are treading out the corn at the threshing-floors, and in exact accord with Levitical law, they are not muzzled, and are eating as they walk round.

The seasons in Central India run somewhat after this fashion; January, hay harvest, and healthy; February, cereals gathered, and healthy; March, wheat harvest, and healthy. The hot winds set in about the middle of March. April, is hot; May, hotter; June, hottest; July and August, heavy rains. In September there are frequent attacks of fever and depression of spirits consequent on the state of the atmosphere. October is unhealthy.

In November the fevers clear away, and December is healthy and invigorating.

The rainfall is from forty to sixty inches in the year. The average maximum temperature is 91° in the shade, and the average minimum is 73°.

A great méla, or religious festival, is held annually at the junction of the river Tawa with the Nerbudda, and the little earthen saucers are still lying on the shore, the offerings of devout Hindu pilgrims, as they exclaim, "long life to Mother Nerbudda."

Crossing the estuary in a flat boat, we find ourselves at the hamlet of Bunderabund, where there is a noted Hindu temple. We enter its precincts, and behold the ugly lewd god. A *charpoy*, or rough bedstead with four posts, is brought from a neighbouring house for the English visitors to sit upon, and a present of milk in a brass *lota*. But we must on no account drink out of the *lota*, or it will be defiled. The milk is poured into our own drinking vessel and the people are satisfied.

"May the *guru* come and pay his respects to you?" they enquire. Their teacher lying upon a bed, and covered with wraps to keep him warm, is then brought to us by four men. The old man is very ill, suffering from fever and dropsy, and has not long to live. The helpless idol-priest entreats the medical skill of the white man. This is the wretched man who is supported with his temple by the grant of thirty-four acres of land from our Government. He puts his hands in the attitude of prayer towards me and says in astonishment, "Have you come all across the great water to teach?" My companion feels his pulse and heart, and lays upon the bed two books for the *guru* to read. His aged mother is a miserable widow, dressed in coarse clothing, and her head all shaven, in mourning for the dead. She sits upon her haunches on the earth and bemoans the illness of her only son. "Through the blessing of Mother Nerbudda," she says she hopes her son may get better, and with a sad heart I turn away home to hear in a few days that the *guru* is dead.

On returning to Hoshangabad I visited the temples of Jagarnâth and Mahadeo. In the former are three hideous figures in the midst of a blaze of golden offerings and surrounded by lesser deities. Opposite to them is a huge and disgusting red figure of the Monkey god. God *hates* these idols. Idolatry is inconceivably abominable and degrading. The righteous indigation of God, as expressed so strongly in Scripture is His mind about it.

The Rev. John Robson, observes, "The Greeks and Romans were quite willing to admit Christ into their pantheon as one of their gods, and to allow worship to be paid to Him along with others. But this concession the early Christians refused. They insisted that He *alone* was God, and that the others were no gods, that He *alone* should be worshipped, and that the worship of the others was a sin abominable in His sight. It is only by a similar process that Christianity can be successful in India. The Hindu pundit does not say that Christ may be worshipped as well as Vishnu. He says Christ is Vishnu. 'He whom you worship under the name of Christ is the same whom I worship under the name of Vishnu. You worship Him after your fashion and I worship Him after mine.' While gladly welcoming the truth that is in Hinduism, there must be no parleying with the great falsehood that characterizes the system. It is needful to have seen some of those whom the Hindus look upon as their most holy men, to understand how loathesome this conception may become." Perhaps there is no way in which we may more surely test the value of a religion than by its effect on its followers. We have plenty of wicked men in England and America. But among the Hindus it is the *most* religious who are the most detestably wicked and unclean, and that in the very name of their religion.

"The lapsed masses in England are either ignorant of what Christianity is, or it has lost its power over them, and they know they are acting in opposition to it. But a Hindu will commit all these crimes, believing that in committing them he is not only not offending against religion, but even performing religious acts. Uncleanness is as much a part of Hindu worship as it was of the heathen worship in Corinth and Ephesus in the days of the apostle Paul. There is scarcely a crime which Hinduism will not allow in some men because it is a caste practice. The lapsed masses then, in the large cities of Great Britain, are low and degraded because they are not Christians. The masses of India are low and degraded because they are Hindus."* As Macaulay truly testifies, "Emblems of vice are objects of public worship, acts of vice are acts of public worship."

We gladly turned from this grossness of idolatry to the little Saturday evening prayer meeting at Rachel Metcalfe's. Outside was the noise of kettle drums and the shouting of a horde of Muhammadans. The Lord's people in prayer, though few in number, have victory assured them, for greater is He that is in them than he that is in the world. "This feature in history," writes Norman McLeod, "constantly repeats itself, a time of long and varied

---

* Rev. Jno. Robson, of Ajmeer, 'Hinduism, and Christianity.'

preparations, with not unfrequently very rapid fulfilments. It seems to me as if the spiritual conquest of India was a work reserved for these latter days to accomplish, because requiring all the previous dear-bought experiences of the church, and all the preliminary education of the world. No such battle has ever before been given to the Church of God to fight since history began, and no victory will be followed by greater consequences."

There is an effort made by Sanskrit scholars in the present day to separate Brahmanism as essentially different from Hinduism. Certain foundation truths in Brahmanism are admired, and passages from Brahmanical writers quoted in proof of the original excellence of Brahmanism. Hinduism, on the other hand, is so outrageously abominable and hideous, that no one who comprehends it attempts to defend it. Sanskrit literature does indeed abound with fine thoughts and lofty aspirations, amid volumes of puerilities; but it is utterly unjust on that account to separate Brahmanism from Hinduism, as though the one was essentially distinct from the other. Hinduism is the natural and full-blown outgrowth of the corrupt root of Brahmanism. We need to remember that it is the Brahman priest who is to-day the very centre and life of Hindu worship. The present defilement of India is the direct result of the religious teaching of the Brahman. It is the Brahmans that thrive and fatten on the atrocious Hindu ceremonial. It is the philosophical and astute Brahman, with his Sanskrit liturgy, that is the object of Hindu worship and reverence, and must ever stand arraigned at the tribunal of justice as guilty of the crime of Hinduism.

Before leaving England, a gentleman of position suggested to me that there was 'but little advantage after all in endeavouring to persuade the Hindu to exchange his religion for the Christianity of the nineteenth century.' One hour in a Hindu temple would utterly dispel such a delusion. It is almost marvellous that, with such a flood of light and testimony pouring in upon English society in our current literature, and in missionary reports, gentlemen at home can remain in such ignorance. But Hinduism is essentially conservative, and makes no attempt to win converts. Of course, any religion that fails to win converts must in the long run die out. A Brahman does not aim to make a single person of any other caste or faith into a Brahman. Such a thought is perfectly antagonistic to his creed. He has privileges which are absolutely limited to his own caste, and it is only children of his own caste that can ever obtain the like privileges. Of the ten millions of our subjects in India, who belong to the Brahmanical caste, probably not one of them would attempt to make a European into a Brahman. Christianity, on the other hand, is in its very nature aggressive. The impulse of every true Christian is to win others to the same faith. When two such faiths are placed alongside, as they now are in India, it is only a question of time as to which conquers.

We are now in the midst of the Muharram festival, the "most sacred" Muhammadan festival of the whole year. For nine days the drums have been beating, apparently growing louder and louder every day, and this is the tenth day, the great day of the feast. This festival is professedly a great *mourning* in celebration of the first martyrs of one of the leading Muslim sects. The martyrs' names were Hasan and Husain ; and these two words "Hasan and Husain" are shouted hour after hour amid wild dancing for ten days. The people erect *taziyas*, made for the most part of bamboos and paper, covered with tinsel work and pictures, and bright colouring and gilding. The *taziya* professes to be a model of the Mausoleum of Husain at Karbala, but it takes all manner of shapes, sometimes like a huge hand eight feet high, emblematic of the hands of Husain which were cut off when he was murdered. Men with kettledrums parade the streets day and night without any cessation whatever. In the midst of the festival the announcement is made "The tigers have come." Some of the people have smeared themselves over with paint, and have disfigured themselves with tails six or seven feet long with a large tassel at the end, and a man running behind each tiger carries his tail for him wherever he pleases to go. They rush about like madmen, calling at one house after another. The people give the tiger almost anything he asks for, and men behind carry the various presents he has received; while others carry caldrons filled with fire, and torches.

Three years ago there were no less than 120 *taziyas* made at one festival at Hoshangabad. Last year there were 75; this year the number is much fewer, so that the extravagance and excitement is losing favour. Meanwhile multitudes come in for miles from the country "to see the fun" while "the faithful" are wailing and beating their breasts with professed grief. "Do they really weep?" we enquire, "Oh yes, the tears stream down their faces." The great *tāmashā*, or show, accumulates in strength as evening draws on. A party approach the Mission bungalow shouting, "Shah Husain! Dulha! Dulha." *Dulha* means the bridegroom, 'Behold the Bridegroom cometh,' in allusion to Husain having been murdered the night before his wedding. As the *taziyas* collect, the mass of the people are dressed in their brightest holiday costume, the prevailing colours being red, yellow, white, and green. The elephant of the rajah, and camels richly caparisoned, lead the way as the *taziyas* approach in front of a Muhammadan tomb. The first *taziya* belongs to the native soldiery, and is beautifully finished. Another has been prepared by the eunuchs of the city, who stand round it dressed as women. Each *taziya* is borne aloft on men's shoulders. The people burn frankincense in little urns in front of it, and the women crouch round muttering their prayers, and chanting some dirge as they sway to and fro. There are all the elements of gross idolatry. Numbers of the people toss sweatmeats and votive offerings into the crevices, others hold up their hands to the *taziya* in the attitude of prayer.

As darkness comes on, thousands of little oil lamps are lit round the holy places and tombs of the Muslims. Fireworks are thrown into the air, and torches are carried in procession. The so-called "priests," decorated in white sugar-loaf hats three feet high, lead the way. Every now and then they halt; fencing and such like games abound. "The people sat down to eat and drink and rose up to play." The immense concourse march past our bungalow to the open *Maidan*, and after taking the valuables off their gaudy effigies, cast the *taziyas* into the river, and the ten days excitement is at an end.

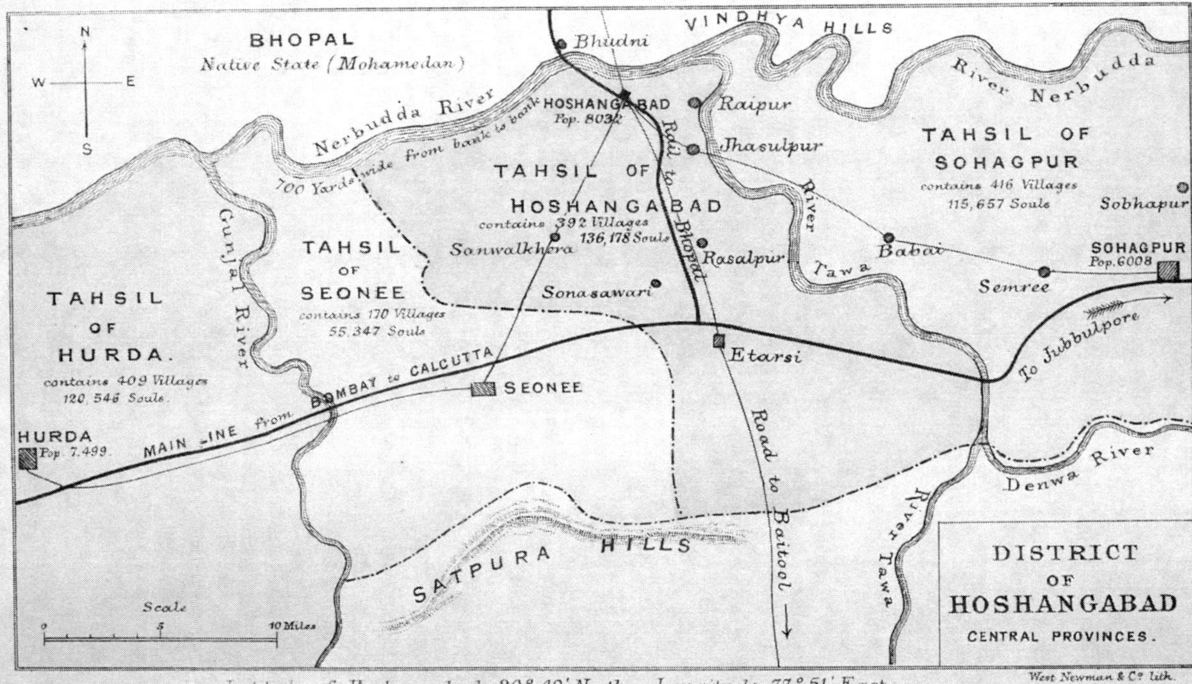

Latitude of Hoshangabad 20° 40' North, Longitude 77° 51' East.

Chapter V.—Sohagpur.

> "Bear railing words with patience, never meet
> An angry man with anger, nor return
> Reviling for reviling. Smite not him
> Who smites thee, let thy speech and acts be gentle.
>
> *Epic of the Mahâ-bhârata.*

Sohagpur is a healthy town standing a thousand feet above the sea on the main line between Bombay and Calcutta, with a population of 7000 inhabitants. It is the residence of a considerable number of Europeans and Eurasians, government and railway officials. All the passenger trains stop here half-an-hour for refreshments; and there is an encampment adjoining the station for the accommodation of troops passing up-country. It is the head-quarters of the *Tahsil* of the same name which contains 416 villages including Babai, Semree, and Sobhapur.

Before entering Sohagpur we pass the Gônd fortress of Bágrá on the banks of the Tawa. The ruins stand high on a spur of the Satpuras, surrounded by dense jungle. The old ramparts look down upon us as the rail crosses the river telling of days gone by when the rajahs of Gôndwana were men of power. In these jungly districts, when and whore there is much moisture, and the temperature persistently high, rank deciduous vegetation generates fever as a matter of course. With abundant tropical rain and tropical vegetation comes inevitable malaria. But as we approach Sohagpur we leave the jungles behind and find ourselves on a firm gravelly soil and fine open country.

As we passed up the streets the natives whispered to one another, "Here are the Christians come." The Friends commenced work at Sohagpur in 1874; and the old Banyan tree is standing under which Rachel Metcalfe held her girls' school with the monkeys frolicking about in its branches overhead. A tall woman stopped us and said, "When will you open school here again, because I want to send my girl for you to teach?" Arrangements have now been made for reorganizing the work, and J. H. Williams and his wife are residing there.

In bazaar preaching it is an immense advantage to the missionary to be able to preach in the vernacular without the medium of an interpreter, yet the effect of speaking English in the Bazaar is peculiar. The audience often doubles in size as soon as the people hear English. As sentence after sentence is translated by the catechist who stands alongside, the interest deepens. Quite independent of the subject-matter, it is a valuable lesson to the young men and students. A knowledge of English, in India, is often a passport to a lucrative position, the more respectable part of the community therefore eagerly gather to hear English translated.

"If Christ is God," queried an old man in Sohagpur, "why does he not come into our hearts and make us Christians?" We had to explain that God does not *compel* converts, but seeks to persuade men to receive Christ. While the catechist and Ali Bakhsh were preaching, some of the people laughed. I admired their patience, and when I questioned the catechist about it, he said, "I was laughing myself when I was converted. I felt the force of conviction, and tried to laugh it off. I was reading a book about Jagarnâth and trying to interrupt Mr. Gayford in his preaching at the very time I was feeling the force of his words, and I tried to make my friend, Jugal Kishore, laugh too; and then Jugal came to me and said he would be a Christian if I would, and afterwards he came all the way to Allahabad to find me." Thus it is sometimes those who are impressed that are the most ready to interrupt. It was in the streets of Sohagpur, in 1875, that Bâl Mukand first made public confession of Christianity. At that time he stood under the verandah in front of our book shop in the town, with the whole street packed with people in excitement because a Brahman was changing his religion. His father stood before him weeping bitterly the 'loss' of his son, and entreating him not to throw himself away; but Bâl Mukand said, "I have left all and become a Christian, not for man, but because I know that the Lord Jesus has died for me. I am not a disciple of man, but of Jesus. I have left Hinduism because I feel it is false, and that salvation is not of it. No one has persuaded me into this. I have of my own free choice become a Christian, and would confess Christ now if thousands of people were added to those already present."

We received a cordial welcome from many of the people in Sohagpur, and when we returned to the *Serai*, or native inn, a young man who had heard us preaching in the Bazaar was waiting for us. He had his difficulties, and as he sat cross-legged on the floor at our feet, enquired, "God made us Hindus, and if He wished to make us Christians, He would have done it when we were born, would He not?" He then became more serious, and said, "I should like you to show me how to pray." He had been reading Christian books that were distributed a year ago, and thus one wave of influence after another deepens conviction, but he was not yet ready to forsake all for Christ.

In the evening we exhibited the magic lantern with Bible pictures to a large concourse in the Market-place.

There is some silk weaving and lac-melting carried on in the town, but one of its most prosperous trades is the manufacture of cotton goods. As we pass through the streets we find the natives working their little rickety machines for cleaning the cotton and preparing it for market. If the farmers would but grow a better quality of cotton in their fields, the trade would be capable of almost indefinite development, for almost the whole population is clothed in cotton fabrics, and there are already forty-one cotton factories in Western India. There is plenty of room for English enterprise and capital if the English merchant will only take the trouble to win the natives to better modes of cultivation and production. We saw sugar-cane and cotton growing abundantly.

Dyeing is also a thriving trade in Sohagpur. Large low vats are lying on the shingle by the river, and the dyed *chadars* spread along the banks in profusion to dry in the sun. An experienced missionary told me that the whole expense of a Mission might be easily earned if some English expert, acquainted with the art, would come out and dye cotton goods the "Turkey red," which is so popular among the people. The trade in dyeing is exclusively in the hands of the Muhammadans.

Close by the dye vats on the banks of the river we stumbled on the goddess of cholera and small-pox. Dr. Hunter says, "The Gônds worship cholera and small-pox, and offer sacrifices to appease the wrath of these divinities," and probably this stone goddess, lying neglected under a tree, is a relic of Gôndi superstition. But this worship of small-pox and cholera does not appear to be at all confined to the Gônds in the Central Provinces. It happened to be a healthy time of year, and therefore the goddess was not just then in request. But we had evidence that the people of Sohagpur were only too prone to this form of idolatry when occasion served.

Perhaps there is no trade in Sohagpur so peculiar as the cultivation of the Betel leaf. To the east of the town there are large gardens devoted entirely to the Betel vine. These gardens are most carefully fenced in with wickerwork. They have a plentiful supply of water and are roofed in from the sun with a sort of light trellis work at the height of eight or ten feet. Stakes are thrust into the ground in long lines, and the Betel vine is trained up these supports. There is just space enough between each row of stakes for a man without much clothing to make his way to cultivate the plants and to pick the flat leaf. I visited these curious botanical gardens and found the Hindus adepts in their own line of horticulture. The arrangement was perfect. It seemed as though every green leaf of every Betel plant *(Piper Betel)* was cared for. The men gather the leaves by thousands, and the *tamolees*, or sellers of betel leaf, have their stand in every bazaar and find an abundance of customers. The leaf is called *pán* (pronounced pawn.) A particle of lime is smudged on it, some bruised Betel-nut *(areca catechu)* is added, also a little katthá *(terra Japonica)*, and one or two aromatics, such as a clove or a fraction of cinnamon. The Betel-leaf is then adroitly wrapped up in a triangular form and chewed. The *pán* is considered so necessary to oriental comfort that many a Hindu would feel miserable without it, and the gift of *pán* from friend to friend is one of the ordinary courtesies of Indian life in the Central Provinces. I found that when I handed the *pán* to the native Christians at the close of the evening meal it was a very welcome offering. The lime and the *terra Japonica* give the mouth a bright red colour, which the Hindu thinks improves his personal appearance, and in the street and in the bazaar we constantly meet the people chewing the *pán*, with their lips deeply tinged.

Near Sohagpur is the large market town of Sobhapur. On our way thither we witnessed the mirage, which the natives call "the deceiver of the antelope."

Sobhapur is the head-quarters of the weaving trade and some cotton spinning. The babies' cradles hang by ropes from the cottage rafters, swinging to and fro, while their mothers sit at their little machines preparing the cotton for market.

The Patel of Sobhapur is a Gônd, and many of the inhabitants are descended from the Gônds. The patel owns some eighty villages, but is an opium eater, and is so deeply in debt that the profits of his villages have been awarded to his creditors for thirteen years.

A band of serpent charmers were in possession of the square as we entered. We accordingly waited our time, and when their performance was over had a good meeting under the large Pipal tree in the centre of the town. The Pipal tree is considered sacred by the natives, and they say, "we cannot tell lies or swear falsely under its shade." While I discoursed on the Creator, and on our own sinful state needing a Saviour, the necessity for forgiveness and a holy life, the people willingly assented, but when I came to speak of Jesus dying on the cross for our redemption there was the laugh and sneer from the more educated natives, illustrating the truth of Paul's words, "We preach a Messiah crucified, unto Jews a stumblingblock, and unto Greeks foolishness." As we came away one man observed, "the truths of Christianity are very good, but it is our *sins* that prevent Christ coming to our hearts."

In this land the harvest ripens faster than in more temperate climes. There may be something analogous in the spiritual development of the country. Professor Max Müller says, "The influence of Christianity in India is felt everywhere. From what I know of the Hindus they seem riper for Christianity than any nation that ever accepted the Gospel." "The very strength of the tremendous system of caste," says Norman MacLeod, "may at last prove its weakness. If on the side of wrong 'it moveth altogether if it move at all,' it may do so also on the side of right. Let the wall be so far sapped that it must fall, it will do so, not by crumbling down in minute fragments, but as a whole, *en masse.*"

The village of Sânwalkhera is eight miles from Hoshangabad on the Seoni road; and receiving an invitation from Mr. and Mrs. Norman De Lange, who were tenting there, we visited it.

It is owned by three patels who are brothers, and is almost exclusively inhabited by Brahmans. The three patels own about 1400 acres of land, but are, in accordance with custom, heavily in debt to the exorbitant money-lenders to the amount of something like 26,000 rupees. They are paying 12 per cent. interest on part of this amount, and 18 per cent. on the remainder; thus the interest alone swallows up most of their annual returns. Their wives and children are nevertheless decorated with jewelry worth something like 17,000 rupees, the

NATIVE LADY OF CENTRAL INDIA.

whole wealth of the wife being often invested in the decoration of her person.

Being a purely Brahman village there are no chickens and consequently no eggs for visitors, as the Brahman objects to take life. Reverence for the Brahman, however, is rapidly decreasing even in these country districts. Ten years ago the patels would often spend 60 rupees on an idolatrous feast in feeding Brahmans. One of the patels says that this year all he gave to the support of the feast was eight annas. "Why did you give so little?" we inquired. "Because it is not worth while wasting a lot of money in feeding Brahmans," was the quiet reply. The patels were cursed by the great pandit because they gave so little, but the people are learning that their curses or blessings are of small avail. A learned Marâtha Brahman told me that the six privileges of a Brahman of his position were (1st), to exercise charity; (2nd), to receive charity; (3rd), to learn the Vedas; (4th), to teach the Vedas; (5th), to perform sacrifices; (6th), to receive sacrifices. He looked ashamed as he quoted the sixth privilege, but many of these men deliberately claim the right of having sacrifices offered to them as though they were God.

The twice-born man conceives with some truth that every man is a debtor. He divides life into three portions, the student life, the family life, and the forest life. He owes a debt to the wise men of past ages, this he repays by a careful study of the Sanskrit Vedas and Purânas. He owes a debt to his parents and to the gods, this he repays by becoming a married man, teaching his children, and offering the sacrifices of a householder. Having paid these debts he is a free man; and the third portion of his life he may retire to the forest to hold communion with the Divine Being, being himself divine.

When gray hairs come, or when he has seen his children's children, he gives place to younger men. Up to this time his life has been bound up with ceremonial observance. He now has liberty to perform his devotions spiritually and is no longer bound to carnal ordinances; he is henceforth called a Vânaprastha. Thus we read in the Mahâ-bhârata, "The enjoyment of a man who lives in the village is a rope to bind him; good men cut it asunder and are free. The forest is the abode of the gods, so the scripture teaches. There is no such treasure for a Brahman as solitude, equanimity, truth, virtue, kindness, and righteousness. What does wealth profit thee, O Brahman, when thou art going to die? Seek for that which is hidden in the heart." They recognise that a man may live in a forest and yet have the heart darkened by passion and evil desire. Thus we read: "The hermitage is not the cause of virtue. Wherever a *self-controlled* man dwells, that is a forest, that is an hermitage."

But this was just the point where Brahmanism utterly broke down. Archimedes might move the earth if he could find a fulcrum on which to rest his lever, but in man himself there is no fulcrum for efficient self-control apart from Christ. Earth and all that is earthly gravitates downward. I have seen the wicker-work hut of the hermit on the rocky banks of the Nerbudda, and can bear witness to the lovely scenes of nature's grandeur where within constant sound of the torrent the Brahman had chosen his hermitage. But this forest life is a thing of the past. It has failed, as of necessity it must fail. Man was not born to be a hermit, and the Brahman of to-day lives among men, looks to his fellowmen for support, and appears never to release himself from the perpetual round of ceremonials.

There is a weekly market in Sânwalkhera, but so

primitive are the people in their habits that the whole trade on market day is conducted by barter, without money of any kind being used.

After refreshing ourselves in the comfortable tent under the mango trees, we proceeded to the house of the patels. A carpet was spread for us, and to our astonishment we found the wives of the patels, and their mothers and grandmothers and children, assembled to meet us. Of course it was the presence of the English ladies with us that alone secured for us the privilege so rare in India of being introduced to the women of an Eastern household. They were all decorously seated on one side, and were evidently well pleased to peep through their veils at the strangers. The timber of the house was of stained hard black wood. There was a good deal of *tamāshā*, or finery, over the doorway. Parrots were hanging over our heads in cages, and the children were ordered to be quiet, although it was as much as they were equal to on such an occasion. The bow and the spear hung on the wall, and the cocoa-nut palm waved its plumage in the courtyard in the centre. To the right of the court-yard was the family altar with the sacred *tulsi* plant growing on the top. But still more strange was the motley throng of people that at the invitation of the patels now entered and sat cross-legged before us. The young men had chains of coloured cowries round their necks, and were not only decorated with bracelets, but had ornaments round their wrists. The women had diminutive looking-glasses fastened in the centre of their foreheads called *tîka*, reflecting everyone who looked at them. As they became accustomed to us they were quite willing to exhibit their jewelry. One lady took off her huge nose-ring with its jewels for us to feel the weight of it. Another of the ladies handed us an enormous necklace of silver which was literally weighted with a long string of rupees, and the ornaments on their heads were also freighted with silver portraits of Victoria.

We proceeded with our errand, and the catechist read the 11th chapter of John, and explained the Gospel. A couple of Christian *gîts* were sung, and the people crowded in at the low doorways as I told them of a Boy twelve years old who was lost in a great city, how his mother sought him with tears, and found him at last among the doctors in the Temple hearing them and asking them questions. Prayer was offered amid the most profound stillness, and the people evidently realized something of the presence of God. Although the buffaloes and the bullocks with their tinkling bells came into the outer court while the meeting proceeded, nothing was suffered to disturb us, and it was a privilege to witness for Christ to such an audience. A large bronze dish of sweatmeats was then presented to us, of which we partook and withdrew. As we sat down again under the shade of the mangoes, which were loaded with fragrant blossoms, we found ourselves surrounded by the villagers. I sat on a camp stool, and opening my watch exhibited the 'living wheels,' and quickly secured an audience.

"Why have you those marks on your forehead?" we enquired of a young man. "I am a Brahman," he replied, "and I have put those marks on my forehead that the people may feed me." "Are you not ashamed," we answered, "with such strong hands and arms not to work for your living?" He showed us his hands, and replied that he did work sometimes, "for the people do not give me enough to eat without." Mr. Williams saw one little boy presenting an offering at a wretched *chabûtra* near the tent. These *chabûtras*, plastered with cow dung, are places for sacrifice. Mr. Williams asked the lad what he was doing. The boy explained that he had a bad sore, that another boy who had a bad sore had presented an offering at this *chabûtra* and recovered, so he came to present his offering in the hope he might also be healed. Such 'logical' conclusions are not easily dispelled, and the boy continued his offering in faith.

An idolatrous feast had been held in the village a few days before our arrival. Eight young men were sitting cross-legged in front of us, with a group of children in the rear, and among them one fair-complexioned child, a daughter of the patel, very different from the rest, and we enquired, "Now tell us what you did the other day at the feast?" They replied, "At the feast one man, who was a Gônd, wanted the Spirit to rest upon him, and brought mango leaves, and the products of the fields, and presented them at the *chabûtra*. He then walked three times solemnly round the place of sacrifice where the idol was, and the Spirit came upon him." "What happened when the Spirit came upon him?" we exclaimed. "Why then he could *divine*," replied the villagers, "and the people came to him and enquired respecting the prosperity of their crops, what sort of harvest there would be, and the welfare of their families, how their distant relations were, and so forth, and he professed to tell them how it would be." "And were his answers true?" "No, they were not *all* true. Sometimes he gave the right answer and sometimes the wrong." "How was it they were not all true answers?" "It was because the man was *only an instrument* in the hands of the gods, therefore he sometimes made mistakes, but when the great God himself comes, as *He will come some day*, then He will make no mistakes."

Oh, that people with such strange guesses at truth, and yet in such darkness, might have Gospel teachers settled among them to lead them to Christ, the Saviour! Of all the delusions in the world, some of the worst have been those which have claimed the inspiration of the Spirit. The actual guidance of the Spirit is the glorious inheritance of every Christian believer, but it has had its counterfeit in all ages, leading into spiritual pride and dogmatism. Unless we hold the truth in reverent humility we are infallibly led into error. The gift of God is no delusion but is the Spirit of power and not childishness, the Spirit of love and not bitterness, and the Spirit of a sound mind and not an uncertain impulse.

HINDU JEWELLER.

CHAPTER VI.—CENTRAL PROVINCES.

> " Do good TO-DAY, time passes, death is near
> E'en to foes who visit us as guests
> Due hospitality should be displayed,
> The tree screens with its leaves, the man who fells it."
>
> *From the Mahâ-bhârata.*

UNTIL the Great Indian Peninsular Railway created the main route to Calcutta through the Central Provinces, this part of our Indian Empire was comparatively a *terra incognita* to Englishmen. This may account for the singular fact that the Hoshangabad District was left so long without a single missionary, reserved for a Missionary Society which has but lately entered the field. Englishmen had heard indeed of Nagpur, Indore, Narsingpur, in the annals of military achievements. Jabalpur had for years been an important European station, yet the fertility of the Nerbudda Valley as the finest wheat-producing district in the whole of India was unknown, and even now is scarcely appreciated.

The district of Hoshangahad is divided into four *tahsils*, each under a native *tahsildar*. These four divisions arc Hoshangabad, Sohagpur, Seoni, and Harda. Two of these we have already visited, and there remain the two important centres of Seoni and Harda, two towns on the main line of railway.

Seoni is frequently visited by the missionaries from Hoshangabad, though not so accessible as Etarsi, where there is bazaar-preaching regularly established at the weekly market. The neighbouring villages of Sonasawari and Rhasalpur are also frequently visited.

In Seoni there is an active cotton trade, and it is a convenient centre for the native corn merchants. The town existed in the time of Akbar, and about 1750 a fort was built there which was taken by the British in 1818. There is a *serái*, but not much accommodation for travellers, and we had to forage for ourselves. One of the native Christians lighted a fire under a tree near the *serái*, borrowed a tin plate, and proceeded to make *chapátís*. Two stones supported the tin plate over the wee fire and completed the kitchen range. A little flour was made into dough, then thrown from hand to hand by the cook. Men do the cooking in the East, and are adepts at the art. This process of tossing the dough produces what we should call in England a round small pancake. This is cast on to the hot tin plate, and in a minute or two is cooked sufficiently to make way for its successor. When a little pile of these cakes was ready they were brought to us for our dinner. Each *chapátí* bore visible marks, by its variegated surface, of the different experiences it had passed through in the hands of him that fashioned it. But hunger covers a multitude of faults, and the *chapátís* were eaten. They are not digestible but are satisfying. They form the common meal of the country. A Brahman makes them for himself rather than have his food defiled by the touch of a man of lower caste, and any evening, by the roadside, may be seen the solemn man slowly at work preparing his meal.

Our open-air meeting in Seoni was well attended. We stood where four ways met surrounded by grotesque native shops, and opposite the open idol temple. David, our Bible colporteur had received rough handling in the town a few days before, and when the people saw the English missionaries they concluded it was the wisest course to give us a thoroughly courteous reception. Some of the more wealthy inhabitants desired us to send a teacher to reside there and offered to pay his expenses, but when we offered them a man on these terms they deferred their conclusions.

The shopkeeping class, or *baniyas* of India, sell cloth and piece goods, grain of various kinds, crystals and *ghi*, which is a disagreeable kind of butter. There are no shop windows, and the front of the open store has usually two or three rows of round open baskets containing cloves, cinnamon, pepper-corns, chillies, nutmegs, cocoanuts, &c. The *baniya* sells his articles by weight and not by measure, and wraps what he has sold in leaves. He sits cross-legged behind his little display of goods, and appears to be quite indifferent as to whether any one buys of him or not.

Our visit to Harda was enlivened by the friendly greeting of Mr. William D. Brown, of the Episcopal Methodist Mission. His work is for the most part with the English-speaking portion of the population. He gladly accompanied us to the bazaar when he found our companions were intending to preach in the vernacular. As at Seoni a crowd gathered to listen in the centre of the town where four ways met. Harda was under the Marâtha Government previous to its cession to the English. Sir John Malcolm established his head-quarters here in 1817, and it is now a thriving town of 7500 inhabitants, surrounded by 409 villages.

In Harda we made the acquaintance of Mr. Snuggs, the naturalist. At his house was a large collection of stuffed birds, bucks, antelopes, and serpents. He had recently killed a large tiger and had its head stuffed with artistic effect. Large numbers of people are killed every year in India by wild animals. In 1878 it was found that 816 people had been killed by tigers, 845 by wolves, and 1773 by other wild beasts. No less than 16,812 people had been killed by snakes. In that year 48,700 head of cattle had been destroyed by wild beasts. When we remember the importance the Hindu attaches to his bullocks and cows for his sustenance, this destruction of cattle is no small item. In the Central Provinces alone there are 5,196,681 bullocks, cows, and buffaloes in the hands of the people. The English Government, amid the many other benefits it confers on India, offers rewards for the destruction of wolves, tigers, and snakes. In four years 6554 tigers have been destroyed, and the people who destroyed them received £15,860 from Government for delivering the country districts of one of their greatest dangers. During the same four years, 1875, 1876, 1877, and 1878, there were 84,600 other wild beasts killed by the people, and 727,809 snakes, and the total amount of reward paid by the Government was £44,679. The districts that are most inhabited by the wolves are the North-west Provinces and Oudh. In these two districts 600 people annually lose their lives by wolves. The districts most frequented by tigers are the Central Provinces and the western part of the Madras Presidency. One curious fact is that in Bengal there are twice as many people killed by tigers as in Assam, while in Assam there are more tigers killed by the people than in Bengal. In the Punjab alone there were no less than 144,000 snakes killed in 1875, and in the Presidency of Bombay 153,000 snakes were destroyed in 1876.

At Raipur, a Sanskrit scholar, and the chief

pandit of the district resides, named Govind Rām. The Hindus regard him with reverence as their religious teacher. We were courteously received as we sat down in his house, surrounded by a group of natives. Bâl Mukand explained to them the Gospel of Jesus Christ. Govind Rām answered, "God is in every man. God is a Spirit, and God's Spirit is in everything, in the trees, in the animals, God is everywhere. You say you are to love your neighbour, but you kill the goat and eat him. God's Spirit is in the goat, why do you kill him? If you love your neighbour you should not kill the goat. The Sanskrit language was given us from God. It is the divine language, therefore the Hindu religion is from God, because it is from the Sanskrit." Again he said, "I do not believe in all the Hindu deities, there is but *One God.* You Christians say that Jesus Christ is God, if so, you make two Gods, I say there is only one God." Bâl Mukand replied, "God was manifest in the flesh, and Jesus revealed the *one* God to us. We who believe in Jesus are the children of God." Govind Rām at once replied, "If you are the children of God, so are we the children of God. If Jesus was a Son of God, we are also sons of God." Bâl Mukand replied "Oh! there is a great difference; Jesus was all good, we are all sinful. We are not equal to Jesus, the Son of God." The light seemed to play on Govind Rām's face as he spoke, and his eyes sparkled with intelligence and enjoyment as the discussion proceeded. He pleaded earnestly for the working of God's Spirit in the hearts of all men, and one could not but appreciate his evident sincerity, yet the truth he has grasped is so entangled with error that it is hard to unravel the tangled skein. His view is, "God's Spirit is in all, therefore God is in me, and so I am God. I am a Brahm and need no other God to believe in, for I have God in myself." Thus the Brahman becomes full of conceit believing in his own inspiration and trusting to his own intuition.

We passed on to the Boys' Day-school in Raipur and gave tracts to the children. When a Hindu boy first comes to school he brings with him three requisites, a little wooden slate, a reed for a pen, and a bottle of ink, which is white instead of black, being composed of pounded chalk mixed with water. His father bows to the schoolmaster and says respecting his son, "I give his flesh to you, but I keep his bones for myself," that is "You may flog the boy as much as you please, but there are to be no broken bones." The scholar's first lesson consists in repeating the words *Onam sidhang*, a prayer to the gods, "May I succeed!" and with this prayer for success he commences to climb the hill of knowledge. From the school we passed on to the wheelwrights and carpenters. We sat down on a mound, they stopped us and said, "You must not sit there, that is Rām's house, the house of our god." It was a *chabutra*, about three feet high, carefully daubed over with cow dung in honour of their divinity. One man, a Brahman, was anxious to receive a tract, but would not take it out of our hand lest he should be defiled, so we put the tract on the ground and then he eagerly picked it up. An eclipse of the moon had occurred the previous night, and, consequently, thousands of the people had gone down to the sacred river to bathe themselves. Surrounded as we were with carpenters' tools, probably the very counterpart of those in the carpenter's shop at Nazareth, we spoke of the despised Nazarene, who humbled Himself for our sakes. Before leaving the village we called on Bala Rām, a wealthy brother-in-law of the patel.

As we told him of the love of God he pointed to the Hindu temple and said, "I like to *see* God. There is my god, I cannot see your God;" and then turning with a sneer to Bâl Mukand, he said, "you were a Brahman once, but you have changed your religion." I explained to Bala Rām that the people of England were at one time idolaters and had changed their religion and become Christians. I reminded him that when a foreign prince once had an audience with Queen Victoria, her Majesty handed him a Bible and said, "This is the secret of England's greatness." Our bullock tonga rested for us in a grove of mangoes surrounded with bamboos and palms, and on regaining it we struck across the country to Jhasalpur, starting groups of monkeys and birds-of-paradise on our *kutcha*, or second-rate, track. The Patel of Jhasalpur died four weeks ago, and his family gave us a cordial welcome. He had been often visited by members of the Mission, and died calling upon the name of Jesus Christ.

At the first Monthly Meeting for church affairs after my arrival, the catechist informed us of a fakir in Jerrapur in the Bhopal State who was reading Christian books, and we concluded to visit him. On the Bhopal side of the Nerbudda we found cocoanuts, and wheat, and bales of Manchester goods, *en route* for the interior. Numbers of bullock-carts, with two quiet patient bullocks yoked to each, were waiting for freight. Men were bathing in the river, and women washing clothes. Here a bronze-coloured Brahman with his *jamjam*, or Brahmanical thread, and his brass *lota* has just been performing his morning ablutions in the sacred river, and as he passes us he mutters incessantly the name of his god "Rām, Rām, Rām." Three fine elephants under the trees belong to the Begum of

Bhopal. The fakir's house stands on the left above the river. We walked up a rough staircase to find shelter under his verandah, and there he lay asleep, for he had been on the Hoshangabad side of the river during the night. When he is roused and has regaled himself with his *hookah* we enquire for the books. A mat is spread for us and we sit as nearly cross-legged as English limbs permit. The old man produces a parcel wrapped carefully round with string containing the New Testament and other books he has purchased. They have evidently been read and are well cared for, the binding of one of the books having been scrupulously mended in a land remote from all bookbinders. I remind him that there is but "one way of salvation, not two ways." "Yes," he answers, "a man who says there are two ways is still in uncertainty." My companion explained that Christ is "the Way." "Yes," replied the fakir, as a motley group of men, women, and children climbed up into the verandah and crouched round the wood fire at his feet, "Yes, if I wanted to go to see Sahib Baker at Hoshangabad it is no use to wander about among the hills here, I must cross the river; so Christ is the only way to God. If I do not go to Christ who am I to go to?" Bâl Mukand, the catechist, then took out his Hindi New Testament and read one of the parables, and the fakir followed verse by verse in his own Testament. Samuel Baker urged that we must pray in the name of Jesus. "Yes," answered the fakir, "unless we pray in the name of the Guru it avails nothing." But then he added, "You are a Guru, and this Sahib from England is a Guru." We pointed out to him the utter distinction between ourselves as teachers, and the Lord Jesus Christ. Christ was much more than a Guru, and died on the cross for all men.

A little dirty stone idol stood in a niche of the wall, and a wee lamp was suspended in front of it, where an offering had apparently been made to the god the previous night. "You take a stone," said Bâl Mukand, "and with part of the stone you make a god, and with another part of the same stone you grind your corn, what is the use of such gods as these?" "Well," replied the fakir, "I will make an open confession to you, I am a Christian." At the word of the fakir a man then brought a sword out from the interior of the house, for in this native State the men carry swords when they go a journey, to protect themselves from robbers. Then the fakir showed us a cage full of beautiful little birds hanging above us, and as the men put on their shoes to depart, Samuel Baker tested the fakir, saying, "Will you give my friend this stone idol to take back with him to England, as you say you are a Christian?" He laughed, and the men round him were amused as he replied, "No, I cannot give it you," and so we parted.

Bâl Mukand says, "We cannot make men Christians in one day," and while the fakir evidently understands so much of Christian truth he still holds fast to his idolatrous practices.

We proceeded to the shop of a *buniya* to buy some "gram," a kind of small grain the people roast like chestnuts, and good eating. For two pice we got as much as we desired.

We passed on to the Gun-jhery Ghât, where there is a little temple by a Banyan tree, and in the village near poles are erected, with flags and inverted earthenware *chattis* on the top, to frighten away the *Bhûts*, or evil spirits, that are supposed to have haunted the place. The people pay much more respect to evil spirits than they do to any good spirit, for "the evil spirit can do us harm," they say, "but what harm can a good spirit do?" In the evening a native thinks he sees something

HINDU BANIYA.

under a tree. He supposes it is an evil spirit, and forthwith a red strip of a flag is put on a pole at the top of the tree to frighten it away. The same signal is often put on a tree where the people perform *puja*, or where they have an idol. Every village has its own god, often consisting only of one or two boulders smeared over with red ochre.

At the river's edge, we find the boat loaded with a company of *hadjis*, pilgrims returning from Mecca. A haggard old woman shouts out "Unclean! unclean!" as she steps on shore. A babe, a fortnight old has been born on the miserable voyage home, and just as in the days of Moses, the mother is supposed to be ceremonially unclean for forty days; and this old woman, taking care of mother and child, warns us lest unwittingly we become defiled by contact with the poor woman. After a few minutes shouting, the ferry boat is ready for a fresh cargo. I sit on the prow of the vessel, under the shade of a green umbrella, and a sola-topi to protect the head from the sun. The topi is invaluable to the European, the pith of the sola tree being an efficient non-conductor of heat. There is water inside the boat as well as outside, but what boots it, with all these brown naked legs that stud the bottom? The native with a *dhoti* round his loins has all the clothing he requires, although if he is a Muslim he probably has a loose *chadar* thrown over his head and shoulders. The coloured horns of the bullocks, painted for the festival, tower up among the turbaned heads of the Hindus—but what now? one of the bullocks does not like his new quarters in the boat, and with one bound is overboard in deep water. The gondola sways about a bit, and the men attach a rope to the head of the bullock to keep its head above water, and the animal has to swim or flounder alongside till we land. The ferry contractor pays government 3,500 rupees a year for his little monopoly, and makes a handsome thing out of it, for there is an abundant traffic, and whatever India lacks, there is no lack of men.

On the 14th December we started for the Birmân méla, one of those great religious fairs that form important episodes in Hindu life. We took our tent and four natives with us, and tent-life in the East has its marked characteristics, enjoyments, and difficulties. We had thirty-four packages when we mustered at the Etarsi railway station. Twenty-seven of these must be labelled for the luggage van. The clerk had to write out each label for Kareli. The imperturbable slowness of these officials is good discipline for a European. I remember a missionary telling our committee in London that a "tropical climate has the tendency to develop the worst side of our nature." The patient spirit that seems so natural to the Hindu is just one of the elements of character supremely essential to a missionary's success if he would exert much influence in India. He must bear all things for Christ's sake, and avoid all *gâlee* and *zabbardast*, or bad language and tyranny.

Railway travelling in India is cheap if people are inclined to be economical. Most of the carriages are crowded with natives. We booked our servants from Etarsi to Kareli, a distance of ninety miles for nine annas each, *i.e.*, for about one shilling.

On arrival at Birmân we took up our quarters for the night at the Dâk bungalow. These Dâk bungalows are provided by Government in lieu of hotels. They consist of a large sparsely-furnished house with a *khansamah*, or head-servant, to wait on you. The last comer has the privilege of turning out the previous occupant when necessary, if the rooms have been occupied for more than two days. They contain two or three sets of apartments on the ground floor, with verandahs in front. In the bedroom there is often nothing but a *charpoy* or cane bedstead and a chair, with a series of Government regulations on the wall, and an adjoining bathroom furnished with two or three *chattis* of water. The charge is one rupee (1s. 8d.) a-day for sittingroom, bedroom, bathroom, and attendance. The attendant gets some profit out of the victuals he sells. The next morning our tent was erected on the top of a hill commanding a magnificent view of the surrounding country with the broad Nerbudda flowing below. Birmân is situated on an island in the river and is held sacred among the Hindus. The fair or méla is spread out on the level sands formed by the overflow of the river. There are some 1500 native tents pitched below us in the valley. These are carefully arranged in streets, and each quarter of the fair has its own characteristic merchandise. There is the magistrates' court, the police tent, the post-office tent, telegraph office, and all appliances for the maintenance of good order. There is real commerce going on the whole day long. The fair lasts for weeks, and many of the tents contain merchandise of great value. There is the buying and selling of grain and farm produce, the annual purchasing of cloth and cotton goods, brass lotas, and the thousand and one oddities of Indian life.

A writer in the *Nineteenth Century* observes:— "Generation after generation has attended them. Hindu or Muslim or Christian the rulers may be, but the *mélas* are still the same, and, looking back into the vistas of vanished centuries, we still see the same crowds, the same devotions, the same amusements, food, clothing, and attendant animals. When Britons were painted savages, it was so, and now that Victoria, Queen of England, is Empress of India, it is so still."

Such an assemblage, from hundreds of widely-spread villages, presents an exceptionally good opportunity for Mission-work. We took our stand in the midst of the fair and sang a hymn. The people congregated, and a chapter from the Gospels was read respecting the young man who enquired, "What shall I do to inherit eternal life?" Samuel Baker followed in fluent Hindi. The crowd thickened and drew closer, listening attentively. There was the tall bearded Afghan from the North, the pliant Madrasee from the South, the proud grey-headed Brahman, the coolies and sepoys, the astute scholar from the city, and the wayfaring men from the villages.

We can always distinguish the Muhammadans from the Hindus; whereas an Englishman has his coat open in front, the coat of the Hindu always opens on the right side, and a Muhammadan's on the left.

Immediately in front of us, high above us, was the White Temple on the sacred island, standing out against the bright blue sky, to our right were the magnificent domes of the Temple of the Rajah, and to our left, across the river, the huge ghât towards Saugor.

Sir Richard Temple observes, in speaking of Indian perception of the beautiful;—"There is hardly, throughout the whole continent, a fine and effective position on summit, eminence, river bank, junction of waters, or commanding point of prospect, which the natives have failed to occupy with some structure."

Hardy, a Madrasee catechist from the Chindwara Mission, now joined us. His work lies among the Gônds. He says, "They are a people easily persuaded, but too readily relapsing into idolatry." Hardy and his companions took eleven or twelve days *en route* from Chindwara, preaching day after day in the villages they passed through. They bring no tent with them and fare simply and humbly. They sleep where they can. Hardy had been sleeping in the Rajah's Temple at the top of the hill where there is an open door for every one.

In a few minutes he is in the midst of controversy. He has attacked the heathen gods by name and has, of course, excited opposition, one answer after another is given with all the vivacity of orientals. Good humour, however, prevails and another Hindi hymn is sung,

> "I heard the voice of Jesus say,
> Come unto Me and rest.."

Jugal Kishore follows. His theme is, "The Hindu gods and incarnations were all selfish ; what they did they did for themselves, but Jesus Christ lived and died for others, even for our sakes." He speaks respectfully and again the crowd press round to hear. The men have garlands of flowers round their necks, others have for necklaces a string of nuts. A young Christian student, with fine figure, gives the concluding address on "Christ the way of life." Tracts are freely distributed and several portions of Holy Scripture are sold. At four o'clock next morning I left for Kareli in a bamboo cart with the "southern cross" shining straight before me in the heavens, but the sun rose long ere I reached my destination.

The Swedish Missionary Society have recently established themselves at Baitool to the south of the Hoshangabad district, under the superintendence of Mr. N. E. Lundborg. They have also missionaries stationed to the east, at Saugor and Narsingpur. The Rev. John Wilkie of the Canadian Presbyterian Mission is at work at Indore, and there are thriving Missions in and around Nagpur. The most important centre to the eastward is Jabalpur. It stands 1460 feet above the sea, has a population of 56,000, and a large number of European residents. It is well laid out with good roads adorned with clumps of feathery bamboos.

On visiting the compound of the Church Missionary Society we had a chat with the native pastor, Mado Rām, and made the acquaintance of Dr. Mendes, a leading solicitor in the town.

A few years ago Major Oldham and a few other Christian gentlemen held a prayer-meeting here on their return from the Allahabad Missionary Conference, praying specially that a Mission might be established in the Nerbudda valley; and that prayer has now been answered.

It was from Jabalpur that Elkanah Beard first made his itinerating expeditions into the villages of the Nerbudda valley in 1871. "At one place," he writes, "I took my stand near the old village priest, sitting on the bank of the Nerbudda with seventeen small idols at his side, sheltered from the rays of the sun by a large umbrella. I was soon surrounded by a strange-looking congregation who were delighted to hear me talk and read, while the old priest sat with a dignified air and apparently stolid indifference as to what was going on until I had nearly concluded. He then suddenly turned to a young priest at his side who was seated in front of the idols and said to him, 'That man is like God.' 'Why? why?' said the young priest in astonishment. 'Listen!' replied the old man, 'his words are full of love, so I say he is like God.' Then he sent his little grandson, and the boy came, and making a low bow, said, 'Please sir, will you give me one of the little books that are so full of sweet words? We never saw any books like yours, and we want one to read at home.'"

At the farther end of the village Mr. Beard found about fifty people sitting at the roadside, who, when he drew near, at the beck of a Brahman, all rose and saluted him, and the Brahman, on behalf of the company, then said: "Peace be to you, God bless you." Then bowing at his feet, he asked for each of the company a little book that was full of good words. As we visited the empty bungalow, surrounded by bamboos, where Elkanah and Irena Beard resided, we could not but long for more such labourers to evangelize the thousands of villages still unvisited in this great valley.

Having some hours to wait for a train, we visited the Marble Rocks. These rocks form a deep gorge of solid white marble, eighty to one hundred feet high, between which the Nerbudda forces its way. Hiring a boat, we plunged into this giant solitude. The blue sky above, the tall wall of white marble on both sides, carved into fantastic forms by the force of the water, and the depth below us, all tended to impress the mind with solemn awe, and as the men rested on their oars, not a sound was to be heard save the screech of some wild bird that was startled from its haunts. The boatmen tell imaginary stories of the visits of the gods, and elephants transformed to stone; and the grotesque outlines of the marble give force to fancy, and make it easy for imagination to carve out the forms of other worlds. But there is some self-asserting life above us. Dense black masses lie encamped under the white slabs of nature's architecture. They are huge hives of bees, three to four feet long, pendant from the solid rock. These bees are not to be trifled with. Some time ago, a party of gentlemen were shooting, and disturbed them; they attacked the man nearest at hand, and so stung him that he plunged into the water to escape; as he rose to the surface, they attacked him again, and he lost his life. Under other ledges of rock close by is an assemblage of round swallows' nests, neat and well arranged row upon row, as if they lived under good magistracy. There are also king-fishers and rock pigeons and teal, all at home in the solitude. Here and there we are startled by the splash of a fish, and as we round a corner, a huge crocodile lies full length on the shore. Is he asleep? No. As the boat makes towards him, he takes one plunge into the depth and is seen no more. On landing, a walk through the rough jungle takes us to the Badaghir Waterfalls. We pass the hut of some Hindu recluse, who chooses to live in sound of the perpetual roar of the waters, and then springing from one rocky ledge to another we are at the edge of the fall, and see the Nerbudda pour over the precipice into the white foam below.

There are large coal-fields and iron ore between Jabalpur and Hoshangabad. The Warora Colliery alone yields 40,000 tons of coal a-year. Thus, whether we regard the mineral wealth of the Central Provinces, the magnificent rivers and their tributaries, or the tropical fertility of the soil, there is scope for indefinite development and enterprise, while the great village population presents an abundant field for the Christian missionary.

CHAPTER VII.—AMONG THE MARATHAS.

"Thou canst not gather what thou dost not sow,
As thou dost plant the tree, so will it grow."

Code of Manu.

As soon as the festivities of Christmas were over, I started for Nasik, in company with my friend Samuel Baker. The "Nasik Boys" are well known in connection with Dr. Livingstone's expeditions in Central Africa. It was here that the Rev. C. P. Farrar lived, and wrote many of the beautiful native hymns that are to-day in use in the native churches, and Canon Farrar, of Westminster, was born at Nasik in the midst of foreign missionary enterprise. The Mission is really located about a mile out of town, at the Christian village of Shâranpur, or "City of Refuge." The Marâthas are a fine, strongly-built race, who lived for generations by plunder, exacting "*chout*," or revenue contributions, from the farming population, and for centuries were the terror of Western India. In the midst of the Marâthi population are the Mângs and Mâhars, who rank low in the social scale. Many of the converts of the Church Missionary Society around Nasik are from the lower castes, and form a body of Christians rather peculiarly difficult to elevate. At Shâranpur there is a congregation of about 300 persons. In the village there is a Training Institution, an Orphanage, a Poor Asylum, an excellent Library, and Schools. The boys work on a large

H

farm belonging to the Mission, containing a vineyard, an orange grove, and sugar-cane and guava plantations.

Aurangabad, 120 miles from Nasik, is another important station of the Church Missionary Society, with some 300 members enrolled, mostly gathered from the Mângs.

A Christian Festival or Conference for the whole of the Marâthi Church Mission was in session when we arrived at Shâranpur on the 28th December, and many of the native converts from Aurungabad, and other stations, were present. At eleven o'clock the Conference was opened by the Rev. H. C. Squires, of Bombay. Mr. Carss gave an address on Unity, observing, "We object to the Pope, but we may sometimes get a notion of our own infallibility, every man acting as though he himself was a pope; this is dangerous to unity and to our own welfare." Several of the native brethren followed. In England it is often hard to get converts to make an open confession, but it is comparatively easy for Eastern races to speak fluently of what they feel deeply. What is needed is that they learn to speak wisely and concisely, and conferences such as this, in which the meetings are kept in thorough order, are most useful discipline to native preachers and catechists.

We dined with the Rev. W. A. Roberts, at the Mission House. The Bishop of Bombay, Major Jacobs, of Poona, and others, were with us. Major Jacobs is the Inspector of Military Schools for this Presidency, a staunch teetotaler and an active Christian worker. It is heart-cheering to see so many Government officials in India devoting themselves to the welfare of the natives. The amount of genuine hard work many of these men do shows that they are not only able administrators, but conscientiously endeavouring to study the true interests of our Indian Empire.

Mrs. Roberts says that the Mâng children are dull scholars, and unreliable, and are always below the Brahman boys in mental power. Mr. Roberts has the oversight of the Orphanage. It is entirely supported by separate funds, and not by the funds of the Church Missionary Society. The Orphanage is conducted with rigid economy, the children live very simply and work hard. Mr. Roberts observed to me, "It would be a great mistake to spoil them for the position they will have to occupy in after life." The girls make the clothes for the boys as well as for themselves. "I do not think it will be the fault of their training," added Mr. Roberts, "if they fail to turn out the good industrious housewives we hope to see them."

I had some conversation with the Bishop of Bombay on the desirability of introducing the Bible into the Government Schools, but he says it is a question beset with difficulties. Another of our companions at the same table was Ruttonji-nowraji, a converted Parsi, and now pastor of the native church at Aurangabad. Ten of his catechists and native helpers were with him at the Conference. At my side sat a German missionary, the Rev. J. G. Deimler: He regards Wurtemberg as a centre of religious life, especially Stuttgard. He has been in the mission field since 1855. His present work is among the Muhammadan population in Bombay. He finds it very hard to win converts from among the Muhammadans, but works with a brave heart and true faith. His wife has forty houses among the Muslims open to her visitations.

Although the Church Missionary Society has worked here so long, there is only one native Christian family in the town of Nasik, among a population of 30,000 people. This one family is that of the catechist who has been placed there from Shâranpur. I went through the Christian village and visited some of the cottages. The village system has some advantages, but it is doubtful whether the plan of isolating a Christian community in this way is altogether the best for promoting independent vigour and healthy development. The work of the Church Missionary Society is genuine and thoroughly evangelical. They work in excellent harmony with other Societies, and economically husband their resources.

Nasik stands on the Godavery, and its rocky bed and banks are the scene of a fearful amount of gross idolatry. The whole place is the object of the most superstitious regard of Hindus. As I passed one idol sanctuary after another, it might seem as though their motto was, "Vice is godliness," the Linga being everywhere to be seen. Mr. Baker assisted in preaching to the people in the open air at the crowded Ghâts of the Godavery, while a clever Hindu was preaching in favour of Hinduism at a short distance. It is rocky ground to work upon, but as the Church Missionary Society observes, the cave-temples of Ellora, cut to the depth of 80 to 130 feet, and carved with such care, are a fit emblem of the patient labour now needed in hewing out a living temple for Christ amid the hard prejudices and caste systems of the proud Marâthas.

The last day of 1880 found us housed at the Mission-house of the American Board at Ahmadnagar. This Mission was commenced in 1831. Dr. Bissell met us at the railway station, and gave us a hearty welcome. Dr. Fairbank, who has been at work here for thirty-four years, was also staying at the Mission bungalow, though he resides at

Wadale, where he superintends the country work. "When I reached Ahmadnagar in September, 1846," he says, "and saw it from the hillside, I thought there was little hardship in settling in such a beautiful spot." Dr. Fairbank has the joy of a man who is in his right place. With regard to the spiritual welfare of his own children in America, he said, "It is more to their advantage that I should be here than there."

The pastor of the native church, the Rev. Anaji Kshirsāgar, is entirely supported by the natives. The success of the work has been largely owing to their system of working the country districts. As Dr. Bissell says, "The Hindus love to go in companies," and whole villages seem preparing to receive the truth. Bible-women are actively employed both in the city and the surrounding villages, and Mrs. Bissell has fifteen Bible-women under her oversight.

The native members have been carefully trained in systematic giving, and the Marâthi congregations contribute from 1500 to 1600 rupees a year for church purposes. Even the children in the schools give their mite toward the support of their pastor. They put some of their daily portion of grain into what they call "the pastor's vessel;" two girls collect this and sell it, and at the end of each month give the money to the church treasurer. There are now 153 villages where converts reside, and the native churches form an ecclesiastical union. These native church councils work vigorously. Some time ago, one of the pastors forsook the Mission and joined the Society for the Propagation of the Gospel. At the end of a year he was anxious to return to his former home. The American missionaries received him, but not so the "Aikya," or Native Church Union. They said "No, he forsook his position from unworthy motives, and he must be suspended for one year from the pastorate." Another pastor was suspended by the "Aikya" because he married a person they thought unsuitable. Another pastor, a Brahman, of the name of Ram Krishna Modak, came to the Church and said he had been troubled in mind because some years ago, when he was a schoolmaster, he had obtained money under false pretences by passing boys in one standard, and then sending them to change their clothes, and presenting them again for examination in another standard. He publicly made restitution of forty rupees he had thus obtained.

Dr. Fairbank seldom finds among new converts that deep conviction for sin which we look for among converts in America and England. Conviction for sin is largely a question of religious teaching and training under the influence of the Holy Spirit, and such conviction developes in the Christian character in after years. A much clearer understanding of what sin is, comes as light increases, and it is a great mistake to judge of a man's sincerity or ripeness for admission into membership by any European or American theological barometer. Dr. Fairbank says it is commonly the affections that are influenced in the first place, and that just as it is the intensely strong family feeling of clanship in India that so commonly influences men's motives in other respects, so it is the *love* of Christ that wins the convert, and as the convert learns to love Jesus, because He first loved us, the basis of a true religious experience is formed. I asked whether the line of thought that President Finney advocates in his *Lectures on Revivals* was the best line of thought in dealing with the natives of India, namely, enforcing the subjection of the will. Dr. Fairbank answered, "No, though of course the will must be subjected to Christ in every conversion, it is not at this point that you specially need to impress the mind of the Hindu in the first instance. The English and the Americans are a strong-willed race, and it is on the question of the surrender of their will to Christ that their conversion commonly depends, but the Hindu is different. He is easily persuaded. His will-power is weak. He naturally yields to the impress of a master mind. It is therefore better to secure his affections and preach the *love* of Christ." "Such deep contrition for sin is rarely seen among the Marâthas as we find exhibited among those who have known the Bible from childhood. A convert's knowledge of doctrine may be very limited, and yet he may be a true Christian. If there is evidence of a change of heart, his ignorance ought not to debar him from the Church. Native church members will often judge more correctly of the character of a candidate for church membership than the missionary. Coming as the missionaries do from a country where there have been so many master-spirits of theology, they may too much distrust native experience, where *love*, *consolation*, and *joy*, are out of proportion to *conviction*. But a more careful perusal of the history of the primitive Churches and the Epistles of John, in connection with the manifestation of God's grace in oriental converts, brings us to the conclusion that true piety, in some of its beautiful developments, may exist with either form of experience."* But this brings us to another important point, and that is the absolute necessity for holiness. One missionary after another says that the great trial of his life in India is, not the isolation from home joys, but the disappointment often experienced in the lives

* Report of American Board.

HINDU PEASANTS.

of converts. The same thing constantly comes to the surface in the missionary experiences of the Apostle Paul when dealing with new converts from heathenism. Hence it becomes a matter of intense importance that the standard of conscientious conviction in the native Church be steadily maintained.

Year after year of patient toil will help to set right that which is wrong. Delinquencies become fewer, the light shines brighter, the witness for Christ is freer from blemish. And the line of action usually adopted by missionaries in India respecting delinquents appears sound and scriptural. It is a great mistake to suppose that true charity consists in ignoring the sin. While the object in view is the restoration of the offender, sin must be witnessed against, that the standard of holiness may be upheld.

The villages we saw in this district, consisting of a few square heaps of mud with flat roofs, present a miserable appearance. More than anything else they are like the "Dirt Pies" that the juveniles of England are pleased to spade together in their seaside holidays. Round a group of these mud houses the villagers of former times have erected a mud wall to defend them from the Pindari robbers who infested the country. The Pindaris exercised a kind of wild rule, and in the midst of the village there is often one square heap of mud stronger and higher than the rest, in which the robbers formed a sort of citadel, where they could deposit their ill-gotten booty. Near the village wall there is usually an open staircase, forming a 'Look out,' where a man stood and warned the people of the approach of an enemy. From village to village Dr. Fairbank and his teachers wend their way. One morning he had baptized twelve converts in one village and in the evening arrived at another village where seven more awaited him. They happened to be mostly women, and had probably never seen a white face before, and were consequently very shy at the approach of Sahib. They were however persuaded to squat on the floor, and the native catechist, instead of commencing with any theological formula, began by telling the story of a Swiss mother who rescued her child from an eagle. The women soon forgot their shyness in their awakened interest, and Dr. Fairbank followed, "I had a mother once who loved her boy. I was her firstborn, and when I was a little boy, my mother gave me to the Lord. When a young man in Illinois, I went to her and told her the Lord called me to be a missionary to the heathen. She loved her boy very much, yet she did not hinder me, but said, 'Go, and the Lord go with thee.' I came to India, and for more than thirty years I have been trying to persuade the people of India to love Jesus, and this evening I am come to baptize you in His name, and my mother would be very glad if she could see her boy among you. You are to become with us like one family, and to try and help each other." The women had lost their timidity, they quietly and modestly lifted the veils that covered their heads, and the missionary poured water on them in the name of the Lord.

The bell now sounded from the chapel of the American Board, calling the people to the Watch Night service on the last day of the old year. At nine o'clock in the evening from two hundred and fifty, to three hundred people were gathered together. No missionary faced the meeting, and the service was conducted for three hours in excellent order by the native Christians. Anaji Kshirsāgar presided, and the interest was well sustained throughout.

Although the converts are mostly from among the Mahârs, there are many fine men among them well qualified for leaders. They have risen to office by the suffrages of their fellow members, and I was struck with their open countenances, their dignified bearing, and governing faculty. Long prayers were avoided, a large number took part, vigorous Marâthi addresses and hymns being freely interspersed. At eleven o'clock a native hymn was struck up, accompanied by a drum and triangles and cymbals, after the fashion of the Hindu *Kîrttan*.

The *Kîrttan* is an old national mode of impressing religious truth, or historic fiction and poetic romance. A *gosavi*, or religious teacher, celebrates the praises of some god in a kind of chant, with the aid of three or four musicians and singers, who join him vociferously in the chorus. It is partly didactic and partly song.

In 1862, a young native Christian poet, of the name of Krishnarow, introduced the *Kîrttan* at Ahmadnagar, chanting a narrative of the Man of Sorrows in native poetry. The plaintiveness of the native *gîts* or songs tells with force on a responsive audience, and it has proved a powerful means of evangelizing the masses. It is in thorough accord with the national tastes, and large and attentive audiences are easily secured.

As midnight approached, Dr. Bissell was asked to speak. He concluded with a thrilling address on "Time past, present, and to come," and the whole audience bowed their heads in prayer, as the great Father in Heaven ushered in the New Year.

Mrs. Bissell has an excellent school for girls. New premises are now in course of erection, and the work has not only taken firm root, but is spreading to the right hand and the left. The compound of the American Board is within the city walls. Adjoining it, just outside the city boundary, are the premises of the Christian Vernacular Education Society. This Society is working in thorough harmony with the American Mission, and in the absence of Mr. Jas. S. Haig in England, Dr. Bissell was acting as superintendent in addition to his other duties.

This Society was established in India in 1858, as a memorial of the Mutiny, and as such is a beautiful monument of the Christian spirit of forgiveness. The institution at Ahmadnagar contains forty-four students.

Another active Christian agency in Ahmadnagar is the Society for the Propagation of the Gospel, under the superintendence of the Rev. T. Williams. The work is not much developed in the town, but in the villages a large number of schools are established. We spent a pleasant evening with the missionaries of this Society at the bungalow of the Rev. T. Williams and his wife, with the Rev. Percy Ellis and Mr. King. They publish a monthly periodical in Marâthi, called *Prakashah*, or the *Enlightener*, which they sell to their catechists and native teachers, or "masters," as they style the men who act in the threefold capacity of schoolmaster, preacher and pastor.

Once a month, Mr. Ellis and Mr. Williams gather these men together, and thoroughly catechise them on the different articles in the *Prakashah* of the previous month. Thus the *Enlightener* becomes a text-book for the instruction and education of the native agents, and the articles in it are written with this object in view. The principle of thus stirring up the teachers to the constant acquisition of knowledge has an excellent effect on them, and prevents them from settling down in a spirit of self-satisfaction at their former attainments. This is equally necessary for the missionary. If he does not study he stagnates. "If he rest satisfied with what he has attained, he will, in a land where the tendency of everything is *downwards*, become mentally impoverished, and lose the power of production."*

Mr. Williams is an enthusiastic Sanskrit scholar, and we were not long in his house before he produced the bulky volumes of the *Rig-Veda*, the *Mahâ-Bhârata*, the *Rāmāyana*, and the *Sakuntalā*. It is doubtful how far the masses of India are affected by a dead language like the Sanskrit, but as Norman McLeod observes, "In that language the Hindus produced an heroic and philosophic poetry centuries before the Christian Era, a language which scholars tell us is the fullest, the most flexible and musical in existence, to which Greek, although its child, is immensely inferior ; a language capable, as no other is, of expressing the subtlest thoughts of the metaphysician, and the most shadowy and transient gleams of the poet." The oldest hymns of the *Rig-Veda* are supposed to date from 1400 years B.C.

The *Rig-Veda* consists of ten books containing 1028 hymns, *veda* simply meaning sacred knowledge. Thus we have from the same root the Hindu *veda*, the Latin *videre*, and the English *wit*, wisdom. As early as 600 B.C. every verse, word, and syllable was carefully counted in the theological schools of India. Many of the authors imagined that they received divine help and inspiration in their utterances. "O God, have mercy. Give me my daily bread," says one of these poets. "Sharpen my mind like the edge of iron. Whatever I now may utter, longing for Thee, do Thou accept it ; make me possessed of God." These Aryans of the East who

---

* Professor Christlieb on Foreign Missions.

drove the aborigines to the hills, are the same race as ourselves, and like our own forefathers they worshipped the sun and the moon, the storm-cloud and the dawn. In the *Vedas* we have, it may be, the very thoughts of our ancestors three or four thousand years ago. Once in the end of the æons they meet, and the Aryan of the west rules the Aryans of the east.

In these early writings the unity of God is proclaimed, "There is in truth but one Deity, the Supreme Spirit, the Lord of the Universe." With this truth was inculcated the worship of the powers of nature, but the gross idolatry of the present day is of later date.

If history repeats itself, does not deep answer to deep in the intuitions of east and west? The Brahman has the same notion of infallibility that many others have assumed, though differently expressed. Has not the Brahman a scripture and a language, even Sanskrit, which he believes to be God-given and inspired? He may be unable to explain even his own *Gāyatrī* but it is enough to him that it was given of God. The *Gāyatrī*, from the *Rig-Veda*, which the Brahman repeats 3000 times to obtain freedom from guilt, is as follows:

> "*Tat Savitur varenyam bhargo devasya dhīmahi,*
> *Dhiyo yo nah prácodayāt.*"

> "Let us adore the excellent glory of the Divine Author of life,
> May He enlighten our understandings."

Hinduism is spiritual Pantheism. It supposes that God may manifest Himself variously, in the rainbow, in the dawn, or in the storm-cloud, and thus God is in every thing, and in one sense the Hindu will say, every thing is God. Most educated men among the Hindus regard the names of Brahmā, Rāma, Krishna, and Siva as convenient symbols for different manifestations of the One Supreme Being.

But the practical outcome of it all is a grinding priestcraft and despotism on the part of the Brahmans, and a degrading idolatry among the masses of the people.

These missionaries all speak of the utter weariness of Sanskrit literature as a whole, that though here and there fine thoughts find expression, the student must wade through page after page of the trivial and the commonplace to find thirty or forty lines of really fine poetry or sound philosophy. Mr. King thinks that much that we find in our English translations from Sanskrit is the result of the free and poetic rendering of clever scholars. But the historic value of such a language, as a permanent record of the thought and life of millions, is unquestionable, and its intrinsic beauty must ever command admirers among those who have more leisure for study than usually falls to the lot of the missionary.

On New Year's Day, 1881, we reached Poona, and were welcomed by the Rev. John Small, of the Free Church of Scotland Mission.

"We have nothing very great to show you," were the words of this unassuming man. A large proportion of the native population of Poona are Brahmans, and the converts of the Free Church are from all classes and castes, high and low. "It is easy to get preachers, it is hard to find pastors," is the experience here as elsewhere. Many of the converts are willing to speak, but few are really qualified for the responsible charge of congregations. As years run on and the work developes, the quality of labourers improves.

At seven o'clock on Sunday morning we made for the Free Church. The house was full of natives, scarcely a seat vacant from top to bottom, and the boys and girls seated on the floor to the right and left of the preacher's desk. This church has recently received a whole family of Jewish converts, first the father and daughter, and finally the mother and two other daughters.

As soon as the service concluded, a Sunday School commenced in the same room. The girls from Miss Bernard's Zenana Mission were present, and the children from the Boy's and Girl's Orphanages of the Free Church. The native boys had their round heads carefully shaven, except a little tuft of black hair left on the top. Each boy has a printed text in Marâthi given him, which he is expected to repeat the following Sunday. In the adult class there were gentlemanly-looking Brahmans, with their red and white turbans, ready for an argument, and quick at repartee, yet courteous and naturally polite. Alongside, on the same forms, were Jews and Madrasees, old men with spectacles, young earnest enquirers, and established Christians. One of them, a Beni-Israel, began questioning me about the Christian Jews in England, "What do they do when they become Christians?" The man was evidently thinking of coming out boldly as a Christian himself, and he wanted to know about others of the same kith and kin. The teacher did not sit down to teach as in Sunday-schools in England, but stood the whole time while his adult scholars were sitting round him. The lesson was from "Little-faith" in *Pilgrim's Progress*, first, how Little-faith got into unnecessary trouble because of his lack of faith; secondly, how a little true faith is far better than none at all, and that Little-faith was right at last because he had *some* faith in the Lord Jesus Christ. As the good Scotch minister gave two or three vivid illustrations from life, the faces of his scholars shone with pleasure, and as he asked one question after another they fairly laughed with glee, as they saw how much they themselves were like Little-faith. The heathen would not venture inside the building, but were listening attentively outside at the windows, and seed thus sown may spring up after many days.

In the afternoon we found the Mission Room again crowded, and there were six baptisms at the conclusion of the service.

In the evening we attended the English service in the Scotch church. In the adjoining compound there is a Girls' Orphanage under the care of Miss Small, who has been working for some time at Chindwárá among the Gônds. Mr. Small has a Famine Orphanage for boys. These boys, with their black hair and faces, and rows of white teeth, are evidently thriving. Their coats are a brown sandy colour, a colour half-way between their dark faces and the mud floor they sit on. As a counterfoil they have rose-coloured buttons, and the costume looks appropriate. These Indian Orphanages are rare specimens of domestic economy. Four walls of sun-dried bricks, and a tile roof with bamboo rafters, provide shelter day and night, answering for school house, roosting place, and play-room. None of the Orphan work is supported by the ordinary funds of the Mission. The older boys work in the printing office, under the guidance of skilled compositors. The Sunday-school children of Scotland have sent £400 for the purchase of new type and machinery to fit up the Orphans' Printing Press, and Miller & Richard have just sent out some excellent machinery.

One room after another of the bungalow has been absorbed by the printers, and Mrs. Small finds all her spare space, even sitting room and verandah, monopolized by Mr. Small's missionary hobbies. It is such men that succeed.

The American Episcopal Methodists have a Mission in Poona, resulting from the evangelistic work of the Rev. Wm. Taylor, who visited India in 1870. The working of these Missions is different to many others, the settled aim of their organization being to work in the first place among the European population, and to form an English-speaking congregation. Each of these English congregations is to support its own pastor. A nucleus thus formed, is itself to become an agency to reach the outlying masses of the people, and with a view to develope the largest amount of indigenous help, it has been resolved to accept no aid from foreign missionary societies, and it is hoped that in due time native churches will be organized on the same basis. To use the words of Dr. Thoburn, "The result of this policy has not thus far fully met the expectations of those who inaugurated it, yet it has been sufficiently encouraging to comfirm our faith in its final success." Their pastor in Poona is the Rev. W. E. Robbins, from Indiana, who is endeavouring to leaven the European and Eurasian population with Christian influences.

A large number of Eurasians reside in most of these Civil stations, and naturally look to the English for support and sympathy. Sir Ashley Eden observes, "The great defect of men thus brought up in India is the want of self-reliance, self-dependence, and a certain hardness of character that we may call backbone." This by no means applies to all the Eurasians we meet, and many of them are now occupying most useful positions in society, yet Sir Alexander Arbuthnot says with some justice, that the two defects in the character of the Anglo-Indian are, "first, a want of independence, and secondly, a seemingly constitutional aversion to manual labour." Christian work among them is consequently beset with difficulties. There is undoubtedly wisdom in the aspiration of the American Episcopal Methodists to "settle the business," as Mr. Robbins expressed it, "with the European and Eurasian population first," before devoting their energies to evangelizing the native population. Every missionary who travels in India must be struck with the large number of our fellow-countrymen engaged in railway and Government service, who are almost entirely separated from religious associations.

The Anglo-Indian Evangelization Society is an earnest effort on the part of our own English churches in the same direction. "OUR COUNTRYMEN IN INDIA; what anxiety do these words express in the hearts of many Christian fathers and mothers, sisters and brothers," who have relatives scattered in different parts of that great empire. "Thousands of them are absolutely destitute of religious associations. Their interest in religion declines, they influence each other injuriously, and become an element of danger among the native population."*

Our countrymen in India marry, and from the necessities of the case, often marry half-caste women or Eurasians. Their children, with weaker bodies and less elastic minds, cluster round centres like Poona, looking for education, for employment, and for help. It is essential to the honour of the Christian name that they should be Christianized, but it is found that the work among them, to be efficient, monopolizes the energy of the worker, and the missionary is able to do but little in evangelizing the heathen. "To every man his work," is the motto of our Lord and Master, and it is a mistake to

---

* Appeal of the Anglo-Indian Evangelization Society.

expect any one man to do every kind of work. Dr. Thoburn of Calcutta, is an exceptional man, and he very rightly sums up the history of the Episcopal Methodist Mission in these words, "The claims of the purely English part of the Mission absorb most of the time of the missionaries, and hence some of them have done nothing in a direct way among the heathen. Meanwhile a native church is slowly growing up, and the proportion of native to English members steadily increases from year to year."

In Poona we attended the native Marâthi service of this Mission in the verandah in front of Mr. Robbins' bungalow. A young catechist took the direction of the meeting, and expounded the 10th chapter of Luke. My companion, Samuel Baker, followed with a discourse in Urdu. The congregation was small, and the work is in its infancy.

Miss Bernard's Zenana Mission and Orphanage is a thriving undertaking. She has from thirty to forty native houses thrown open to her visitations, and has continual opportunities of making fresh acquaintance among the native women.

In Poona the native gentry do not maintain *purda*, that is, the seclusion of the ladies of the household, so rigorously as in the north of India, and only the Muhammadans and a few high families strictly observe it.

The system of employing native Bible-women does not answer so well as among more agricultural populations. Only native widows and married women can be employed. These are apt to be indolent unless carefully superintended, and very few native women have the necessary qualifications for gaining access to the higher class of native ladies.

The girls in Miss Bernard's orphanage clustered merrily round us as we examined their cook-house where the dinner of curry and rice was being prepared, and the little stone mills on the floor where the girls grind the corn. These mills, with the upper and nether millstone, are easily turned by hand, and have been in use in the East for thousands of years.

Last, but not least, of the missionary enterprises we visited in Poona was the Free Church Institution, or Scotch Mission Marâthi School for the education of the upper classes of boys. Nearly two hundred young men and Brahman boys here receive a good education. The school is in the old palace of the native chief, Phadke.

The whole district is surrounded with traditions of Marâtha warfare and conquest, and this fine old residence abounds in beautiful carving and panelling. The central courts are open to the sky, and are environed with a labyrinth of rooms where Phadke maintained his wives and suite. These are now converted to holier purposes, and form excellent class-room accommodation, where Sanskrit, algebra and mathematics are taught by experienced masters. From the flat roof there is a fine view of Poona and its suburbs. At the appointed hour, the whole of the classes filed off from the class-rooms to the central hall, with its ebony columns and decorated ceiling. The order and precision with which each took his allotted place spoke well for the directors of the school. The teachers are orientals, many of whom have matriculated. They are for the most part Marâtha Brahmans, and walk every man of them like a prince. Very few of these teachers of secular subjects are Christians. In this princely hall Phadke held his *durbars*, and now we gathered in the name of the King of kings to a Christian *durbar* to hear the Gospel. Phadke himself probably never had more high caste Brahmans ranged around him than were now gathered before the Christian teacher to hear the message of God's love to man unfolded from the Scriptures. As I watched the fine intelligent countenances of these young men who must soon take leading positions in native society, I rejoiced that Christian love had devised a plan for systematically giving them, day by day, the glad tidings of great joy.

It is by a great variety of methods that the missionary enterprise in India can alone be accomplished, and we act unwisely if we attempt to compare one department of service with another to the detriment of either. Rather may we admire the way in which different men by different means are working in the same great conflict of light with darkness, and knowledge with error.

INDIAN WATER CARRIER.

CHAPTER VIII.—AMONG THE TELUGUS.

> "Be patient if thou would'st thy ends accomplish,
> For like to patience there is no appliance
> So effective of success."
>
> *From the Kirātārjunīya.*

ON bidding farewell to the Rev. J. Small, at Poona, we providentially met in his parlour an Oxfordshire man, the Rev. James Smith, of Belgaum. He was going to Cuddapah, where the Annual District Conference of the London Missionary Society was about to hold its session, and invited us to accompany him. It was six years since Mr. Smith had attended one of these district conferences, and such gatherings are a great refreshment to isolated workers. As we ran south, catechists and native helpers were on the platforms at the stations with words of greeting, and before we arrived at Cuddapah both sides of our railway compartment were occupied with missionaries eagerly comparing notes and making enquiries, and as lively as a lot of schoolboys let loose from school.

Mr. Smith's work is among the Kanarese, and no true conception of Indian Mission-work can be formed without a careful study of the absolutely distinct races and languages of India. The language map at the commencement of this book may give some idea of the distribution of these peoples of many tongues.

We find, for instance, that there are about 180 million Hindus in India, over 51 million Muhammadans, and, including Roman Catholics, about 900,000 professing Christians. But the Hindus speak various languages in different districts, and the Muhammadans are not confined to any one part of the country. About 100 millions speak Hindi and Urdu, 36 millions speak Bengâli, 16 millions Punjâbi, 15 millions Marâthi, $14\frac{1}{2}$ millions Tamil, $15\frac{1}{2}$ millions Telugu, nearly 10 millions speak Kanarese, 7 millions speak Gujerâti, nearly 4 millions speak Malayalam, and one million Santâli. There are ninety-eight different languages spoken in India, not including the dead languages, such as Sanskrit and Pali, or the intrusive languages, such as English and Arabic.

The Kanarese work of the London Missionary Society was commenced at Belgaum, in 1820. They have now 241 native Christians, four Vernacular boys' schools, and an Anglo-Vernacular high school, containing 547 scholars.

Mr. Smith had to travel thirty hours in the mail cart to get from Belgaum to Poona, and all night and the next day to reach Cuddapah.

The line runs through the recent Indian Famine districts and we saw the villages in ruins, whose inhabitants had died of starvation. But now we passed through abundant rice fields, and the fire flies were darting through the air from bush to bush.

The Telugu language is the Italian of the East, liquid and melodious, abounding in vowels. Many of the villages in this wide district are becoming Christian, and it is the village work that is especially prosperous. There is no limit to its expansion, except the lack of men and means. One missionary told me that out of forty villages asking for help he was only able to supply six with teachers, and yet these teachers require but some six or eight rupees a month, with the rice the villagers provide. The teachers do not learn English, and are only taught the rudiments of knowledge. The entire character of the population is very simple.

In accord with Bishop Patteson's motto, "That only is to be changed which is incompatible with the simplest form of Christian teaching and life," and it would be a mistake to introduce among them European customs alien to the needs of their country.

We breakfasted with the band of missionaries at the Rev. J. R. Bacon's beautiful bungalow. The two patriarchs of the company were the Rev. Benjamin Rice of Bangalore, who arrived in India in 1836, and the Rev. Joseph Coles of Bellary, who came out in 1843.

One of our companions was Mr. Edwin Lewis of Bellary. Half of the Bellary district is Kanarese and the other half Telugu, so that the missionaries have to work in both languages. Mr. Lewis has been very successful and persevering in his itinerant work. "Some years ago," he says, "I was itinerating in a remote part of my district, and to my astonishment in one village called Bookapatnam, in the Pennakonda Taluq, I found a number of people who were holding meetings, reading the Scriptures together, and praying, but had never seen a Christian missionary. A young man of that village of the name of Seeta Rām had become possessed of a Bible which he had read diligently himself, been converted to Christianity by its perusal, and had then read to his relatives and neighbours. Seeta Rām, after some months, fell ill and died rejoicing in the consolations of the Gospel. His little congregation consisted of his mother, his wife, two men, and two women of very respectable position, and several boys connected with the family. I could not send them a catechist, but took them into my tent and encouraged them all I could. The unaffected way in which every one of them spoke of 'our Father in Heaven,' of Jesus as 'our Saviour,' and of the Holy Ghost as 'the Comforter and Teacher,' shewed that flesh and blood had not revealed these things unto them. I saw them afterwards and found they were still holding their meetings and growing in grace. I had further conversation with them and at last asked an old man of the name of Mullapah about baptism. 'What do we need to be baptized for?' he replied. 'We have Christ. What does the Bible say about baptism? We find a good deal about it in the history of John the Baptist, but what is John's answer when he is questioned? 'There cometh One mightier than I after me, the latchet of whose shoes I am not worthy to stoop down and unloose,' and then he contrasts his own baptism by water with the baptism of Christ, saying, 'I indeed have baptized you with water, but He shall baptize you with the Holy Ghost.' Seeing then that we have Jesus Christ, why should we go back to the baptism with water?'" Mr. Lewis concluded not to press the matter further, and the little band went on searching the Scriptures and learning. But Mullapah was visited with heavy affliction. His house was burned down. The Brahmans told him it was a curse on him because he had forsaken the gods of his fathers and was worshipping a strange god. He stood firm and bore their taunts patiently. A second great trial came. His wife died. This was a great blow to him, and again his Hindu neighbours taunted him saying, "It is because you have changed your religion." He replied, "I will still trust in the Lord my God!" A third time he was visited with affliction. His eldest son died. This well nigh crushed him. He could not face the taunts of his neighbours. He shut himself up in his house, and would let no one see him. At last after many days he ventured into the street. In the bazaar he was met by a young woman who belonged to their Bible-class, and she said to him, "Mullapah, where have you been? we have seen nothing of you for days. Are you going to give up your God now? Do you not remember the last lesson you gave us in the Bible out of the book of Job, how God permitted Job to be sorely tried, and to lose one thing after another so that his wife said to him, 'Curse God and die,' and Job held fast his integrity, and was not forsaken, for God gave him a greater blessing than ever before?" Mullapah raised himself upright, and with his hand stretched up to heaven exclaimed, with reverent faith and joy, "Though He slay me, yet will I trust in Him." And thus the little band of Bible readers at Bookapatnam still holds on its way, and forms an out-station of the London Missionary Society.

In the afternoon, pastor Mason introduced us to several of the native Christians at their own houses in Cuddapah. There are three hundred converts in the town, and some three thousand to four thousand in the villages round. Two fresh villages were received last year, sixty-nine persons being baptized on one occasion and seventy on another. The Rev. Edward Porter was formerly at this station, and is still spoken of in terms of intense affection by the natives. "He was more than father to us," they said, with tears in their eyes. His portrait hangs on the walls of their little cottages, with portraits of Moody and Sankey, the Queen and Prince of Wales. "Where is Mr. Porter, now?" I enquired. Their hearts were full as they laconically replied, "At Reading, Berks."

The Rev. E. Porter, during his thirty-three years

of active service, had many experiences of the development of the village work at Gooty, Nundial, and elsewhere. He spent twenty-three years at Cuddapah.

Many of the converts were from among the Mâlas, but not so with all. The first seed of divine truth sown in the village of Velavely was a tract, left by a catechist in the hands of a Sudra weaver, and another tract left in the hands of a smith. Both read the tracts carefully, and were convinced of the folly of heathenism. They also read them to their neighbours. They came to Dhúr and asked for a teacher. One of their elders at last came forward and said to the villagers, "Come, let us pull down our dumb idol which we have served in vain so many years, and embrace the new religion, which shows us our sins and the goodness of God in sending a Saviour who came and gave His life for sinners." The people pulled down their stony god, it now forms part of the wall of their new schoolroom, and forty of the villagers were received into the church at one time.

Another native pastor, of the name of Moses Williams, joined us as we walked to the bazaar. He resides in the country to the north of Cuddapah, and has three hundred native Christians under his care. He spoke feelingly of the large number of his flock that had died of famine and cholera. In the bazaar preaching we had a Telugu congregation of at least two hundred people, and S. Baker addressed the Muhammadans in Hindustani.

Perhaps no work of late years among the Telugus has more remarkably developed than the Mission at Ongole on the east coast, and I had the privilege of making the personal acquaintance of that veteran missionary, the Rev. Dr. Lyman Jewett, of the American Baptist Telugu Mission, and hearing from him some details respecting it. He landed in Madras in 1849, in company with Mr. Day, *en route* for Nellore. For five years they worked amid discouragement. A deputation visited them in 1853, but had little to report of success, and the committee in America was well nigh ready to give up the Mission altogether. The Rev. J. L. Burrows, however, pointing to Nellore on the map compared it to a "Lone Star" in a dark land, and the Rev. S. F. Smith caught up the words and put thought into verse.

> "Shine on, 'Lone Star,' thy radiance bright
> Shall spread o'er all the Eastern sky ;
> Morn breaks apace from gloom and night,
> Shine on, and bless the pilgrim's eye.
>
> "Shine on, 'Lone Star,' till earth redeemed,
> In dust shall bid its idols fall :
> And thousands, where thy radiance beamed,
> Shall crown the Saviour Lord of all."

In 1852, Mr. and Mrs. Jewett made a tour in the villages round Ongole. On New Year's Day, 1853, before the sun was up, they ascended a hill with three companions, where they had a magnificent view of the surrounding country. There they each prayed to the Lord to send a missionary to Ongole. That prayer was answered twelve years afterwards by the arrival of the Rev. J. E. Clough.

In 1862, a resolution was again urged for abandoning the Telugu Mission. Mr. Jewett was then on his way to America, and the corresponding secretary said, "Let us wait and hear what brother Jewett has to say on this question." When Jewett was asked respecting relinquishing it, he replied with an emphatic "No, the Lord has much people to be gathered among the Telugus." The secretary replied, "Well, my brother, if you are resolved to go back, we must at least send some one with you to bury you." But now the light was breaking. Four converts were baptized in 1862. The first of these was a Mádiga, at Ramapatam. He has since been ordained and preaches in Telugu. He cannot read, but knows much of the Bible by heart, and has been the means of very many conversions.

In 1868, the Church numbered 148, and from that day forward there has been a constant increase. Dr. Jewett tells me that for many years, in the Nellore District, there was an average of fifty baptisms annually. These converts were mostly from the Mádigas, or shoemakers' caste, and the Málas.

Some have supposed that the recent great accessions are the result of the famine, but when carefully examined it is evident that there has been a great and genuine work of the Lord. The origin of the revival was before the famine came. Since 1866 the Gospel has been preached in almost every village and hamlet in the Ongole field. Thousands of Bibles, New Testaments, and Scripture portions have been annually put into circulation, but the relief works of 1876 and 1877 had undoubtedly an important bearing on the movement. For the purpose of finding employment during the famine for those who were able to work, the Rev. J. E. Clough took a contract to cut three-and-a-half miles of the Buckingham Canal. This brought thousands of coolies from all parts of his Mission field. The *gumastahs* who overlooked the work were his preachers, teachers, and colporteurs. These gathered the people in the evening and read and conversed with them concerning salvation. The coolies were frequently changed; and after earning a few rupees returned to their villages and others took their place. Thus for six months thousands were brought under the influence and teachings of Christianity, most of the time under the direct superintendence of the missionary. It was a grand opportunity, and God blessed it. For fifteen months all applications for baptism were postponed. But when the relief work was for the most part completed, the missionary felt he could no longer reject those whom he believed God had saved. He commenced baptizing on the 16th June, and by the end of December in the same year had received on profession of faith in Christ 9,606 converts, making a total membership in the church at the end of 1878 of 12,804. A few have gone back to heathenism, some others may be nominal professors, but the missionaries give clear testimony that for the most part the converts are standing firm. They have seventy elders or lay preachers at work in the district. These elders receive nothing whatever for their services. They are volunteers and pay their own expenses, and are entertained by the people at the native houses as they itinerate. There are now more than fifty native preachers and 17,000 church members.

The Americans aim steadily at the self-support of their native congregations. "I have seen a tree at Boston," Mr. Jewett observed to me, "with props to keep up its branches, and many Mission churches are very much like that. What we want is to train the native churches to stand alone. I came from Maine, where they saved twenty-five million dollars in one year by prohibition, and all our converts are expected to be total abstainers from all intoxicating liquors." The following is the Church Covenant adopted by the churches of the Telugu Baptist Mission on this subject: "We covenant with each other to abstain from all intoxicating liquors, and from the use of narcotics, such as bang, hemp, and opium, except as medicine. We will also avoid theatrical amusements, dancing, cockfighting, and gambling. We will not go from house to house talking against our neighbours. We will abstain from filthy language, from immoderate anger, and from quarrelling. We will not eat food offered to idols, or carrion."

Dr. Jewett is now engaged in the revision of the Telugu New Testament, and in the translation of the Old Testament from Hebrew into Telugu, and in grey hairs rejoices to see the aspirations of his manhood crowned with success, and the patient labour of faith abundantly rewarded.

HINDU SERPENT CHARMER.

Chapter IX.—Among the Kanarese.

Most fatherly of Fathers, we are thine,
Thou art our Guardian, Advocate, and Friend ;
Oh, let Thy pitying soul turn in compassion,
And slay us not for one sin or for many,
Deliver us to-day, to-morrow, everyday.

From the Védas.

The Rev. James A. Vanes of the Wesleyan Missionary Society, met us at Bangalore station on our arrival, after a long ascent from the plains. It was refreshing to breathe again the air of the hills. Bangalore is a lovely and invigorating residence for Europeans. The Annual Conference of the Wesleyan Missionaries of Mysore was in session, and afforded us an excellent opportunity of mingling with them, and understanding their work in this large native state.

Mr. Vanes is the superintendent of the High School at Bangalore, and has 407 boys under his charge. The Rev. Henry Gulliford, another Somersetshire man, has charge of the High School for boys at Mysore City, with 300 pupils. At the Mission-house the Government maps were spread out upon the parlour table, and these men, as they clustered round, pointed out the many different centres of operation which the Wesleyans are occupying from one end of the province to the other. Kanarese is the language of the people. The Rev. H. Haegh, who was one of our party, has been diligently itinerating in the north-west of Mysore during the past year. He takes with him a catechist, a colporteur, and a servant. His bullock tonga is unique. It has an expanding roof, which enables him to use it like a tent. He lives, sleeps, eats, drinks, and travels in his tonga. He finds many signs of vitality in the village churches.

The senior missionary in Bangalore is the Rev. J. Hudson, of Westmorland. He has charge of the Theological Institution, and is chairman of the Wesleyan Mysore District. Their entire native membership contributes at the rate of one and a half rupees each annually towards the funds of the society, and it was pleasant to see the collection made morning and evening at their church services in true Methodist fashion. There are 2000 children in the Wesleyan day schools in Bangalore, and 5000 in the whole province. At eight o'clock on Sunday morning we attended Kanarese service in the *Pettah*. About 200 were present, including the native pastors and catechists, and the Kanarese orphan girls. At eleven o'clock we were at the Tamil service in the cantonment, an English service being held close by at the same hour in the Wesleyan Chapel, which is attended by many of the English troops. There are 115 men in the barracks who are declared Wesleyans.

The Tamil service was conducted by the Rev. D. Manuel. About 200 Tamils were present, including the orphan children. Mr. Manuel, who is the native pastor, took for his text Psalm xlv. 10th and 11th verses, "Hearken, O daughter, and consider, and incline thine ear, forget also thine own people and thy father's house. So shall the King greatly desire thy beauty, for He is thy Lord and worship thou Him." It was an Oriental text, such as these fluent Orientals appreciate. Manuel handled it with his whole soul. The men and women sat on different sides of the house according to Eastern custom. The tall bamboos were swaying gently to and fro with the wind outside, and Manuel swayed his audience throughout, rivetting their attention. Not half-a-dozen Europeans were present, and these orderly native congregations, under entirely native management, are a fine witness to the conquering power of Christ in leavening the hearts of all men into one church with one accord.

Mrs. Hudson has eighty-two Kanarese orphan girls under her care. The children sang to us a native lyric, "The call to repentance," and the Kanarese translation of the hymn,

> "There were ninety and nine that safely lay
> In the shelter of the fold;
> But one was out on the hills away,
> Far off from the gates of gold."

The Rev. A. T. Riddett and his wife have another vigorous orphanage for famine children at Hassan, and thus the Wesleyans have shown themselves ready to meet emergencies, and to throw themselves into the breach wherever a great need constituted a divine call. Mrs. Riddett explained to me that when a child has suffered from famine, and taken to eat roots and rubbish, there is very little chance of its life. Some will even swallow clay at the roadside to stay the cravings of hunger. They may live on for six months, or one or two years, with their large heads, large stomachs, fearfully thin legs and arms, and hollow sparkling eyes, and then they die. This makes the famine-orphan work very trying. Mr. and Mrs. Riddett are wise kind people, but out of 490 famine orphans they have received at Hassan, 340 have died in two years, and they had 150 remaining in January, 1881.

At half-past four in the afternoon I went to the chapel of the London Missionary Society. Again the minister was a Wesleyan, Mr. Wesley Samuels.

Only three Europeans were present. Mr. Samuels took for his text, "What think ye of Christ?" He had caught the fire of the early Methodists, and it would have done John Wesley's heart good to see the flame burning brightly among these swarthy sons of the tropics. It is quite possible for a missionary society to try to cover too much ground, and to "occupy" too many stations. It is much better to work systematically within a given area, and to do the work well. The area must bear some relationship to spiritual and numerical strength, and it is better to do as the Wesleyan Missionary Society is doing in Mysore, take up one district and endeavour to work it thoroughly, than to be dotted about hither and thither in a great empire like India, squandering resources and occupying more ground than can be efficiently worked. The principle adopted by the missionary societies in India is a very important one, for each society to work its own ground.

I was pleased to make the acquaintance of the Rev. Job Paul, the native pastor of the London Missionary Society. He is a many-sided man. He does a little watchmaking, a little photography, and a good deal of evangelistic work; and with his three undertakings provides a very comfortable dwelling for himself, with the tall plantains clustering round his home. He is also an author. That he does not neglect work may be seen from the fact that in one year he sold 2,495 Scriptures and 20,589 tracts, which must have cheered the heart even of Dr. Murdoch, the great book evangelist. As Mr. Paul reviews the present development of the native church in South India comparing it with the pioneer difficulties of half a century ago, he exclaims, "Blessed are the eyes which see the things that ye see, for I tell you that many prophets and kings have desired to see those things which ye see and have not seen them, and to hear those things which ye hear and have not heard them."

Bishop Cotton's large Schools for European and Eurasian boys and girls are also at Bangalore, the boys under the care of Dr. Pope, and the girls under the charge of Mrs. Smith. The aged Rev. E. Marsden occupies the Baptist Chapel with all the enthusiasm of youth. He knows no such word as retirement in his vocabulary, and intends to die at his post.

In giving some account of Miss Anstey's FAITH WORK AT COLAR, I adopt the name Miss Anstey has appropriated, and her work and modes of work justify her in adopting it. She is a woman of mental power and extraordinary energy, and is probably better adapted to work alone than in conjunction with any committee ; but there is abundant room in the Lord's wide field for all. The words "Have faith in God" might fitly be inscribed over the portals of her Orphanage, as on Dr. Cullis's Consumptive Hospital in Boston. Faith, however, knows no monopoly. Dr. Miller among his students in Madras acknowledges his to be essentially a work of faith. Miss Bernard in her Zenana work among the women of Poona goes forth in faith. Dr. Murdoch with his books and tracts and colportage is engaged in faith-work ; and it is by faith that Mr. Lewis of Bellary with a joyous heart itinerates the country and preaches in the open-air.

Out of a population of five millions in the Province of Mysore one million died of starvation and consequent disease during the recent famine. Twenty-four to twenty-six bodies were picked up morning after morning on the Bangalore roads. Relief works, and the Mansion House fund, and the distribution of rice were organized later on through the benevolence of the British public, but all came *too late.*

Miss Anstey has thrown her doors open for the admission of every child however far gone in famine. "I am always hungry for children," was one of her first remarks to me, "but I never ask any one on earth for money; if we have not a cash left we ask God, but we do not make our wants known to man." Miss Anstey has received 1,400 destitute children into her orphanage. Of this number about 1,000 have died, a few ran away, a few others left from various causes, and she has now 330 under her care. She has received "unasked," from the Mansion House fund 10,000 rupees, from the Chittur famine fund 5,000 rupees, and again from the Mansion House fund another 1,000 rupees. The cost of an orphan child is about £3 a year, or 36 rupees, and the Government at one time were offering a certain amount per head for each child sheltered, which the Wesleyans and other missionaries accepted, but Miss Anstey would never ask for this capitation grant as she desired to rely wholly on the Lord.

There are two farms on which the boys work, containing some eighty acres; one is called Bethany, and the other Nazareth, and a great deal of interest centres in these farms. "Our strong boys are away on the farm," was Miss Anstey's reply to me. Six couples of her young people have recently been married, and we saw two of the young brides. The present well-arranged group of buildings is near the mud ruin where the first house stood, in which the great battle was fought with hunger and disease in the crisis of the famine. It was a house altogether unsuitable for such a mass of suffering humanity. Miss Anstey's neat little bungalow stands on a separate plot of ground. The orphanage costs a thousand rupees per month; the children have two meals a day. We saw them sitting in rows in their playground, with their tin plates or bowls, partaking of their red pepper-water and rice at five in the evening. Each boy had a large ball of cooked rice and a ladleful of pepper-water out of a pail that stood by. Miss Haynes, Mr. Kirk an American, and others, help in their departments, but Miss Anstey has had considerable difficulty in obtaining efficient assistance.

After visiting the children's quarters we all met in the Central Hall for prayers. Over the entrance were the words "God is love," and "The blood of Jesus Christ His Son cleanseth us from all sin." The boys were ranged in rank before us and the girls to our left-hand, the little ones in front, the older in the rear. Some of these little ones have been baptized in the river as converts, and I have no doubt many of them are true Christians. There is a strong religious atmosphere present. But it is painful to see ranged together such a mass of sorrow and child-suffering as stood represented in that hall by those groups of thin children with famine-fashioned limbs. An experienced doctor as he passes through a crowd of these famine orphans will tell by their very look, "This child will live," "That child will die," "This may recover," and in most cases his verdict will prove true although they may receive kind nursing and good nourishment for months or years.

Miss Anstey believes in the power of healing sickness and disease by faith and prayer, yet this does not forbid the use of means, for true faith consists in the use of appointed means, and Miss Coleman, who is a believer in homeopathy, has the care of the Children's Hospital.

But now Miss Anstey is at the piano, and the hundreds of child-voices join with hers in singing in Kanarese,

> "The Great Physician now is near,
> The sympathizing Jesus;
> He speaks the drooping heart to cheer,
> O hear the voice of Jesus."

The sun was shining brightly without, but there had been little sunshine in those young lives so prematurely old. One of the boys of the name of Enoch gave a Scripture exposition in Kanarese, and the children listened to the child-sermon attentively. It was a genuine children's service, and the love-song of Christ's presence seemed hovering over them. We bowed in prayer, but who prayed? Hundreds of young hearts. But who uttered those words of prayer that rose from that assembly? It was the children themselves, first in low tones very humbly, and then waxing bolder as they proceeded. One boy after another prayed, and then two or three of the girls. These children a year or two ago were heathen, now they are Christians. They have a weekly prayer-meeting of their own as well as this daily family prayer. But what are their prayers about? Just such things as they need. Sometimes Miss Anstey's exchequer runs short, and the prayer to their great House-Father is for rice. But when I was there they were praying that an opportunity might be given for presenting the Maharajah of Mysore with a copy of the Holy Bible. Yes, God hears the prayer of famine-stricken orphans, not selfish prayers, but for the prince who rules the millions of Mysore; and He that is no respecter of persons, has royal answers to His children's cry. Men may criticise such work as this and think they discover faults, but the Lord is with it and is able to make it stand.

As I leaned back in the coach kindly sent to convey us to the railway station I turned in thought to the 11th chapter of Hebrews, to the glowing list of men and women of faith. I remembered how some were called to leave home and kindred and sojourn in a foreign land, and through faith obeyed; others by their faith laid hold of means and wrought mighty deeds. It is not for us to draw comparisons between one class of the Lord's workers and another. All are of God. Whatsoever is not of faith is not of God.

INDIAN CONVEYANCE.

EASTEKN JEWS.

CHAPTER X.—MALABAR.

> "Return unto thy Home, O soul! Thy sin and shame
> Leave thou behind, refined
> And from all taint of sin set free."
>
> *From the Védas.*

ON our journey to Beypoor we found ourselves in the company of a Syrian Christian from Malabar, of the name of Potham, and we soon made friends. These Syrian Christians dwell on the south-west coast, and profess to have received the Gospel from the apostle St. Thomas, about the year 70 A.D. There is a considerable colony of black and white Jews living in the same district, and our companion told us that every Saturday these Jews meet together, and look up to heaven, and pray for the speedy coming of the Messiah.

The Syrian Christians were evidently on the Malabar Coast at the time of the Council of Nicæa 325 A.D. Cosmas of Alexandria found them there in the 6th century. Our own King Alfred, in the 9th century, sent an embassy to visit the shrine of St. Thomas in India. The Romanists tried to persuade them to join with Rome in 1599. The cruel inquisition was established among them, and a wholesale burning of Syrian manuscripts of the Holy Scriptures took place, and their bishop was burned as a heretic at Goa, in 1654.

In 1661 the Dutch took Quilon, and the Church was again free, and there are now 335,000 Syrian Christians in Malabar and Travancore.

As we approached the coast, the exuberance of tropical vegetation was exquisite. The railway passes under the spurs of the Nilgiris, among which Ootacamund lies nestled, and we swept past groves of date and areca palms, sugar palms, and cocoanuts. Tree ferns, with their lovely fronds, grow on the embankments, and plantations of cinchona on the hill side for the production of quinine.

There are no less than 1,718,185 cinchona plants growing at the present time on the Nilgiris. These plantations stand as a living monument of the untiring skill and perseverance of the late Mr. MacIvor. On the heights of Dodabetta one hundred and fifty acres of cinchona now gladden the eye, while along the Nedawathun slopes two hundred and eighty-four acres have been brought under cultivation. Here the jungle has disappeared, and in its place are miles of long and regular rows of cinchona trees. Another successful plantation has been opened near the Paikava Falls, while far away to the westward on the Kenidah Hills two hundred acres are already planted, and much land is being cleared for the extension of this cultivation. Of the eighty-five persons who purchased land under the waste land regulations of 1863, fifty have undertaken the cultivation of cinchona. The first batch of seed, being of the grey bark, reached Ootacamund early in 1861, and this was closely followed by a consignment of red bark seed. Quinine is so essential in India to assist in withstanding the periodical attacks of fever, that we may rejoice when the wilderness and the solitary jungle are thus converted into the fruitful garden and plantation. The people offer us fresh cocoanuts and pine-apples in profusion. They have jet black hair and hardly any clothing except a white cloth or *dhoti* round their loins. When we arrived at the terminus on the coast, we found ourselves jostling in a crowd of Malays, talking Malayalim. Five stalwart copper-coloured men seized our luggage, put it on their heads, and at the one word "Calicut," took us to a boat. Two more extemporized a sedan chair with their arms, took possession of me, and carried me into the water, two others courteously treated my companion in the same fashion, amid a storm of voices and shouting the baggage was safely deposited, and in about two minutes our boat was pushing off from shore, while a hundred natives stowed themselves in other boats to our right and left.

The boat was urged forward with two primitive paddles, moving like a duck's wings when it tries to fly fast, and a third broader paddle was worked in the rear of the boat in lieu of rudder. On one side lay the wide ocean towards home, with the setting sun playing on the breakers as they rolled in, and on the other hand we looked up the estuary to forests of palm trees at the water's edge, many of the trees eighty feet high, loaded with cocoanuts. In the foreground were boats loaded with fragrant spices, manned by nearly nude sailors. Higher up were the distant coffee plantations of Coorg and Mysore.

On landing, a bullock-coach conveyed us through the woods. The men carry umbrellas made of leaves, and the women have broad sunshades fastened on their heads instead of hats, so that their hands and arms are at liberty to carry the luggage for their husbands. We drove seven miles along a red road, the whole distance lined with a dense mass of palm trees, a thriving population walking to and fro, and every policeman under orders to touch his hat and salute an Englishman.

A hearty welcome awaited us as we entered the compound of the Basle Mission at Calicut, and ascended the steps to their comfortable bungalow. We were not long in learning to appreciate our kind host, the Rev. Julius Knobloch of Baden. The missionary society with which he is connected has more than one hundred missionaries at work in China, India and Africa. As early as 1834 they sent out three men to the Malabar coast, among whom was the well-known Hebich, a man endowed by the Spirit of God with an extraordinary power for winning souls. He was the Moody of that day. At Cannamore he produced such an effect on one regiment of soldiers, that every officer in the regiment became a devout Christian, and the regiment was named "Hebich's own." On one occasion, when the Bishop of Madras was passing through the place, he dined at the mess. At the close the officers proposed that the Bible should be brought, and the Bishop was requested to conduct family worship, which he cheerfully did, but said it was a thing he had never been asked to do before.

One day when Hebich came home from a large fair he remarked, "They tried to put me down to-day. A man on an elephant tried to ride me down, but I had a long stick and stood my ground." Years afterwards, a Brahman in Travancore applied to a missionary for Christian instruction. "What led you to think of Christianity?" enquired the missionary. The Brahman replied, "One day I went to a fair, there was a missionary preaching. They tried to ride him down with an elephant, but he stood firm, and I thought there must be something in that man's religion." Of course, such men prosper, and the Rev. E. Schrenk told us at the Mildmay Conference in London, that they have now between 6,000 and 7,000 native Christians in connection with their work in India, besides very many others under instruction for baptism, and 2,654 pupils in their schools.

As we sat down to dinner at the Mission-house, a group of Christian Malayan girls gathered in the dusk of the evening, under the mango trees, and sang to us in English the old missionary hymn,—

> "From Greenland's icy mountains, from India's coral strand,"

and in that land of spicy breezes we realized as never before, the words

> "In vain with lavish kindness the gifts of God are strewn,
> The heathen in his blindness bows down to wood and stone."

One part of Calicut is practically inhabited by Christian families, and the Mission has considerable estates, and rents land to the native Christians. Calicut is so named from the "crowing of the cock." A former king of Malabar, Seramen Perumaul, concluded to retire from the burdens of state and divide his kingdom among his friends. When he had done so, a poor man's voice was heard claiming a portion, reminding the king of services he had rendered. The king listened and acknowledged the cowherd's fidelity, but said "I have now little left, but what I can I give. Take this sword, and with it I give you the title of 'Lord of the Rajahs,' and as much land as a cock in that pagoda can be heard crowing over." The poor man grasped the sword, and took a cock to the pagoda, and its voice was heard over the neighbouring fields. A town was built, and the Zamorin, or Lord of the Rajahs, made great use of his sword in acquiring more, so that for hundreds of years the Zamorins of Malabar were powerful princes in southern India.

A special feature of the German Mission is its industrial work, and in this respect it differs from almost every other Mission in India. To use Mr. Knobloch's words, "We began by employing our converts as coolies on our farms and paying them regular wages, but it did not answer. Many of the converts were out of employ; we did not incline to pay them to be idle, so we commenced industrial work for them, and this was the origin of our tile business."

The Rev. B. Græter mentions four classes of people for whom this industrial work was needed—first, for the apprentices who had been brought up and educated in the Christian orphanages, and with whom it would be a dangerous experiment to apprentice them to heathen masters; secondly, for converts, who often lost their means of livelihood when they made profession of Christianity, or whose previous means of livelihood was unholy; thirdly, for the very poor whose wretchedness excited sympathy but to whom it was unwise to give money; fourthly, for enquirers who wished to place themselves under instruction, whom it would be entirely unsuitable for the Mission to support in idleness.

On the morning after our arrival, we directed our steps to the Tile Works. The clay for the tiles comes from the rice fields which are lowered for the purpose of irrigation. The clay comes to the works in boats, and the Germans pay 12 annas, or 1s. 3d., for a boatload. It lies in heaps near the water side for about a year seasoning, and is not fit for use till the climate has told upon it. Among these heaps we found a palm growing with 132 cocoanuts hanging on it. After the clay has matured during the monsoon, it is broken up again and mixed with one-third sand, and pounded. It is then passed through a crushing mill which breaks all stones and makes it of an even consistency. Thence it passes to a large machine with the interior fashioned like a screw worked by four fine bullocks. The clay is tossed in by a boy at the top

RESCUED FAMINE ORPHANS.

L

and the screw presses it into a compact mass so that at the bottom it is solid and is cut by wires in thin layers ready for the tile mills. Two boys are watching it. Each boy seizes four of these layers as soon as they are the required length, and runs off with them. One man turns the tile mill while two other men are passing in the clay, and with one turn of the wheel the tile is fashioned in the required shape and fully stamped. Other boys are ready to receive these newly-fashioned tiles and rush with them to eight little round tables where each is trimmed after having been oiled.

The people of India believe in oil. The Malabar children are oiled from head to foot, and their copper-coloured skins shine with oil ; and every tile is oiled also.

The tile is then carried by the boys to tiers of shelves to dry in the shade before being exposed to the sun. Here they lie in perfect stillness for six days after all the activities to which they have been subjected. They are afterwards exposed to the sun for two or three days when they acquire colour. They are now ready for the furnace. Huge brick kilns are waiting to receive them. For two days they endure the fire, and then lie quietly for seven or eight days to cool, if cool they can in such a climate. These huge kilns have to be rebuilt once a year, and thus new ones are preparing while the old ones are wearing out with the heat. The kilns are supplied with wood for thirty-six hours after the tiles are put in, but no coal is used. Each tile is so constructed that it will fit in exactly with the tile next to it on the roof, and thus with the Basle Mission tiles no wet is able to penetrate in a torrent of rain. Every tile is stamped "Basle Mission Tile Works." The Mission makes 400,000 tiles a year, sells them at 45 rupees per thousand, makes 2,000 a day, and gets a good profit out of them, besides finding employment for eighty-five persons, fifty-two of whom are Christians and a number of others are "under convincement." "When people come to me and want to be Christians," says Mr. Knobloch, "I send them for twelve months to Mr. Feuchter at the Tile Works," where they remain under the eye and under the instruction of the missionaries.

But this is not all. We pass on to the Mercantile Establishment. Here are two other German missionaries residing with their wives. It is a huge store where they seem to sell everything, from German clocks and drapery down to tea and buttons. It is the most commanding house in all Calicut, looking out on the public tank in the square; and this establishment also pays its own way.

Hard by is the Girls' Day School with 107 children, and the large Chapel calculated to seat 800 people which is being decorated for the honourable reception of their secretary, Mr. Schott, from Europe.

We next drive to the Carpenters' Establishment which is on French territory. Here the Mission Bungalow faces the ocean, and the verandah hangs with festoons in honour of the arrival of the missionary's bride. The said bride appeared on the verandah amid the festoons, and after pleasantly greeting us, disappeared with the words "I do not speak English," and we passed on to the timber yards where teak and rosewood and wendeck lie ready to be carved into tables and chairs. A quantity of attractive-looking furniture awaits the Indian public; and twenty-seven men are at work, twenty of whom are Christians. The same account is given as before, "It pays its way."

Passing along the sea shore, and through the bazaar to the Kinder Garten, we found thirty-four little ones lying fast asleep in rows on mats on the floor. The jet black hair and brown faces do not stir one inch as we enter. The mango blossom fills the air with fragrance. The cacao *(cocoa)* trees are hanging with their rich masses of fruit. The chillies are being gathered, and the coffee bushes have just been cleared of their berries. Below us the pine-apples luxuriate as if they enjoyed growing, and the great " chack " trees overhang us with their odd bunches of huge fruit springing from the main trunk like parasites. We now enter the weaving establishment where thirty-four looms are crowded together and all briskly at work. Here are 127 people in full employment, of whom 121 are Christians, and like all the rest, " the weaving pays." We edge our way from loom to loom, and watch the towels, tablecloths, trowserings, check patterns, and so forth, in the meridian of manufacture. These Germans are busy people, and the proverb in Malabar respecting their work at Mangalore and Calicut is, " What the Germans make, they make well," and consequently they get a good demand for all their manufactures. One secret of their success is that they let a missionary be a missionary, and a merchant a merchant. If the merchant consecrates his trading-faculty to Christ, well and good, only let each man be apt at what he undertakes and not a novice. Put the right man in the right place. This is of course a question of time. It must be perfected slowly, like the Basle Mission tiles, and perhaps some of the initial steps are failures. But it is by our failures that we make a highway to success, and the work of the Germans of Calicut succeeds all round. We rose at four the next morning. The Mission-coach was ready for us, and we passed once more through the dark forest of palms till the glimmering light of the rosy dawn peeped in upon us through the tall stems.

CHAPTER XI.—MADRAS.

> "Revolving in thy mind the certainty
> Of retribution in a future state,
> Be pure in thought, in word, in deed."
>
> *Statutes of Manu.*

THE populations in the South of India are essentially of different temperament to those in the North. They are more settled and contented, and more thoroughly in accord with the English Government. They have been much longer under our rule, and realize the advantage it is to them, more than the vigorous races to the north of the Vindhyas. There is not the same *fear* of the English that we meet with in the Central Provinces, or the same degree of *scorn* that we occasionally meet with from Brahmans and Muhammadans in the North West Provinces.

Madras is very inferior to Bombay in position. There is no efficient harbour, the port is unprotected from the north-east monsoon, and a heavy rolling surf fringes the coast. The city covers an area of twenty-seven square miles, stretching nine miles along the shore. Its present population is 405,948. Our first call was on the Rev. D. Sinclair, of the Church of Scotland Mission. At the disruption of the Scotch Church in May, 1843, all their missionaries in India adhered to the "Free Church," and their converts went with them. The Church of Scotland Missionary Society consequently suffered a temporary cessation, but has since gained ground and they now occupy ten centres and have seventeen European missionaries. Mr. Sinclair's work is to a large extent in connection with higher education.

The Scotch are great educationalists, and in this way reach the highest ranks of native society. While Mr. Sinclair works in connection with the Established Church of Scotland in Madras, the Rev. William Miller is in connection with the Free Church. This gentleman has left his family mansion and estate in Scotland to devote himself to the welfare of the sons of India, and the Christian College is a monument of large-hearted Scotch philanthropy. The Christian College in Madras was commenced in 1837 by Dr. Anderson, and within a year there were 270 scholars. He then admitted two Pariah boys of low caste and the rest of his scholars left in a body. Dr. Anderson was entreated to dismiss the Pariah boys, but he stood firm and gained the victory. By-and-bye his scholars returned, and now all castes sit together at the same lessons. It was a blow to caste prejudices which is felt to the present day in South India.

We found Mr. Miller in the midst of a crowd of attentive students to whom he was talking and giving instruction in that easy way which showed at once his marvellous power of winning boys and control over them. He has about one thousand students in the institution, and is the soul and life of the whole, and the college is manned with an exceptionally good staff of competent professors and teachers. What would not some of the grouse-shooting, billiard-playing gentlemen of England give for the honest joy and pleasure Miller finds in this work for Christ in the tropics! The young men were anxiously waiting the result of their Government examination. Mr. Miller took hold of one young man, and pleasantly catching him by the shoulders, said, "You need not think you have passed." It was a hard saying for the lad, but as we passed on, Mr. Miller said to me, "He is a good young man, but not clever," and the young man looked as though he was ready to try again for another year, or do anything else, if he could only please Mr. Miller. "Where are the naughty boys who came late?" enquired Mr. Miller playfully of another group, and a student who was late once would evidently learn, without punishment, not to be late again. We followed Mr. Miller from one class-room to another commencing with the lower classes of boys to the upper sections for young men that actually constitute the college. There are good lecture rooms, a chemical laboratory, an excellent reference library, and a large lending library. In the registry of the books that the students select for their own reading I noticed that many were books of Bible illustration and exposition. There were comparatively few historical books selected, much fewer than would be the case in England, for the Hindu does not appreciate history as we do, and his own historical records are enveloped in myth, but there was a decidedly large proportion of metaphysical and philosophical works and books of an argumentative character.

Another feature of this college life is that the Hindu develops earlier than an Englishman. He does not pass through the stage of "hobbledyhoyhood" that the young Englishman encounters, or at any rate, he recovers from it earlier. He acquires a suavity of manner and a gentlemanly courtesy that our islanders lack. As some counterpoise to this, the Hindu is "used up" much sooner than an Englishman, and becomes an old man earlier in life, but the young man of eighteen in India is a remarkably promising and receptive scholar. It is doubtful whether he turns out the man of thought that we find in English colleges. The Hindu saves himself the trouble of thinking by his immense faculty of memory. His naturally meditative turn of mind does not necessarily make him an acute thinker. He will learn long passages by heart in a way that would astonish an English boy, but his deductions will often be illogical, and he will not reason accurately. The consequence is that these Hindu students pass splendidly at their examinations and do not expect to fail like English boys, but are unable to make such good use of their learning in after life. A number of boys will give the same answer *verbatim* to an examination question without conniving with each other in the least; but the whole answer has been learned word for word. For instance, the question stands on the examination paper, "Give the history of Luther, Calvin, or Knox," and several boys will give a most complete answer exactly alike. An English teacher would suspect unfair play, but no, the scholars have primed themselves beforehand, and have learned the whole thing ready for the emergency, from a biographical cyclopœdia. They fail to make the men of mark in after life that their college life would indicate, but in certain directions they excel, especially in the law courts, with their faculties developed in the direction of the Laws of Evidence and of Public Enquiry. The Hindu has a great capacity for litigation, and is only too apt to embroil himself in law-suits.

The English student will turn out a more practically useful man than his college life predicated, while the Hindu student will take some subordinate Government employ, and settle down into a very ordinary man.

The affection of these students for Mr. Miller is

something beautiful, yet nothing but the power of God can make them Christian converts. Though only a small proportion of them actually make an open profession of Christianity, Mr. Miller tells me that there is an immense change going on in the feeling of the people in favour of Christianity. I enquired of Mr. Miller what proportion of the scholars were Christians. He replied there were about one hundred Christians to nine hundred Hindus! Who can measure the influence for good exerted upon these nine hundred Hindus as they daily receive systematic Scriptural instruction from Christian teachers in their respective class-rooms? Some may imagine they endure the Bible lesson for the sake of the privileges of the college. On the contrary, Mr. Miller says, "The Bible lesson is one of the most popular lessons we have." It happened to be the hour for Bible study when we visited the college. We entered one class-room after another with Mr. Miller, quite unexpectedly. We found the young men sitting thoughtfully at their desks with their Bibles before them, the teacher sitting below at his table giving the lesson and questioning them on it. In England we may call such men "heathen," but I never saw more reverent attention at a Bible class anywhere, or more complete evidence of sustained interest than in these classes where nine-tenths of the scholars profess Hinduism. But this college has been in operation for forty years, and such results are not attained in a day or two. The present annual cost is about 51,000 rupees. Of this amount 23,000 rupees are contributed by the students themselves, some 7,000 rupees are received by Government grant, and the remaining 21,000 rupees come from home, or by subscription.

Mr. Miller pointed out to me a young Karen

from Burmah, and scholars come from all parts of South India, the Church Missionary Society and other societies cordially giving it their approval and aid. It may seem a bold thing to call such an institution in a heathen land "The Christian College," but such men as Mr. Miller may safely do bold things. The well-known maxim ever holds good, "Christian things done in a Chistian manner will never alienate the people of India." "Above all," as Sir Herbert Edwardes said in India, "we may be quite sure that we are much safer if we do our duty than if we neglect it, and that He who has brought us here, with His own right arm, will shield and bless us, if in simple reliance upon Him we try to do His will."

Mr. Miller's thoughtful testimony at the Bangalore Conference is in these words, "I cannot claim for myself any special faculty for teaching Scripture. Where the teaching is earnest and efficient, there is no lack of attention on the part of students, no unwillingness to prepare earnestly for the instruction, and no lack of interest. To me, at least, the hour when I am most conscious of enlivened thought in those to whom I speak, most conscious of an interest in a subject being awakened for its own sake, has commonly, though not always, been the hour of Scripture teaching." "Looked at in the light of experience, and of the Word of God, higher education is among the most valuable of Christianizing agencies. It is valuable because it has already added to the Indian church some of its brightest ornaments. It is valuable because it will yet add to it many more, a number that will steadily increase as its influence extends. Yet it is only as *one* among many agencies that its priceless value comes clearly out. It is thus that all agencies produce, and are divinely intended to produce, their full effects, *not* as isolated things, but as parts in one harmonious whole."

An important Medical Mission in Madras is under the care of Dr. W. Elder, also of the Free Church of Scotland. He was an active mission worker in the Cowgate, Edinburgh, before he gave himself to medical mission work in India. "I have now over 21,000 patients in the year," he remarked. "We have service with them daily before attending to them at the dispensary. Our hours are from 7 to 10 a.m. We have a girls' school, and teach them to sing Christian lyrics. We get tambourines and native music, and then I have a Poet, who composes native renderings of the Scripture narratives, and we often have 400 or 500 natives listening to them here in Madras. We have an English and a Tamil congregation, with two schools and two native assistants, brave fellows, who assist me. There was a time when I began to wonder what was the use of my work here, and then I took a journey through Tinnevelly and Travancore, and saw the work that was being done there, and came back to Madras with a new inspiration."

The Rev. P. Rajahgopal was a convert of the Scotch Church who afterwards joined the Free Church, and is now pastor of their native church in Madras. He has a congregation of about two hundred people, and, ably aided by his wife, has the care of four girls' schools for caste children, as well as a Ragged School. "Why are we Hindus to pin ourselves to all the divisions of the churches at home?" was one of the pertinent questions he put to me as I sat in his house, and I could only answer "Why? indeed!" Rajahgopal believes with all his heart in independent native churches, and he is equally assertive against the iniquities of caste. He has protested earnestly against the admission of caste prejudices into the church, and there is no doubt that such a protest is urgently needed. With regard to caste in native society at Madras, Rajahgopal says that "Unquestionably caste has lost that rigid and firm grip which it once had. When the system of caste which has for ages held Hindu society together, breaks up, Indian paganism must go with it." Rajahgopal speaks somewhat discouragingly of the present attitude of the educated natives towards Christianity. He says "An utter *indifference* to all moral and religious truth, and an all-absorbing worldliness at present prevail among them. Of late there has been imported into the country a great deal of low and infidel literature, which saps the foundation of all religion. These books are no sooner advertised than they are eagerly sought after and devoured. Some of the educated natives make it their boast that they are infidels and atheists, the disciples of Bradlaugh. If left to their own course unimpeded, they will reach yet lower depths of moral darkness."

With respect to the high-class education in the large missionary colleges, which are affiliated to the universities, and pursue the same curriculum of studies prescribed for university tests, Rajahgopal says, that in not a few cases when students leave the missionary colleges their attitude towards idolatry is one of marked and thorough antagonism. They have completely swept away every vestige of idol worship from their houses, and are found years after clinging to their Bible tenaciously, but the numerical strength of those who have been morally and spiritually benefited is not to be measured by the number of baptisms or public professions. The majority lack the courage to altogether sever themselves from their early sympathies and surroundings. They live false hypocritical lives. There is the fierce struggle between conviction and self interest. It tends to a terrible searing of conscience, and as a final resort they too often sink into Deism or Neo-Vedantism.

The present intellectual and moral fermentation is tending to a general break-up of the system of Hindu life, and then many of the higher classes and their families will readily become Christian professors. "We seem," as Rajahgopal observes, "on the verge of a great crisis in the history of India. Old things are passing away and the nation is in a state of transition. Such a change comes but once in a nation's history, offering alike glorious opportunities of moulding the character of the people, and impressing upon them, while still in a plastic state, the stamp of Christianity."

The Church Missionary Society has an old and well-established Mission in Madras, of which the Rev. A. H. Arden is the Madras Secretary. After calling on him we proceeded to the Rev. W. T. Satthianadhan's, the pastor of the Madras Native Church in connection with the Church Missionary Society. He has about nine hundred members under his care in two congregations, of whom four hundred are communicants. He is supported by his own congregation, but the church that is linked with it still needs help. They have a native church council, consisting of delegates elected by the four native congregations in Madras, with the native pastors as ex-officio members.

In these councils no Europeans are present. The council meets every two months to conduct church affairs. There are schools, cottage meetings, prayer meetings, lectures, and the usual accompaniments of aggressive work. Mrs. Satthianadhan has five high caste schools in Madras under her care, supplied with native teachers, having 450 girls under tuition. She is a welcome visitor in fifty Zenanas, in which she regularly instructs more than 100 Hindu ladies in the Holy Scriptures. As I entered the simple native chapel I found it as plain as a Nonconformist Meeting House in England, and the words are inscribed in large native characters in front of the congregation, "God is a Spirit and they that worship Him must worship Him in spirit and in truth."

After a call on the Rev. George Fryer at the Wesleyan Mission-house, we went to the Memorial Hall, where there is the dêpot of the Madras Auxiliary of the British and Foreign Bible Society. This active organization has no less than forty-five colporteurs engaged in scattering the seeds of eternal truth in the cities, towns, and villages of the Madras Presidency. Some time ago the Madras Bible Society presented Bibles to 150 heathen schoolmasters. For two years no result appeared. At the end of that time the schoolmaster from Kalugu-Mali came with his Bible marked from Genesis to Revelation. He had read it all through. "But," he said, "I find it full of difficulties." For three years a native catechist went with him step by step through all these difficulties. In five years he came out clearly as a Christian and was baptized. He continued as a schoolmaster, and the Hindus had such confidence in his teaching-power that they still sent their boys to his school. He began to preach the Gospel, but would receive no money for preaching. One of his first converts was the leading Brahman of the district, and thus the good work spread.

Large meetings for prayer were being held in the Memorial Hall every night during the week we were

SOUTH INDIA.

there, which was the first week in the New Year. It was heart-cheering to see such large numbers in Madras wending their way to these united prayer meetings. The Week of Prayer originated in India, and marks an epoch in the history of the Church of our times. At Ilkstone in Derbyshire, lived a Christian woman whose son was sailing as a soldier to India. She was poor and gave him a bundle of tracts as her parting gift. A group of soldiers on the voyage met on deck and wiled away the time by reading young Slater's tracts. The truth took hold of their hearts and they commenced holding prayer meetings. Arrived at their destination, they erected a little chapel and worshipped together. Called to separate, they agreed that wherever they were they would, at a stated time each day, pray one for another. Other chapels were built by their instrumentality, and it was from one of the faithful band of worshippers in one of these very chapels that the request went forth for a week of united prayer throughout the world.

Adjoining the Memorial Hall is the large Book Depository of the Christian Vernacular Education Society. The master spirit of this movement in Madras is the Rev. Dr. John Murdoch. He was born at Glasgow in 1819. In 1849 he resigned his connection with the Government schools in Ceylon in order that he might devote himself to the publication of Christian literature, and has ever since consecrated his energy and zeal to this cause. Mr. Murdoch was supported for a time by the Wellington Street congregation, Glasgow, and probably there is no more healthy form of missionary help than for a Christian congregation at home thus to maintain some special work and worker abroad. It forms a close bond of interest between home and foreign work. In 1854 Mr. Murdoch went to India to obtain catechists for the coolies working on the Coffee Estates in Ceylon. This led him to Madras, and in 1858 he became the agent of the Christian Vernacular Education Society, and afterwards of the Religious Tract Society. The former of these societies has now 42 colporteurs who sold 141,656 publications in 1879, including 6,615 Scriptures, and in 1879 the society printed 636,440 copies of 147 Christian publications. The name by which the Holy Scriptures are known through the Madras Presidency is the *Sathia Vedam*, the true Veda.

When we remember that not a Bible was sold in Madras prior to 1809, and scarcely a copy to be found in the city, we cannot but rejoice in the progress that has been made. In 1812, when a missionary landed in Madras, he received an order from the police to quit the country instantly. Now missionary enterprise receives encouragement, is protected by the authorities, and receives thoughtful attention from thousands of the inhabitants.

The Rev. Dr. Chamberlain, in reviewing the work in South India says, "I may not live to see the day, but my sons now in the university preparing to come to India as missionaries may see it, when there shall be organized a 'Church of Christ in India,' not American, not English, not German, not Danish, but of India, and suited to India, in which we shall not see Scotch Presbyterianism, nor English Anglicanism, nor German Lutheranism, but the best features chosen out of all denominations incorporated into one visible church."

Seldom has it fallen to the lot of a city to have such a band of men grouped together consecrated to its highest welfare, as are now found in Madras. Some men may honour the past, others may have illimitable hope in the future, but we do well to acknowledge God's present endowments. Dr. Murdoch for books, Mr. Miller for college life, Dr. Jewett for revival work, Dr. Elder at medical missions, with all the accessories of native churches, mission schools, Bible societies, and Zenana visiting, each running out its solid block-work of concrete masonry, will surely form a compact breakwater of truth to withstand every surf that can beat against it.

The dissemination of a healthy literature is of growing importance, for as Rām Chandra Bose observes, "Young men leave Mission schools not only with a thorough knowledge of, but often with a deep reverence for the doctrines and precepts of Christianity. But their life after leaving school militates against the convictions generated, and they often slide down into the abyss of scepticism, audaciously pointing their fingers upwards, saying, 'There is nothing above,' and forward, saying, 'There is nothing beyond.' The iron conservatism of our country has melted like wax before the onward march of occidental education. Time-hallowed beliefs and long-standing customs, hereditary convictions, and institutions held in superstitious veneration from time immemorial, are being driven as chaff to and fro by forces mightier than any brought to bear on India before its contact with European civilization."

Chapter XII.—Madura.

> 'The Universal Spirit regards no creature with contempt."
>
> *Upa-ni-shad.*

A long railway ride lay before us ere we could reach Mad-ura, and we unrolled our bedding and reposed ourselves. Our companion was a native gentleman in Government employ. I lent him one or two pamphlets respecting the Brahmo-Somaj, but said nothing whatever to him about idolatry, for he would have felt insulted at the suggestion that he worshipped idols. "The whole intelligent and informed mind of India is convinced," said Norman McLeod, "that come what may in its place, *idolatry is doomed.* If a man occupies a position halfway between the valley and the mountain-top, that alone cannot determine whether he is ascending or descending. We must know the point from which he has started on his journey. Thus departing from the low level of the Puranas, the Hindu pupil, who has reached the theism of the Vedas only, has ascended *towards* the purer and far-seeing heights of Christian revelation." Norman McLeod asked some of the more intelligent people at a heathen festival in southern India, "Do you believe in all this idolatry?" They replied, "We do." But from the smile of the man who answered, McLeod judged otherwise, and said, "My friend, I candidly tell you that I don't think you believe a bit of it." He laughed, and said, "You are right, sir, we believe nothing." "What! nothing, not even your own existence?" "Oh yes, we believe that," replied the man. "And do you believe in no existence higher than your own?" again queried McLeod. "Yes, we believe in a great God who has created all things." "But if so, why this idolatry?" "We wish to honour our fathers," was the reply; "we keep up these customs while our people believe in them, yet if you educate the people, they will give them up of themselves, and so they will pass away."

In the course of conversation I asked my fellow-passenger, "Do you not feel the need of a God?" "No," he answered; "my intellect teaches me all I need to know at present; and how can any of us know the future?" I urged that we need a revelation from God, both respecting ourselves and respecting God, respecting the present and the future. "I can write a book," he replied, "you can write a book, or anybody else, but that does not make it a revelation." "But," I again queried, "do we not every one of us recognise in our present helplessness the need for some superior power to aid us?" "Yes," he replied, "there are many who may be above us at present, but the time may come in our development when we may be independent of them all." "But," I said, "we need a God who shall be a Father to us." "We have had fathers and mothers," he answered, "and needed them for a time, but the time comes when we can do without father or mother." "Then you really think you can do without God?" I asked. "Yes," he answered, "I do not feel the need of Him at present, and we can none of us tell what shall be. We have read the works of your Stuart Mill and Herbert Spencer."

"You are a kind of god," said a Brahman to my friend Mr. Baker. "Not so," he answered. "Yes you are," the Brahman replied; "you go into a

SCHOOL.

crowd of people, they make their salaams to you, you can return their salaams or not, just as you please. If I go into the crowd they take no notice of me." Another said, "The reason you have such power is because you were a very faithful worshipper of Rām in a previous state of being." And thus a host of wild opinions contravene the truth of God.

As we swept past the tall telegraph posts made of solid slabs of stone to protect them from the destructive white ants whose hillocks stand six or eight feet high by the road, we could not but long for some solid foundation among these Hindus that might never be undermined and eaten into by all the many-footed imaginations that cast up their earth-heaps against the true knowledge of the Most High. It is no light matter for the thinkers of a great empire like India to be effectually loosed from their old moorings by the inroads of education and to be left drifting about on a sea of uncertainty, but it is better thus than that they should sleep in ignorance, for it is impossible for such a race as the Hindus to remain long in a mere quagmire of negations. They *must* adopt some faith, and having lost all faith in Hinduism, many of them will eventually in all probability accept Christ.

One of the strange thoughts of the people in South India is with regard to the horse sacrifice. A row of ten or twenty terra-cotta horses are seen standing as large as life in a pool of water by the roadside. The people of South India are devil worshippers, and have a dread of evil spirits. They therefore have "guardian spirits," the most popular of whom is Ayenār. This Ayenār is supposed to delight in riding about the country on horses, and in times of sickness and distress the people propitiate Ayenār with the offering of a terra-cotta horse.

The Bishop of Madras was travelling in the same

train with us to open a new church at Madura. He well remembered the visit of Russell Jeffrey and Henry Hipsley many years ago. He enquired about our Missions, and rejoiced to hear of the work in Madagascar, in Syria and Hoshangabad. If one of the characteristics of a good bishop is "distributing to the necessity of saints," the Bishop of Madras is worthy of double honour. A large proportion of his income is consecrated to the Lord's work, and he thoroughly espouses the great missionary enterprise.

As we entered Trichinopoly a dense crowd of people occupied the station, and one of those wild scenes occurred that exclusively pertain to oriental life—the demonstrative mourning for the dead. The European is bowed down with grief and seeks retirement when death enters the house, but the loud wailing of the Asiatic is utterly overwhelming. The beating of the breast, the tossing of the arms in the air, the wail that goes on hour after hour, and the wild confusion, are awful. Trichinopoly is head-quarters of the vigorous Roman Catholic Missions. There are 48,889 Romanists in the neighbourhood; and in South India their number is 1,053,000. In the Pondicherry Vicariate alone there are 100 priests, and 878 priests in the Madras Presidency. They have 40,000 children in their schools, but the Government census report states that "the Christian population is usually badly educated where Roman Catholics preponderate."

Schwartz laboured in this district one hundred years ago, making Tanjore his head quarters. He had been preceded in 1705 by Bartholomew Ziegenbalg and Henry Plutschau of the Danish Mission, who had established themselves at Tranquebar, and who owed so much of their success to the faithful prayers of Francke of Halle.

Much of the blessing that has descended so

abundantly upon the Missions of South India was initiated by these pioneers. They were thwarted continually by the inconsistent lives of Europeans, but their influence was great. Schwartz was the only man whom Hyder Ali, the terror of South India, would receive as ambassador from the English. "Let them send the Christian," exclaimed the Rajah, "he will not deceive us." Schwartz kept back from the din of war and from all political schemes, but when the Government of Madras entreated him to act as peacemaker, he consented.

The Europeans scorned the missionaries, yet in the hour of peril were glad of their help. Schwartz travelled on this embassage from Tranquebar to Mysore, and was well received, and Hyder Ali gave him a special safe-conduct on his return, in these words, "Permit the venerable Father Schwartz to pass unmolested, and show him respect and kindness, for he means no harm to my Government."

But Tanjore was besieged, and the natives refused corn to the English, except for ready money. Supplies were falling short and the money was not forthcoming at the juncture. The British officers came once more to Schwartz in their extremity. Schwartz sent letters by his native Christians to all parts of the country, promising payment for all corn that should be sent in. Immediately hundreds of bullock-carts with stores of grain were sent to the needy city. And thus, as so often in history, the servant of God had more power with men than regiments of soldiers.

At Dindigul we were attracted by the cleanliness and cheerful appearance of several young men on the platform. They proved to be a little band of Christians from Dr. Chester's American Mission. They have 200 members in their church. Some of the more promising students attend the Christian College at Madras.

On arriving at Madura we drove to the American Mission-house, and received a most kind welcome from the Rev. J. Rendall. The missionaries of the American Board in the Tamil country were sitting in council as we entered. Our introduction from Dr. Clark, secretary of the Board in Boston, was read, and Dr. Chester of Dindigul welcomed us to their council. The missionaries all rose to greet us. Here were the Rev. T. S. Burnell of Melûr, J. E. Chandler of Pulney, and his son J. S. Chandler of Battalagundu, G. H. Gutterson and J. E. Tracy of Tirupuvanam, J. Herrick of Tirumangalam, W. S. Howland of Mandapasalai, J. O. Jones of Manamadura, J. T. Noyes of Kodikanal, Dr. Washburn of Pasumalai, and others. All these men are teetotalers, and insist on temperance among all the converts. They have a sanitarium at Pulney where there are three double bungalows for the missionaries and their families. Each missionary can have two months a year at this hill station. Several of these men have been twenty-five, thirty-three, and thirty-six years respectively in active service in the South Indian Mission, and the average length of service among them, including new comers, is $20\frac{1}{2}$ years.

We did not detain the Americans in their council, but drove to the great heathen temple. A visit to this temple conveys a vivid idea of the vitality of heathenism. Madura is the metropolis of South Indian learning and religion, and here we find the masterpieces of Dravidian architecture. The *gopuras*, or gate pyramids, of which there are nine in the monster Pagoda of Madura, are 200 feet high. This huge temple, covering many acres, dates from the 3rd century, B.C. It is dedicated partly to

Minâkshi the fish-eyed goddess, and partly to Siva. Many masons are still at work upon it.

The most elaborate architecture in the world has been raised in honour of the most hideous idols and the most degrading idolatry. The gorgeous architecture is a strange contrast to all European models. There is a broad base, and each storey as it ascends recedes and diminishes, and each is made the opportunity for a profusion of external decoration and fresco modelling, loaded with gold and vermilion, until the twelfth or thirteenth storey rears its pinnacle against heaven. Monier Williams says "The temples at Madura are as superior in magnitude to those of Benares as Westminster Abbey and St. Paul's are to other churches in London." The interior consists of long ranges of colonnades with thousands of hideous idols of Vishnu, Siva, Ganesa, &c., carved on the walls and columns. There is a succession of inner temples where the people assemble for their grotesque worship. But it is in the deep recesses of the temple that the principal idols dwell, inlaid with gold and jewels, covered with gorgeous drapery, amid the flicker of oil lights and tapers, hovering priests, and prostrate devotees.

The arrangement of these temples illustrates one singular expression of Solomon which must have appealed to the oriental mind as it scarcely does to a European—"The Lord said that He would dwell in the thick darkness." It is in the thick darkness that the most sacred gods dwell, while the more Christian thought of Jehovah is, "He dwelleth in the light."

We pass through the idol colonnades to a spacious quadrangle surrounded with porticos, with a large tank in the centre for the sacred bathing.

In one place the horrid idol is being carried

about in a palanquin as though it was the procession of a prince. Some of the idols are clothed like men and women, in other places the stone elephant-god is draped in gay trappings. But here we meet the huge sacred elephant himself with splendid tusks, and tossing his trunk as he strides among the people like a monarch. Hundreds of stone columns are arranged with the most geometrical precision, so that they form a complete series of slanting avenues from all points, centering in the dim recess where the great god dwells. As the worshipper comes up any of these avenues he sees the dim light of the tapers, and faces the idolatrous sanctuary.

Here is the accumulated wealth and art of centuries. In the midst of one avenue stands a golden horse, so arranged that a man could get inside it. The rajahs of South India are persuaded by the Brahmans to present the god with a golden horse or a golden cow big enough for the rajah to go in at one end and out at the other, in order that the rajah may have princely privileges. This is called "being born of the cow," and promotes a rajah to stand in the presence of a Brahman. Sometimes the rajah prefers to weigh himself against gold. He sits in one scale, with his heavy clothes and sword and shield, while the Brahmans receive in the other scale an equivalent weight of gold. If the rajah is a small man they persuade him to give the golden cow, if he is a heavy man they prefer that he should weigh himself with gold.

King Tirumalai contributed perhaps more than any man to beautify the massive temples of Madura. He had spent lacs of rupees on their decoration, but came under Christian influence, and the teaching of some European gained such an ascendency over his mind that he would give no more to the temples. The Brahmans were enraged at this, and came one day and told him that they had discovered a secret treasure-vault under the great Temple of Mînâkshi, which they wished to show him. He went, they took him down into the underground vault, covered it again with a large stone, and left him to die of starvation, reporting that he had been translated to heaven while worshipping the goddess Mînâkshi.

Singularly different in architecture to the Madura temples is the magnificent Palace of Tirumalai in the same city. The lofty pillars round its central court appear to be of European design, but the interior decorations are thoroughly Hindu and Saracenic. The Prince of Wales visited this palace in 1875, and the Government of India is now restoring it to its original splendour. Several of the Audience Chambers are used as Law Courts and Government Offices.

In the course of time we returned to partake of the hospitality of Mr. Rendall and spent a Sabbath among the American missionaries. They say that the natives constantly acknowledge the benefit of English rule. "Fifty years ago," exclaimed a wealthy merchant at one of their meetings, "I dare not travel home out of Madura with fifty rupees in my pocket, now I can travel without fear with 50,000 rupees."

Because of the justice of English rule the natives say,—

"*Sher aur bakrí ek ghát páni píte haìn.*"

"The lion and the goat quench their thirst side by side at the same brook."

That is, the interests of high and low are alike protected.

The native judge, Gopāl-rāo says, "This country for many centuries had no Government deserving the name. There was neither internal peace nor security. There was no power in India which could put a stop to suttee, infanticide, religious suicide, and human sacrifices. But now the case is different. Under the auspices of a beneficent, civilized and strong Government we have become progressive. Light and knowledge are pouring in upon the country, old prejudices and errors are vanishing. We therefore count it a great privilege to be loyal subjects of the Empress of India."

The diminished offerings and lack of reverence to the idol-temples shows the direction in which things are drifting. Formerly as the Brahman passed down the street he was honoured and worshipped, now he is allowed to pass unheeded. We are often told that the Hindu is essentially religious, and if the mingling of superstition and ritual with all the ordinary details of life is religion, then they are doubtless religious; but if the essence of religion is conviction for sin and change of heart, then of true religion they know little. Hence the opposite apothegm is expressed by the Rev. T. P. Jones of Manamadura, "Our chief difficulty lies in the *supreme indifference* of the people to religious things. They do not seem to feel any definite religious wants." Yet the American Mission has been very successful. They have 11,372 adherents, including their vigorous out-stations, with an average attendance on the Sabbath of 6934. They have 340 villages under their care and 126 catechists.

On Sunday morning we attended service at the Eastgate Church, and listened to a sermon by Cornelius on "Behold, I come quickly." In the afternoon Mr. J. E. Tracy took us to the Boys' Seminary at Pasumalai, where a number of the older students are preparing for the pastorate, under the superintendence of Dr. Washburn. I gave them an outline lesson on "Early Christian life at Lindisfarne." The students have twenty little chambers where they can retire alone and study their Bibles and offer prayer. Dr. Washburn has compiled a volume of Native Lyrics, some of which the boys sang to us. One was on Christ, "He humbled Himself to be born among the lowly." Another was a Tamil's appeal to Christ, "Whither, whither, bearing thy cross?" Dr. Washburn has charge of the printing office, and is what the Americans call a "live man."

Mrs. Capron has 370 women in Madura whom she regularly visits at their own homes. Six Bible-women assist her; and she has three high-caste girls' schools under her charge. She teaches no needlework in the Zenanas "relying solely on God's word," and 133 of the ladies she visits are reading the Scriptures for themselves. On entering a Zenana Mrs. Capron thinks "I am a King's daughter; I come in the name of the King of kings." I enquired respecting the conversion of the women. She replied, "We must remember the great natural *timidity* of the people. There may be much true work of the Spirit in their heart that does not show itself in outward profession. The women often make remarks which show clearly the power of God's word upon them. The common way in which the truth operates on their minds is like the first glimmering of light that shines brighter and brighter as they understand more. This light shows itself in a quiet acquiescence to the truth taught rather than in any very deep conviction. An understanding of what sin is comes slowly. My stronghold is God's word. I rely on that for result whether we see result or not. Not long ago I came across an old man at one of the women's houses. He said 'May

BAMBOOS.

not I have a talk with you? Will you not talk to me?' 'Certainly,' I replied; and then he told me that in the year 1829 he had been a scholar in a London Mission school in another part of the country, but had never become a Christian. He however repeated to me one text after another that he had learned in early life. God's word had taken hold of him, and those early impressions had never been lost. He had risen in life and become engrossed in worldly engagements and in his own success; he had aimed at pleasing those above him, and had neglected God. Now he felt a need in his soul that had never been satisfied, and listened to the renewed message of the Gospel."

I asked Mrs. Capron respecting the continuous training of her Bible-women, how far they retained religious life and vigour. She replied, "I find it very much according to myself." If the missionary gets into a stolid routine condition, those who are most closely connected with him will reflect the same mind and tone. Christian helpers will take their cue from his spirit. Those who most loudly deplore the lukewarmness of their flocks will find the fault lies close at home.

Mrs. Capron takes one of the parables of our Saviour and goes round among the high-caste ladies and expounds it to them from house to house. They know when to expect her and are ready for her visit so that there may be no waste of time. She does not ask to have the privilege of visiting a Zenana, but they send to her and ask her if she will be kind enough to come. "Your words make me all aglow," said one of them. Another said, "I am learning to love the Saviour you tell us about." She finds they often repeat the Bible lesson afterwards among their friends with all the animation of a Tamil story. Sometimes the women come from one house to another to hear, and Mrs. Capron stops them, saying, "I am only going to tell these people just the same that I told you the other day." "Yes," reply the women, "that is just why we are come, because we want to hear the same again."

The Spirit of the Lord is similarly at work in the Girls' Schools. Once when the teacher happened not to be at school as early as the girls, he found eight or ten of them had assembled and were all kneeling in prayer while one of their number was asking for Heaven's blessing. "We thought we should like to thank Jesus and ask Him to help us all by ourselves," was their remark to him as they rose from their knees.

One of the means Mrs. Capron has used to win her way and open new doors has been the Medical Dispensary. There she has a room to receive special cases. Muhammadan women and high-caste ladies thus visit the dispensary who would never mingle with others, and she can extend her influence indefinitely. Her testimony is, "I feel it a great privilege to live, and to be allowed to work here for the Master, where there seems no limit whatever to the amount of work that is waiting to be done." The movements of some labourers may attract more attention in our religious periodicals, but it is the quiet steady light that burns year after year that effects so much for the welfare of mankind.

IN THE JUNGLE.

CHAPTER XIII.—THE TAMILS OF TINNEVELLY.

"The turtle swimmeth far to lay her eggs upon the shore,
She buries them in sand and swimmeth back again,
Yet doth her mind adhere to them;
The young ones break their shell and feel that mother's tie.
Her love draws them along their mother's path,
At last they meet. Just so hath God placed us.
We wander here while He is far above,
Yet in His mind we ever stay.
The tie doth reach to earth from highest heaven,
If we but follow it, we cannot fail to reach and live with Him.

From the ancient Tamil Poet, Sivavâkayar.

WE travelled southward from Madura in the company of the Rev. H. J. Shaffter of the Church Missionary Society. As the train drew up at the railway stations in the hot noon-day, a row of passengers held out brazen vessels and lotas for water from the carriage windows, with loud cries of "Pâni! Pâni!" which a man at each station is set apart to provide.

In North Tinnevelly the Native Church Council has the entire control of the Christian community, without a single European being present at its deliberations. The native Christians support their own pastors, and the missionaries have wisely left the management in their hands. The European missionaries are withdrawn, and the Church of Christ in North Tinnevelly is now self-supporting and indigenous. It was commenced by Ragland, Fenn and Meadows, in 1854. Ragland's great forte was itineration. He lived in his tent the year round, and steadily went from village to village preaching the Gospel. There are now 5000 native Christians in the district. The Rev. V. Vethanayagam is the superintendent pastor. In North Tinnevelly the Christians are from no less than twenty-nine different castes, while in South Tinnevelly most of the converts come from one caste.

Most of the Christian converts in South Tinnevelly have been from among the Shanárs, or palmyra climbers. This tree covers hundreds of square miles. It strikes its roots some forty feet below the surface and gathers up moisture, and daily gives forth quantities of sap which is collected in small vessels, and is manufactured into sugar. The sap is also largely used by builders to give consistency to their chunam or mortar. The leaf supplies the roof for the houses, or cut into strips serves as paper for writing on. Its fibre is manufactured into string, its trunk is used for timber, while its root is scooped out, and with a sheep skin stretched over it forms the drum in universal use at festivals. The Shanár climbs thirty or forty trees, each sixty or eighty feet high, twice a day.

In the large towns the worship of the god Siva prevails, and in the town of Tinnevelly there are 1000 Brahman priests connected with the temple and 150 dancing girls. But the bulk of the people are devil-worshippers, and their sacrifices are almost entirely to avert the anger of evil spirits.

On our arrival at the terminus at Palamcotta, a native Christian was waiting for us at the railway station with a note from Bishop Sargent inviting us to his house. As the church bells chimed in the fresh air the following Sabbath morning, they reminded me of the chimes of our old church at home, that play

> "The heart that has truly loved never forgets
> But as truly loves on to the close,
> As the sunflower turns to her god when she sets,
> The same look that she gave when he rose."

But I was far away from home now, and the morning service began at half-past seven o'clock. Bishop Sargent was at church before us, and stood punctually at the communion rail with an audience of one thousand and fifteen people before him. The whole service was in Tamil. "When I came here forty-four years ago," observed the bishop, "there was only an audience of forty-two, besides a few children. This congregation is an answer to the question 'What have Missions achieved?' Some say respecting the conversion of the heathen, 'It cannot be done.' Here is the answer, It is done. What the Lord has done in one place He is able to do in another." The simplicity of the whole service is beautiful. There is no organ, no piano, or harmonium. The men sit on one side, the women on the other. The bishop did not enter the pulpit the whole time. His text was, "Behold I have graven thee upon the palms of my hands." The sermon was about God's love in Christ, His keeping care and faithfulness. One of the native pastors read the 55th Isaiah, and the words of the English church service expressed the thought of my own heart as I united with that Tamil throng in praising the Lord, "Let us come before His presence with thanksgiving and make a joyful noise unto Him with Psalms."

Bishop Sargent has established a Widows' Fund, for the support of the widows of native agents, to which the members subscribe, and they have now 55,000 rupees in hand. There is another fund for the Sustenance of the Native Pastorate when the Church Missionary Society ultimately withdraws all pecuniary support. The Society reduces its grant one-twentieth each year, so that at the end of twenty years the whole of its churches in Tinnevelly may be self-supporting. In each of the eight districts there are from 3000 rupees to 8000 rupees in hand towards this Sustentation Fund. They also contributed 1400 rupees to relieve the Irish distress.

In no Mission in any part of the world has the native pastorate so developed as in Tinnevelly. In connection with the Church Missionary Society 84 Tamils have been ordained, 70 of whom are still labouring in South India. The four European missionaries who alone remain are for the most part in connection with the educational establishments, and have the oversight of the native pastorate. Mrs. Sargent has Bible Classes for girls. On Sunday afternoon they chanted to us the Scripture, "How beautiful upon the mountains are the feet of Him that bringeth good tidings."

The Tamils are not great at logic, but they love repartee, and Bishop Sargent gave me an account of one of his open air services at Páva-násam, which means, "the destruction of sin." It is a town at the source of the Tambiravarni, or copper-coloured river, which runs through Tinnevelly, where multitudes of people make pilgrimages to wash away their sins. A Brahman priest, after listening to him, took off a string of beads and threw them at Mr. Sargent's feet saying, "I am your disciple, now make me white like yourself." "Am I God to kill and to make alive, to make white or black?" responded the bishop. "In that case!" said the Brahman, "your religion is no better than mine." A native magistrate then said to the bishop, "Sir, why do you condemn our religion? Is it because we worship idols? You say there is no life in a stone." Bishop Sargent replied, "Can you prove to me there is life in a stone?" The man said, "When you strike two stones together, what happens?" The bishop answered, "Why, there is very often a spark, of course." "That is the life in the stone," answered the man, and the crowd began to think the man was right. The bishop remembered the proverb of Solomon to 'answer a man according to his folly,' and replied, "I perceive that you are a learned man, pray can you tell me how many living letters (vowels) there are in the Tamil alphabet?" "Three," answered the man. The bishop then turned to the people and said, "Here is a man professing to teach you and he does not know how many living letters there are in the Tamil alphabet." The people clapped their hands and sided with the bishop. After another open air discourse, a Brahman stepped up and said, "May I ask you a question?" "Certainly," said the bishop. "Have you a Munshi that teaches you Tamil?" "Yes." "Is he converted?" "No," replied the bishop. "And this Munshi of yours has been reading your Bible with you for months, and is in intercourse with you daily and is not converted, and do you think you are going to convert us with ten minutes' discourse?" "That stain has been wiped away," observed the bishop to me, "for curiously enough seven or eight of these Munshis have been converted one after another, and we have now some first-rate Tamil linguists in our congregations." "How many Christians have you?" I enquired. "We have about 55,000 in connection with the Church Missionary Society in Tinnevelly, and the Society for the Propagation of the Gospel has about 45,000, making 100,000 out of a population of about two millions."

"We avoid taking orphans into orphanages. We think it is better to board them in some respectable family, and we have a number so arranged for at a very small expense. We have no beggars. We teach the Christians to support their own poor. A collection is made every Sunday morning for this purpose, and the money goes to the support of widows, and the sick and the aged."

A Brahman was converted some time ago, and and his family raised a great storm against him. At length one of his sons, about twelve years old, persuaded his mother, who is a thorough lady, to be reconciled to her husband, and she ultimately became a Christian. She one day visited a Brahman village where she was known. Five or six of the Brahmans got brooms and beat her very roughly. Her son said, "I will run for a policeman." She answered, "No, think of what Jesus suffered for me, and shall not I be willing to bear a little for His sake?" At a class-meeting the women were talking over their troubles, and at last turned to this Brahman lady and said, "Ah, you have your burden to bear like the rest of us, haven't you?" "No," replied the lady, "I have cast *all* my burden on the Lord."

Captain Hodson was passing through a heathen village and overheard a number of children reading the Bible in the Government school. The schoolmaster was a Brahman and a heathen. "How is it you are teaching them the Bible?" asked the Captain. The Brahman replied, "I found the parents wished me to teach them English, and the Bible is not only an easy book for children to read in English, but it is the cheapest book I can get them, and so we use it regularly."

The Rev. H. J. Shaffter says, as the result of careful observation, he is satisfied the Government has made "a great mistake in forbidding the use of the Bible in our elementary Government schools. Government ought to have left it optional." A learned native said, "You make a great mistake if you think that your different denominations are a stumbling-block to the Hindus. It is just what we are accustomed to ourselves. There are a great number of sects amongst us, and yet we are all Hindus. We can see plainly enough that though you have different sects, you are all Christians, and your little differences do not concern us at all." In India it is really a conflict between Hinduism and Christianity, and there is no doubt that Christianity is winning its way.

On Sunday afternoon we again attended the native service. Two of the pastors conducted it, and the minister asked questions in the course of his sermon, and received prompt answers from the congregation. There were only one or two English in the whole company. Several of the heathen were at the side doors listening. At the conclusion, the whole congregation had a time of silent prayer.

The next day we visited the schools for boys and girls, and the students who are preparing for the ministry. If schoolmasters adopted Mr. Shaffter's motto of doing 'a little more' than the rest they would easily sustain the zeal of teachers and scholars. There are at the present time 413 schools in Tinnevelly in connection with the Church Missionary Society, employing 306 schoolmasters and 141 schoolmistresses, and with one exception these teachers are Christians. Bishop Sargent justly observes, "We are educating our people so thoroughly that though at first they belonged mostly to the Shanárs and were of low caste, they are rapidly rising above the Brahmans, and the Brahmans are finding out to their cost that they are being left behind in the race." Bishop Sargent believes heartily in education. He seeks to train the native church to self-support and independence. He teaches them the blessedness of giving, even of their poverty, to the cause they love; but above all, he says, "the preaching of Christ crucified must be the great lever wherewith to raise the people."

Arrangements were most kindly made for our journey further south, and in due course we found our way in native bullock carts to Edeyengudy, the "Shepherd's Abode," the residence of Bishop Caldwell, of the Society for the Propagation of the Gospel. He gave us a cordial welcome to his comfortable bungalow, and we rejoiced again in the surroundings of civilization. Edeyengudy was designed, years ago, by Bishop Caldwell himself, and is very superior to the ordinary run of Indian towns. The streets lie at right angles to each other, in American fashion. They are broad enough to let in plenty of fresh air, and though the town is environed on all sides with trees, it appears to be healthy. "Peace on earth" was the first motto I saw on one of the houses as we entered. The cottages are built low and are of simple construction, but there is an air of quiet contentment that speaks volumes for the practical benefit of Christian teaching. The bishop is a tall, active, elderly man, of quick eye and lively conversation. After tiffin, we saw the children marching past in procession, and were informed that they were expecting to meet us and hear us talk. At three o'clock we met some 340 of them, younger and older, in a large room which for a whole generation served as the church, until, on the 6th July, 1880, the cathedral hard by was opened by the bishop, and is capable of holding 1500 people. The children sang some of their favourite Tamil lyrics, beginning with the Psalm, "The Lord is my Shepherd, I shall not want." They then sang a hymn to a native tune on the "Glories of Christ," and concluded with a Brahmanical anthem on the "Unity of God." Mrs. Caldwell afterwards showed us her lace-workers in the verandah at the Mission-house.

Bishop Caldwell arrived in India, January 8th, 1838. He commenced work at Edeyengudy in 1841. His wife joined him from Nagercoil, in 1844, and they are both still in vigorous health. "Every tree in the compound was planted by my own hand," remarked the Bishop, as we walked through the grounds, and the tall trees, as they looked down upon us, bore witness to having thriven under his care. A man that is good at swimming, fond of gardening, and a zealous naturalist, can preserve an amount of elasticity of mind that goes far to make a good missionary. We are not intended to be one-sided mortals, and Bishop Caldwell is many-sided. One of the first things he shewed me was his "pre-historic" museum, including ancient Tinnevelly pottery, and a pre-historic human skull. Then he took us to the well, one of those huge wells such as we never see in England. "I have many a time been to the bottom of it," quietly remarked the Bishop, as I made some observation on its size. "But are you not afraid of tumbling in?" I exclaimed. "Not a bit of it," he answered, "it is easy enough when you understand the knack of it, I will send a man down to show you how, if you like." "Look here," he at once shouted to a strong Tamil, and the Tamil came at a word and walked down the well from one stepping-stone to another, using his toes like fingers, and his hands like a monkey, as he went down the perpendicular sides to the water-level. We pass on to the girls' schools, where the girls were having some exuberant game on the playground. They wear a light tight-fitting crimson garment, with a loose check shawl thrown over it, and are "well done by." They have a large bath where each girl bathes every morning. A few steps further we came to the Mission Dispensary, supported by Government, where 4000 patients receive attention annually. In the town we visited the Christian "Choultry," or caravanserai, where strangers find lodging free of charge. As evening drew on, the boys and girls are again moving along under the tall trees, chanting as they go to service at church, making the air musical with their young voices. There were 400 people present at the week-night service. I sat in the chancel with the Bishop. He wore no clerical robes, and when the service concluded, he stood up and introduced me to the Tamil congregation. I told them of the prayer of my childhood, "Oh, God, give me some work to do for thee." I told them of the answer God had given to that prayer, and how orphan children in England were now praying for me as I travelled through India. A native pastor in his clean white dress, stood by my side and translated, and as I saw the earnest faces before me, abounding in goodwill, I rejoiced in that glorious brotherhood of believers which oversteps the boundary lines of denominationalism, and makes the whole world akin as we meet in the name of one Saviour. After we had dined, Miss Caldwell shewed us her white water-fowl, and lawn tennis followed. The girls from the school assembled in the balcony to give us a farewell benediction, with messages of love to the school-girls of England, and in another hour or two the indefatigable Bishop Caldwell, instead of retiring to rest, was off in a bullock cart to visit a distant village in his diocese.

Chapter XIV.—Travancore.

> "Do nought to others which if done to thee
> Would cause thee pain ; this is the sum of duty.
> Enjoy thou the prosperity of others
> Although thyself unprosperous. Noble men
> Take pleasure in their neighbour's happiness."
>
> *Epic of the Mahá-bhárata.*

Two bullocks yoked to a covered cart formed our locomotive power as we worked our way through the mountain defile that separates Tinnevelly from the native state of Travancore. In Travancore there are from 55,000 to 60,000 Christians, more than 35,000 of whom are under the care of the Church Missionary Society, whose head-quarters are at Cottayam. On entering Nagercoil we were hospitably received at the London Mission bungalow by the Rev. J. Duthie and his wife, and son and daughter.

The London Missionary Society commenced work in Travancore in 1806, and in Nagercoil in 1816. Mr. Duthie has been in India twenty-five years, having succeeded Mr. Whitehouse. Mr. Whitehouse is the brother-in-law of Bishop Caldwell, both having married daughters of the Rev. Charles Mault. The streets are named after the different missionaries who have resided there, thus we found Mault-street, Whitehouse-street, and Duthie-street. Mr. Mault remained here thirty-six years without a break and was buried here. He is still called by the natives "the great missionary," and was a principal means of achieving success. The usual accompaniments of Schools, Reading Rooms, Young

Men's Christian Association, and Printing Press are in full vigour.

Devasagayam, or 'Helped of God,' has erected for himself an excellent bungalow, and has done much for the Lord's work in Nagercoil. When he was building his house, the Brahmans were in great anger because a low caste man was building a house with an upper storey to it, the very first of its kind built by a native. "Build away," they said, "finish your house up to the roof as grand as ever you like, and we will burn it down as soon as it is finished." The man had to guard it carefully for three full months, and it still stands secure. Devasagayam commenced a coffee plantation on the hills after he had finished his house, and he promised to give one-eleventh of the profits to the Lord's cause. The first year he gave 18 rupees to the Mission, the second year 180 rupees, the third year 365 rupees, and he now gives at least 700 rupees a year to the Mission work. Lately he bought some waste land by Nagercoil and planted it, and has sunk a large tank for public use. The tank cost him a great deal of money, but is of great service, and when the Maharajah of Travancore heard that the good man's resources were being heavily taxed for the tank, he sent 500 rupees towards completing it.

Mrs. Duthie introduced me to her "lace-workers." This lace won prizes at the exhibitions in London, Paris, and Madras. The women work with 200 to 300 bobbins each. In making the flounce to a lady's dress they have used as many as 900 bobbins at a time.

The chapel at Nagercoil is one of the largest in India. The foundation stone was laid by Mr. Knill, when he had a comparatively small congregation, but he had faith in God and believed the work would grow, and on New Year's Day, 1881, there were two thousand people crowded into the building. Thus faith is right, and unbelief with all its calculations is outrun in the race as one generation succeeds another.

The native pastor's name is Joshua. He is entirely supported by the Nagercoil church, and the

TRAVANCORE.

congregation paid his expenses to the Bangalore Missionary Conference, where he read a paper on the condition of the native converts. Before he started the people had a prayer meeting to ask a blessing on him, and escorted him some distance along the road. He told me that on Sunday they have a regular attendance of about 800 people, and that they have 1285 adherents at Nagercoil.

I enquired of Mr. Duthie whether they had open air preaching at Nagercoil. His reply was, "No, we used to have, but now the people are all Christians here, and when we have open air work it is in the out-lying villages where there are heathen." Could as much be said of many towns in England?

We ascended to the summit of a little hill on which stands the unoccupied bungalow of the Resident of Travancore. From this bungalow there is a magnificent view in all directions. The cloud-capped mountain heights of Travancore rise one behind another, with their wealth of coffee plantations. High among the mountains is the little sanitarium where the missionaries resort in the summer heat. Cradled in another mountain valley is the village of Tittuvilei, where we could see the new church that has just been erected by the natives. There are no less than 1400 Christians in the valley around that village. To the eastward opens out the Pass to Tinnevelly, and to the south rise the bold crags of Cape Comorin against the blue sea line that stretches out towards Ceylon. In the foreground are the abundant rice fields of the Nanjenaud, with tens of thousands of palmyra palms rising up out of the valley. By the all-wise provision of the Creator, these palms produce a plentiful supply of refreshing juice in the hot season, but not in the rainy season. The climbers bring the supply to town in early morning and offer it for sale in the streets, something as new milk is sold at home. The luxuriance of the Travancore valleys is a fitting emblem of the harvest of souls that has been garnered to the praise of God.

One or two episodes in the history of the Travancore Mission claim notice. One of these is the contest known as the "upper cloth riots" of 1858. As Christianity spread among the people, the converts among the women naturally assumed a more complete and modest dress than had formerly been worn. The higher castes resented this, and so fierce was the antagonism that the Christian women had their jackets torn off their shoulders in the open market, and they were spat on and earth thrown upon them. Nine chapels and three schools were burnt in Neyoor and the Christians were plundered by officials of the native Government. Through the prompt and peremptory interposition of the Madras Government, the right of the Shanár women to observe rules of decency in their attire was however finally established.

Caste feeling is very strong in Travancore and it has been found difficult to eradicate it even among Christians. In 1870, it was found at Veeranakavoo that the Shanárs had actually erected a different place of worship for the low caste Pariahs to pray in, rather than mingle with them, and when the missionaries insisted on all worshipping together, most of the Shanárs left off attending altogether. As the missionaries have stedfastly withstood these gross prejudices, the work has grown up on a sound basis. Another source of disquietude was in connection with a remarkable revival which affected the Church Mission to some extent, as well as the London Mission, but especially injured the Syrian Church. This revival commenced in 1873 in connection with the dream of a woman who thought she heard a voice saying to her, "Except you repent you will perish." Another woman had a similar dream, and both became very earnest in speaking to all around them about salvation. There was intense sorrow for sin and for the sufferings sin caused to the Redeemer. This was accompanied by physical prostration, but there can be no doubt that many reformed lives were the result. This revival was followed by what is known as the six years' movement, the expectation that Christ would appear in six years' time. Many relinquished their property, forsook their wives and children, and gave themselves up to excitement, accompanied with vile parodies on the "sealing" of the elect, the "four-and-twenty elders," and "the four living creatures" of Revelation. The time limited by these false prophets has now expired, and the delusion has withered into small compass, but it shows the danger to which ignorant and enthusiastic converts are exposed.

Adjoining the rising town of Nagercoil is Kotar. Here we visited the very chapel where Francis Xavier preached and prayed, and baptized in 1540. The *Roman Chronicle* reads respecting it, "The celebrated sanctuary of St. Francis Xavier is situated at Kotar, where the great apostle lived many years, and performed many miracles. On the day of his feast a great concourse of pilgrims flock there from all parts of Southern India." As he undoubtedly baptized thousands, it is worth while studying his method of procedure three hundred and forty years ago. He says, "I go through all the villages of this coast, with bell in hand, collecting together a large concourse both of men and boys. Bringing them twice a day into a convenient place, I give them Christian instruction. The boys, in the space of a month, have committed all to memory beautifully. Then I told them to teach what they had learned to their parents and neighbours. On Sundays I called together the men and women, boys and girls into a sacred edifice. They came together with great alacrity and with an ardent desire to hear. I began with the Confession of the Holy Trinity, the Lord's Prayer, the Angelic Salutation, the Apostles' Creed, pronouncing them in their own language with a clear voice. All followed me in the repetition in which they take an uncommon pleasure. Then I went through the Creed alone, pausing upon each article, asking whether they believed without any doubt. All in an equally confident tone, with their hands in the form of a cross on their breasts, affirmed that they truly believed it." We may not admire all that Xavier did, or the means he adopted to win converts, but we must all admire his zeal.

As we passed out of Nagercoil we were furnished with two *bandies*, or covered carts without springs, each yoked to two bullocks. The carts had a bed of straw in them over which we spread our cotton *rezais*, to defend ourselves from the severe jolting over the rough roads. Three copper-coloured Tamils were our guides and companions, but we could not talk Tamil and they could not talk English. The horns of the bullocks were painted in honour of some festival, and their bells tinkled pleasantly as we slowly moved along with the accompaniment of lanterns and patience, pineapples guavas and cold chicken, as we wended our way for the "Desert." The natives call it "desert," but it is not what we understand as such. The soil is a red sand. There is plenty of rough grass with shrubs here and there, splendid old banyan trees and groves of mangoes, and many miles of palm trees. There are also lagoons with water fowl, and hard river beds. As night came on, the tall dark guide, with his lantern, led on in front, and we followed the glimmering light as best we could. His dark naked legs, as he strode along, seemed equal to any emergency, and he made much more headway than our heavy carts with their goaded bullocks. By midnight we are in some unknown region, our guide has missed his track, and we are lost! The four bullocks

BULLOCK CARTS.

wisely stand still while the men scramble over rocks and across a river, until the lantern is out of sight. "It is quite impossible to get the carts over these rocks," I exclaim, and we get out of our moving apartments and walk through the river. But the men discover an upright stone, the top half of which is in English and the lower half in Tamil, and we again find our road. We pass on to where the road forks. The men stand and dispute as to which way they shall go. I lie quietly in the bullock cart remembering the good promise, "There shall no evil befall thee, neither shall any plague come nigh thy dwelling," and this bullock cart, in this trackless wild, is my dwelling-place for the time present. There is nothing but a cart rut to tell us where some pilgrim has passed before us, and at last the men lead forward. Their dispute has come to a terminus, and they have chosen their path. It proves to be quite the wrong one, and we are more inextricably lost than ever. In the dim moonlight among the palms we see a wide lagoon. The men have some notion that the path lies along this lagoon. They drive the bullocks into the water, and when we are stuck in the mud, they leave us and go again in search of a track. We cannot get out into this mire and water, and therefore lie in the carts with the plumes of the majestic palms around us, waving to the wind on the borders of the pool. After a long halt we are again in motion. Not that the men have discovered the road, but they have found out the points of the compass and know the direction to take. Presently our bullocks are face to face with a hedge of prickly cactus. It is an encouraging sign of humanity to find a hedge at all. But what shall we do? Our course is effectually barricaded with a wall of cactus. The men cannot tear it up with their hands for it is far too prickly. They proceed however, to dig it up, and we wait until they have dug a path wide enough for the carts. Hour after hour passes. We are miles out of the right track. We are tired enough with the long midnight jolting, that matters little ; but the bullocks are thoroughly tired as well, and they must receive attention. We come to a grove of trees, the bullocks are unyoked, and my charioteer, who has goaded the bullocks for hours, hitches up the pole of the cart to an overhanging banyan tree, and I eat my supper and lie down to rest. Amid such surroundings and uncertainties it is cheering to see the first grey light of dawn. The Hindu knows more about sunrise than we do, for the men of the East rise early. Nature looks very lovely as the sun appears. Everything is fresh and inspiriting. We have left behind us the blue mountains and have been working our way across the plain, and ere long are again in the civilized world.

In returning northwards by rail we passed Arcot and Vellore, where Dr. Jared W. Scudder resides in connection with the Mission of the Reformed Church of America. The Scudder family have worked in the North Arcot Mission for many years, and are a beautiful instance of a family consecrated to Mission-work. Seven members of the family have been doctors, including the father and his grandson. Seven brothers and a sister have worked in the Arcot district. Dr. John Scudder, the patriarch of the family, was born in New Jersey in 1793. He laboured in Ceylon for many years, and there his wife gave birth to six sons, who all became missionaries, namely, Dr. H. M. Scudder, the Rev. W. W. Scudder, Rev. Joseph Scudder, Dr. Ezekiel Scudder, Dr. Silas Scudder, and Dr. John Scudder. Another son, Dr. Jared W. Scudder, was born in

India, and a daughter, Miss J. Scudder, has also given herself to the service of the Mission. A grandson, Dr. Henry Martyn Scudder, has been engaged in the Civil and Mission Dispensary at Ranipett. The Arcot Mission has now 3199 native Christian adherents. Dr. Jared Scudder has forwarded me the following valuable information on the temperance question. "The seventh fundamental rule of our Mission is as follows: 'Whereas this Mission, viewing with the deepest anxiety the awful and rapid spread of intemperance among all classes of the Hindus, feels imperatively called upon to erect a barrier against the overflowing scourge. It is resolved, that no individual can become, or continue, a member of our churches unless pledged to total abstinence from all intoxicating drinks as a beverage, and from gunga, opium, and all other inebriating substances, except when medicinally used.'

"For many years a formal signing of the pledge was required of all seeking admission to the church. That custom has now fallen into disuetude. Nevertheless, it is distinctly understood that all persons uniting with our churches are *(ipse facto)* pledged to be teetotalers. The rule has from the first been rigidly maintained, and the happy consequence is, that until now we have been almost entirely untroubled by the vice of intemperance. All our missionaries are total abstainers, and no native helper would be employed for an hour if he were anything else. In Coonoor only, where we have no resident Missionary, habits of drinking have given us some trouble, but even there such habits, where provable, are brought under church discipline. In one or two of our large stations there have been a few cases of individuals who, being drinkers, have withdrawn from us and attended other churches, but we regard ourselves well rid of all such. The effect of our policy as regards temperance has been to exclude drunkenness from our churches. We have been most happily free thus far, and I pray God we may continue to be so."

Such testimony as this from one in the midst of the battle is better than volumes of theory, and the churches at home may rejoice to know that the preaching of the Gospel in India results, as it ever must result where faithfully preached, in open war with sin, and in a life of practical holiness and godliness.

THE ASPIRATION OF THE BUDDHISTS.

THE world of men and gods to bless,
The way of rest and peace to teach,
A holy law Thy Son shall preach,
A law of stainless righteousness.

By Him shall suffering men be freed,
From weakness, sickness, pain and grief,
From all the ills shall find relief,
Which hatred, love, illusion, breed.

His hand shall loose the chains of all
Who groan in fleshly bonds confined;
With healing touch the wounds shall bind
Of those whom pain's sharp arrows gall.

His potent words shall put to flight
The dull array of leaden clouds,
Which helpless mortals' vision shrouds
And clear their intellectual sight.

By Him shall men who, now untaught
In devious paths of error stray,
Be led to find a perfect way
To final calm at last be brought.

Dr. MUIR's translation from the *Lalita-Vistára*, a prophecy of what the Buddha was to do for the world.

SOUTH INDIAN VEGETATION.

Chapter XV.—Benares.

There is a Stream whose sacred ford
Is self-restraint, whose waters are veracity,
Whose bank is virtue. Here practise thy ablutions,
For by mere water the inner man can ne'er be purified.

From the Hito-padesa.

After a few days travelling and a few days rest, we found ourselves at Benares in North India. The Rev. J. J. Johnson and his wife, of the Church Missionary Society, met us at the station, and we crossed the sacred Ganges on the rickety bridge of boats to the city side. On the high bluff on which the city is built, stands the Palace of Aurungzebe, with its tall minarets pointing to heaven. Near the bridge is the Pahlad Ghât where Elkanah and Irena Beard worked in the midst of the people; and far along the shore extends the city of two thousand temples, with its pilgrim-walk and bathing-places. Benares itself has a population of 175,000 souls. Its environs are also densely peopled, and every one, even a beef-eating Englishman, dying within ten miles of Benares is, say the Brahmans, sure of future happiness. The whole district has 798 souls to the square mile, more than double that of Belgium, the most densely populated country in Europe. "When Babylon was struggling with Nineveh for supremacy, when Tyre was planting her colonies, when Athens was growing in strength, before Rome was known, or Greece had contended with Persia, ere Nebuchadnezzar had captured

Jerusalem, or Cyrus had added lustre to the Persian monarchy, Benares had risen to her greatness."

We passed on through the streets to the Golden Temple, the domes of which are overlaid with gold, but the interior is given up to unmentionable pollution. There is the Well of Knowledge, from which the stench of thousands of the offerings of pilgrims continually ascends, and the gilded pomp and pride of Benares can endure but little daylight. "Ichabod" is written upon it, the glory is departed. The usual offering of the pilgrims at the Well of Knowledge is a bunch of flowers, and bunches of the brilliant coloured gênda are sold at the entrance. Close to the Golden Temple of the Hindus is the mosque of the Muslims, and many have been the conflicts between Hindus and Muslims on this spot. There is now a strong wall built between the two, and both parties have learned to keep the peace. Adjoining is the temple to the goddess of food and plenty. Here are sacred peacocks and bullocks feeding. This is the great rendezvous for beggars. It is considered a disgrace for any to go away unfed, and thousands of contributions of grain are provided for all comers.

We drove on to the Dasásámedh, or the ghât of the Ten-horse Sacrifice. These ghâts are often thronged by apparently devout Brahmans and women bathing in the sacred river, some washing and others drying their clothes. High above the ghât stands a purely Hindu observatory. These ancient people delighted in astronomy, and the Man-Mandil observatory contains a number of very clever scientific designs. Its date is about 1693. There is a huge structure of solid masonry in the centre of the roof, called the Prince of Instruments, which points all the year round direct to the pole star, from three different angles. There are three kinds of huge dials for telling the time of day. There is also a large circular building abounding with curious geographical coincidences, and so arranged as to tell the day of the week and day of the month, by the light of the sun by day, or by the light of the moon by night.*

Below the observatory is the Palace of the Rajah of Jhipur. In the city there is also the Palace of Justice where the priest flagellates the worshippers with a peacock's feather to satisfy the troubled consciences of poor sinners.

One more temple we visited was the Monkey Temple. It is not the temple of the monkey god, but has been taken possession of by crowds of monkeys. Long before we reached the place, the monkeys were perched on the house-tops, and in the streets, and at the water-tank. The priest told us many of them were out in search of food, yet

* "The first instrument you come to in the Hindu observatory at Benares is the Bhittayantra or mural quadrant, which consists of a wall eleven feet high and nine feet one and a quarter inches broad in the plane of the meridian. By this instrument the sun's altitude and zenith distance at noon may be ascertained; and also the sun's greatest declination, and the latitude of the the place. Two large circles of stone and lime, and a large square of stone are close by, with which the shadow of the gnomon cast by the sun, and azimuth were ascertained. Another instrument is the Yantras-amrat, or Prince of Instruments, whose wall is thirty six feet in length and four and a half in breadth, and is set in the plane of the meridian. One extremity is six feet four and a quarter inches high, and the other twenty-two feet three and a half inches, sloping gradually upwards so as to point directly to the north pole. By the aid of this instrument the distance from the meridian, and the declination of any planet or star, and the sun, and also the right ascension of a star may be known. There is also a Double Mural Quadrant, and to the east an Equinoctial Circle made of stone. There is likewise another Yantras-amrat of small dimensions and a Chakrayantra between two walls, used for finding the declination of any planet or star. A gigantic instrument, called Bigansayantra, constructed to find the degrees of azimuth of a planet or star, consists of a pillar four feet two inches high and three feet seven and a half inches thick, surrounded by a wall of exactly its own height, at a distance of seven feet three and a quarter inches, which is again surrounded by another wall double its height, and distant from it three feet two and a half inches. The upper surfaces of both walls are divided into three hundred and sixty degrees, and are marked with the points of the compass. On the south side of this instrument there is another Equinoctial Circle."—*Astronomical Paper*, by BABU DEVA SASTRI.

many remained, and as we fed them with the cheap white sweetmeat of the country, they flocked round us making wild grimaces and crunching up the food as they caught it in their hand. At one word from the priest they thronged into the temple, climbing up the elaborate Eastern carving, and perching themselves in all attitudes and in all crevices. Hindu architecture provides a splendid playground for these agile climbers, young and old. The little ones screamed as we approached them, and their mothers came and folded them to their bosom, and the child-monkey looked comforted and consoled as the mother glanced indignation at us.

In the centre of the city the Church Missionary Society has established a vigorous protest against all this idolatry, in the Mission church. The doors are thrown wide open on all sides when service is held, and large numbers of the heathen come to listen. It is often crowded on the Sabbath.

It was pleasant to turn from the city to the peaceful shelter of the Church Mission compound at Sigra. Here Rachel Metcalfe worked for years in the Girls Normal School under the able superintendency of the Rev. C. B. Leupolt. Mr. Treusch, a German, has now charge of this school. His face beams with joy as he goes about his work ; and the girls gave answers in Scripture promptly and brightly. The girls are of much fairer complexion than those in the south, and belong to superior families, being sent from long distances to be trained as teachers. Their parents or friends pay for their education, and the children are all Christians. To the amusement of the girls and ourselves we watched one of their number give a model Hindi lesson in Algebra. Miss Hœrnle has charge of the girls orphanage, and Mrs. Hooper of the orphan boys. The boys learn trades. There is a Mutton Club for the European residents, with the little flock of sheep belonging to it lying in the compound. The Sigra church is usually quite full every Sabbath, and the Christian colony is thriving.

Mrs. Sherring lives at present with her son-in-law, the Rev. J. J. Johnson, at Sigra. The death of the Rev. M. A. Sherring of the London Missionary Society is keenly felt among the Christian agencies of Benares. He was deservedly held in high honour, and by his blameless life had won the goodwill of his fellow-citizens.

In the afternoon Mrs. Sherring accompanied us to the city, and gave us the thrilling story of her experiences during the Mutiny of 1857. The spirit of rebellion was working among the troops at Benares, and Colonel Neill realized that every day it was allowed to smoulder the danger increased. At that time soldiers could only be brought up in carts from Calcutta at the rate of twenty-five soldiers a day. Neill dare not delay. He had only about one hundred English at his command. He ordered all the men on parade at 4 p.m. The native troops came with their guns loaded, and with many rounds of ammunition. When they were ordered to lay down their arms, they fired upon their officers, and on the very plain on which we were driving, commenced the fearful conflict between the native and English troops. Neill planted his little band of Europeans in charge of the artillery. They at once commenced mowing down the native troops with the cannon. The native troops time after time attacked the artillery and were driven back. Suddenly the native soldiers shouted, "To the Huts!" They ran to the huts. The native troops were beaten back. Neill's handful of men had won the victory, and the slain lay in heaps upon the plain of Benares. Our hearts revolt against such butchery, but we cannot ignore the terrible record of the Mutiny if we would at all grasp the actual position of Mission work in North India. Mr. and Mrs. Sherring were at Mirzapore at the time of the outbreak, and Mrs. Sherring was put on board a little steamer on the Ganges. The steamer came down the river. The captain neglected his charge, and put the ladies on board another boat. This boat was attacked, and the ladies only just escaped with their lives. For several days Mr. Sherring was unable to discover what had become of his wife. At last she was rescued, and night after night Mrs. Sherring slept with a large number of other ladies in long rows upon the floor of the Mint in Benares guarded by English Soldiers. To-day there remains a feeling between Europeans and Hindus in the north of India that is far different from that in South India. There is not the same mutual confidence. The Hindu dreads the Englishman, and the Englishman dare not trust the Hindu. There is smoothness of speech on the part of the Hindu, and plentiful servility, but not the love and goodwill. The persistent effort on the part of the English to maintain good government, and to deal fairly with the natives, is undoubtedly gradually healing the wound, but the remembrance of such a conflict cannot quickly be effaced. At the same time there is in these northern races far more natural strength of character, more manliness, acuteness and independence than in southern India. Many a look of proud scorn greets the foreigner, although it is commonly accompanied with dissimulation. One of the difficulties in depicting character in India is the circumstance that what justly applies to one class and race does not apply to an adjoining race, and therefore what is strictly true as applied to the one is just as untrue when applied to another. This gives rise to

BENARES, WITH MINARETS OF THE PALACE OF ARUNGZEBE.

P

apparent contradictions on the surface, which are no contradiction in reality. As Monier Williams puts it, there is "the spirited Hindustani, the martial Sikh, the ambitious Marâthi, the proud Rajput, the hardy Gurkha, the calculating Bengali, the busy Telugu, the active Tamil, and the patient Pariah."

Mrs. Sherring took us through one class-room after another in the college of the London Missionary Society where her husband so recently presided, and it brought many old associations vividly to memory. In the Central Hall, morning by morning, Mr. Sherring punctually bent the head in prayer and gave the short Scripture exposition. At the close of the day, as at the beginning, the 400 students were gathered for a short prayer and benediction. One peculiarity of the College is that it has a large *ty-khana*, or underground cellar, to live in during the hot weather.

Another earnest Christian worker in Benares is Dr. Lazarus. He is employed by the Maharajah of Vizianagram in connection with a school for high-caste girls, numbering some 600 pupils. No low-caste girl is admitted. There is no Scripture teaching. Dr. Lazarus tells me that 8000 girls have passed through his hands since it was commenced in 1867. The system of instruction is his own. He has four books which practically constitute four standards. They are all in Hindi. Each book contains a little of all the subjects taught to the girls in that standard.

Such institutions, the result of enlightened native munificence, do much to raise the position of the women of India.

We also visited the Government College, where the young men of the city receive a first-rate education, with all the appliances which a powerful Government can easily bring to bear in the form of talented professors and superior accommodation. A number of texts of Holy Scripture are carved on the walls.

The Baptist Mission is another agency for good in Benares. Here we found pastor Heinig, an old German missionary, sent out by Father Gossner in 1838. His wife was brought up among the Friends and was wont to worship at Dame-street Meeting House in Dublin. Her quiet early training may have been a fitting preparation for long years of active service on the hot plains of India. It seemed almost like treading on classic ground to sit by the side of an aged veteran, belonging to the band of missionaries raised up through the prayers and ministry of Father Gossner. Pastor Heinig is seventy-one years old, and his heart is still ready for bazaar preaching, though the earthly tabernacle trembles. He has ten children and thirty grandchildren. He was one of twelve young men studying together in Berlin under Gossner. They worked during the day at their trades, earning their own living, and came to Gossner from eight to ten at night, having prepared their lessons and being expected to repeat them correctly. Heinig worked as a tailor. He says, "I supported myself entirely." The strength of Gossner lay in *prayer* and *discernment.* He quickly saw what a man was made of, detected his weak points, and knew how to deal with him. Gossner also had business power, and was a great preacher. One of Gossner's agents was Mr. William Start, now living, in his eightieth year, at Minehead in Somersetshire. William Start took charge of the young men that came out to India, and notably of this party of twelve. They were for the most part very ignorant of the ways of the world and of the requirements of an Indian climate, having come from the country towns of Germany. Consequently

NATIVE GENTLEMAN.

several of them died from want of proper precautions against heat and malaria, and by trying to live like Hindus. Many joined other missionary societies and became some of the most valuable men of the last generation. Heinig is left, greyheaded and full of years.

In the adjoining bungalow, on the same compound, lives another remarkable man, Alexander McCumby. For forty-three years this East Indian has worked for Christ in the great Mission field. His line of service, like so many of the Baptists in India, is bazaar preaching. "I preach eight or ten times a week," he says; "I used to teach the twelve missionaries under Mr. William Start when they first came to India." Alexander McCumby is probably the most notorious open air preacher in North India. He is no copyist and preaches the Gospel after his own fashion. He is well read in the Vedas, and quotes Sanskrit indefinitely. He uses these quotations largely in his preaching, consequently the Hindus crowd to hear him at the melás and great idolatrous festivals on the Ganges. He is so well read in the Shastras that some of the Hindus declare he must be a Brahman in disguise. He pours scathing denunciation on the gross idolatry of Benares, and brings home his arguments with tremendous force against idolaters. Woe to the man that attempts to dispute with him. The crowd will side with the quick-witted acumen of McCumby, though they hate his teaching. He compels the Hindus to laugh at their own religion and loads them with ridicule. He does not deal so much in the gentle message of forgiving love as the stern denunciation of heathenism. Whether they will hear, or whether they forbear, it is probably in good ordering that there should be in a city sacred to two thousand abominations, one voice raised clear and shrill to protest against the iniquity, but McCumby confesses that he is not aware that he has ever made a single convert, and it is the Glad Tidings after all, that is the power of God unto salvation, to the pulling down of strongholds.

WHAT GOD SHALL WE ADORE WITH SACRIFICE?

WHAT god shall we adore with sacrifice?
Him let us praise that rose in the beginning
Who was born the Lord,
The one sole Lord of all that is, who made
The earth and formed the sky, who giveth life,
Who giveth strength, whose bidding gods revere,
Whose hiding-place is immortality,
Whose shadow, death; who by his might is King
Of all the breathing, sleeping, waking world;
Who governs men and beasts, whose majesty
These snowy hills, this ocean with its rivers
All declare, by Whom the firmament is strong,
Earth firmly planted, and the highest heavens
Supported, and the clouds that fill the air
Distributed and measured out, to Whom
Both earth and heaven, established by His will,
Look up with fear, in whom revealed
The rising sun shines forth above the world.

What god shall we adore with sacrifice?
He whose mighty glance looks round the vast expanse
Of watery vapour—source of energy,
Cause of the sacrifice, the only God
Above the gods. Oh that He may not injure us!
He, the Creator of the earth, the Righteous,
Creator of the sky, Creator too
Of oceans bright, and far-extending waters.
He is, whatever is, has been and shall be,
He is the Lord of Immortality.

Rig Véda.

Chapter XVI.—Among the Santals.

Who in this world is able to distinguish
The virtuous from the wicked? both alike
The fruitful earth supports, on both alike
The sun pours down his beams, on both alike
Refreshing breezes blow. *Not so hereafter,*
Then shall the good be severed from the bad.

From the Mahâ-Bhârata.

When we reached Muddapur, there was no room for us in the Inn, the Dâk Bungalow being crowded with military. On returning to the railway station we found the waiting rooms already quite filled with soldiers lying on the floor, some asleep, others with one eye open. We appealed to the station master, and he told us we were welcome to lie down in a railway carriage. We proceeded to the one indicated, and found it pre-occupied, another carriage however, served our purpose, and we lay down to sleep, and before daylight found ourselves at Giridhi. Three thousand troops were under arms in consequence of the disturbed state of Santâlistan. At Jamtara we passed the ruins of the magistrate's bungalow, which had been burned by the Santâls on the 14th January, 1881.

The Santâls are essentially a simpler and more ignorant population than any we have seen. Not that they lack understanding, but they are naturally timid and credulous, and it is their timidity and their credulity that has resulted in this disturbance. One missionary can do more with them than a troop with bayonets. When the police and Hindu officials come in a language which the Santâls do not understand, and issue Government orders respecting the Census, it quite bewilders them. The poor jungle people get terrified and assemble in crowds, and when they see so many of their own Santâls they think such a crowd is quite strong enough to rule the world they live in, and to have a Government of their own. Then the troops appear on the scene, and at the very sight of them, the villages are totally deserted, and men, women and children are hid away in the jungles. These aboriginal tribes need things explaining to them, and not to be terrorized.

The real origin of the present excitement runs further back than the census, in what is known as Kherwerism. Kherwer is the ancient name of the Santâl people, when they had their own rajahs, were under their own local Government, and were their own landlords. Months ago, a clever Hindu of the name of Dubê Gosain, came among the people above Hazaribagh, and commenced preaching a sort of Santâl millenium, when they should have their own rajahs again, and their own land. Gosain means a Faquir, and Dubê means grass. This Dubê Gosain eats grass before the people, and prophesies there shall be "no land tax," that is, no rent to pay, but a tax on buffaloes and bullocks instead. The tax is to be transferred, he says, from the land to the workers. "Kill your pigs, and chickens, and be clean." The Brahman thinks chickens are unclean, and of course pigs are. "Cleanse your houses and wash yourselves, and become 'Sapha Hor,'" that is, 'clean people.' This would-be prophet continues, "When you are clean and have sold your chickens, bring an offering in money to me, and I will give you a 'Darshan,'" that is, a vision. They pay him their annas, he takes them inside his tent, and tells them secretly that he is God. This man has gained a fearful hold on the people, and professes to work miracles, such as the following, "Here are three trees which we plant to-day, one represents the English Government, the second represents the Zemindar or Hindu Government, the third the Santâl Government, whichever of these trees lives, that Government will live, whichever dies, that Government will die." Next day, the English tree is withered, the Zemindar tree has withered, and the Santâl tree is green and flourishing. "So will it be with you," he says, "you will see the English Government wither, and the Hindus, who have oppressed you, will wither, and you shall have your own Government and flourish." "Wait till the 23rd April, and then I will appear unto you and show you what to do."

The Santâls have killed their pigs and chickens, and turned them into money. They have cleaned their houses with cow-dung, and are now expecting some great deliverance. The Santâls are really Devil-worshippers. They stand in great dread of the "Bongas," or evil spirits, and Dubê Gosain has persuaded them that if they keep their houses clean, the Bongas can never come to "Sapha," or clean people, and that they will be quite safe. This preaching of Dubê Gosain was early in 1880.

The Census came on the top of this excitement, and alarmed them. They fled away into the jungles as soon as the Enumerators appeared, thinking it a most dangerous thing to tell the Government how many wives and children they have.

"What is it the Government is going to do with our women?" they exclaim in horror. A body of these men came to the Mission-house at Pachamba, and said, "We want to go and see your King." Mr. William Stevenson replied, "Oh, but we have no King, it is a Queen." "Then we want to see your

Queen. How much will it cost to go and see her?" "You cannot go and see her, she lives far across the sea, but her representative is at Calcutta, and you can go there if you like." "No," they replied, "we do not want to see her representative." "Why do you want to see the Queen?" enquired Mr. Stevenson. "Why does she want to know our number, and to know about our women?" they replied. "What does she mean to do with us and our children?" And then Mr. Stevenson and the men sat quietly down, while he explained the simple object of the Census, and in a little while they went away satisfied. It is not soldiers but instruction these people want, and Government officials who are able to talk Santâli.

On our arrival at Giridhi we hired a carriage and two horses, but the dust on the soft roads lies so deep that the carriage sunk in and for some time we could not stir. Three men came with us, and while one flogged the horses, the other two worked at the wheels, and we finally arrived at the Mission bungalow at Pachamba.

Mr. William H. Stevenson was born at Dundee, and when thirteen years old felt he must make an open confession for Christ. For months he was in trouble about his soul. At last he went and stood at the corner of a street where he knew that two Christians would be passing, in the hope that they would speak to him and give him an opportunity of confessing Christ. But no, they passed the Scotch laddie without a word. They did not know the struggle that had been going on within him and he was sorely disappointed. He afterwards moved to Glasgow and joined the Mission church among the Wynds. This church grew until there were many hundred members, and then swarmed off, and a new Mission church was commenced, some ten or twelve workers calling an Evangelist to be their minister. *Seven* large congregations have swarmed off from this Mission church in the Wynds of Glasgow, and many missionaries have been raised up from among them. These missionaries are still mentioned by name in the prayers of the church at home. Mrs. Stevenson was converted through the plain dealing of Mrs. Joshua Poole of "Fiddler Joss" notoriety, and thus two efficient workers were raised up to carry the good news of free salvation through the blood of Christ to the wild jungle-men of Santâlistan.

We are now in the midst of one of the great coalfields of India. The Kurhurballee mine lies in the valley beneath, 950 feet above the sea level. There are seventeen shafts, mostly in the hands of the East Indian Railway Company. The Santâls work the mines, and the assistant-manager, Dr. Walter Saise, says, "The Kols and Santâls make excellent miners and are tractable men." The cost of working the coal is from 1s. to 1s. 6d. per ton. Wages are very much lower than in England. The shafts are shallow and free from damp, and torches are used by the miners at their work. In the Kurhurballee mine 4500 men are employed, and the annual yield of coal is about 308,000 tons. There are also copper and mica mines in the neighbourhood. The air and temperature of Pachamba is beautifully invigorating, and the English children look bright and rosy, very different to the usually pale faces of European children in India. The sacred hill of the Jains, Mount Parasnàth, 4479 feet high, is immediately in front of the Mission-house.

Every Santâl village has an empty house in it for the spirits of their forefathers to dwell in, and the people provide rice and water in a little vessel in the centre, for the spirits to eat and drink. "If our forefathers went to hell we should like to go there too, for we wish to be with our forefathers," is their ready reply to the missionaries. The Santâls think the sun is God, and it is very hard to divest the Santâl mind of some connection between the sun and God. They think that it is through the sun they get their crops, and that the sun gives them a good harvest. They burn their dead and take a bone or a hand and cast it into their sacred river.

On Saturday evening, at Pachamba, the Christian girls assembled to sing to us. The singing in Santâli is singularly plaintive. It expresses sorrow better than joy. One of their hymns was composed by a Pachamba native catechist as an introduction to his open air meetings in the villages. It runs something after this fashion :

"You are busy with your selling,
You are eager for your pice,
I've good news from God to tell you,
Without money, without price."

This was followed by the history of Adam and Eve, constructed according to the historic Santâli method of telling stories, giving part in prose and part in poetry. Thus we have the account of the birth of Eve, and then a song of praise, "Adam's thanksgiving for his wife." The history of the temptation of Eve, and the entrance of sin is recited, concluding with the most touching "lamentation" of Adam and Eve as they are expelled from the garden, crying "alas! alas!" While we were conversing in the parlour a note was handed in from a native catechist in a neighbouring village to say that a tiger had just carried off a man, and they could not find the man or the tiger.

Dr. Dyer is the medical missionary here, and has many serious cases to deal with at the hospital.

The school has been a fruitful source of converts and is a centre of religious influence. We attended the Santâl services on the Sabbath, and can bear willing testimony to the work of the Lord among these simple-hearted people.

Mr. Stevenson had been itinerating among the Santâls with two of his catechists, proposing to establish an out-station in one of their villages. His catechist, Kanhu, suggested to him, "You had better not go there yourself first, or the people may be frightened away when they see a European coming on horseback." Kanhu and his companion accordingly went by themselves to the village of Saola. When Kanhu arrived, he was surprised to find the people all assembled holding a meeting with their mangee, or headman of the village. The mangee had assembled them together to consider whether the time had not come to give up the worship of the Bongas, or Devils, and said to them, "I have lost faith in the Bongas. They can do nothing for us. It is no use worshipping them any more." Kanhu stepped in and told them of Jesus and the true worship. The mangee replied, "I have heard that before, you told us that two years ago when you were here." For four hours these people continued their meeting. Such a remarkable coincidence pointed to the propriety of erecting a Mission-house there, and Mr. Stevenson accepted it as a token of divine guidance. "Last week," he says, "I went there myself. Night and day the people listened to the truth." Mr. Stevenson asked the mangee whether he was prepared to become a Christian? "Well, I will learn," he replied, "Tell me in a few words what your worship is." "We worship God, and ask His help in the morning when we get up," answered Stevenson, "We worship Him when we sit down to eat, and give Him thanks. We worship Him in the evening when we read His Book." "Why then, you worship God all the day long," responded the mangee. "Yes, that is just the way for the Christian," replied Stevenson, "in all we do to honour God." "Then I will begin to learn the way," answered the mangee, "if you will send a man to teach us," and thus the Free Church Mission is established at Saola.

Several other societies are working vigorously in other parts of Santâlistan and Chota Nagpore. The Church Missionary Society has a very successful Mission with its headquarters at Taljhari, commenced in 1860 by Mr. E. L. Puxley, formerly a cavalry officer. Messrs. Skrefsrud and Boerresen have their well-known Mission at Ebenezer, with about seven hundred native Christians. Both these missionaries came out in 1865 under the auspices of Pastor Gossner, and are not connected with any missionary society. Mr. Skrefsrud employs thirty elders and ten Deaconesses. He says, "We endeavour to get the converts to extend the Kingdom of Christ gratis. We attach ourselves in our preaching to the traditions of the people in which traces are found of the original light of God. We concentrate our labour in a certain limited circle, and we believe in living in the very midst of the people surrounded only by Santâls."

The Society for the Propagation of the Gospel have flourishing Missions to the south of Pachamba in Chota Nagpore.

At Ranchi, Hazaribagh and Lohardugga, the Germans have vigorous Mission stations, numbering 28,000 native Christians.

Another, and still older missionary effort to these hill tribes is at Bhagulpur. This was commenced by Mr. Cleveland among the Paharis on the Râjmahâl Hills. The mail "runners" between Calcutta and Benares had been attacked over and over again by these wild hill-men. Troops were sent to punish the murderers, but the soldiers as they plunged into the interminable jungles fell pierced with poisoned arrows from invisible foes, and to conquer the Pahâris seemed hopeless. This young civilian of Bhagulpur went and lived among them unarmed and almost unattended, and by distributing presents won their confidence and persuaded them to become honorary guides along the post-road at the foot of the hills. In 1784 the Government erected a monument over Cleveland's grave, to the honour of the man who "without bloodshed or terrors of authority, employing only means of conciliation confidence and benevolence, attempted and accomplished the entire subjection of the lawless and savage inhabitants of the Râjmahâl Hills."

SHOPKEEPERS OF CALCUTTA.

Chapter XVII.—Calcutta.

"Do thy appointed work, sleep not in the daytime, obey thy teacher, study Scripture, and every evening and morning collect fuel for the fire."

Instructions in the Sutras to those who are 'born again.'

As we rapidly approach the metropolis of India, passing through Patna and Burdwan, the dense population of Bengal forces itself upon our attention. Over a great extent of country the average population, even in the agricultural districts, is no less than 500 souls to the square mile, whereas in England a population of 200 to the square mile always indicates mines, manufactures, or the vicinity of great cities. Calcutta contains 683,000 inhabitants, including its suburbs, and one singular fact is that there are only thirty-six females out of every hundred of the population. There is a larger proportion of the Non-Aryan element in Bengal than in most other parts of India, and the Hindus in Bengal are singularly different from the Hindus of the Northwest Provinces and the Punjab. Temples to Kâli, the "black" goddess, with her hideous necklace of human skulls, abound everywhere, and the sacrifices offered to her are utterly different to the "nature worship" of the Aryans. At the annual festival to Kâli, the temples literally stream with blood of slaughtered bullocks and goats, and there can be little doubt that the character of the goddess tells injuriously on the character of the people.

On arriving at the railway terminus at Howrah we were met by the Rev. Mr. Macdonald, and crossing the crowded bridge over the Hooghly

FLOATING DOWN THE RIVER.

we proceeded to the Wesleyan Mission-house in South Colinga Street, where we were welcomed by the Rev. G. Baugh, who has worked for many years in Ceylon. We drove at once to the "Monthly Conference of Missionaries," which was being held at the Rev. G. Gillan's, and were thus placed in direct communication with the workers of almost every missionary society in Calcutta. After tea, Mr. Parker read a "Survey of Missions" to a crowded gathering, and Dr. Murray Mitchell, who had just returned from Japan, followed. He believes there are now fully two million converts from heathenism in the world as the result of modern Missions. Ten years ago there were no native Christians in Japan, now there are 4000. In China, a few years ago, there were scarcely any converts, now there are 17,000, and, he added, "after eight years' absence from Calcutta I see a great change and marked progress in our missionary work in this city. I confess I am astonished at the greatness of the change." Dr. Smith of the American Presbyterians, who had just returned from Burmah, was the next to rise. When a boy, he had heard Mr. Ward of Serampore tell in America of Mission work in India. That was in 1820. Now Mr. Smith had just left his own son at the head of a large seminary in Rangoon for training the young Ka-rens for the ministry. Mr. W. R. James of the Baptist Mission Press in Calcutta, told the meeting that hundreds of the educated babus of the city are now week after week attending open air services in the public gardens in Beadon-square, listening to the preaching of the Gospel on the Sabbath, and that the people of Calcutta are stirred on religious topics as they have never been before.*

*With reference to the action of the police in Calcutta interdicting open air preaching, it was decided on the 20th June, 1881, that the order of the Com-

Dr. Thoburn of the American Methodist Episcopal Church was the next to address the meeting with the query, "Have not the missionaries of the last fifty years evaded the strongest positions of the enemy? There is a large force of missionaries at present at work among the aboriginal tribes, I would it were tenfold, but I think it is a little out of proportion. The Hindus proper of India are estimated at 120 millions, and we need to make a more determined effort at the higher castes. We can scarcely be said to have broken the lines in that direction as yet. My enthusiasm in the work has been growing every year I have been in India. I was talking to Keshub Chunder Sen the other day, and he said, 'Since I have known Calcutta I never knew such a stirring among the people on religious questions.' There are now three branches of the Brahmo Somaj, numbering among them some three thousand adherents. This shows that a spirit of enquiry pervades the native mind. We see also that thousands of native babus are ready to come and hear the Gospel, and these things surely should be a voice speaking to us, calling upon us to give a clearer witness for Christ."

The Rev. James Edward Payne of the London Missionary Society replied that in many ways it might be said that we *are* breaking the lines of the

---

missioner of Police was illegal, and the missionaries were discharged. Missionaries had been holding open air services in the public squares every evening. Muslim and Brahman preachers also appeared on the scene and created some disturbance, so that the police interfered and prohibited all preaching. The missionaries appealed against the prohibition, and some of them defied the new police regulation. One or two of the missionaries, by want of tact, were the cause of some disturbance. The bench of magistrates who decided the case in favour of the missionaries was composed of two Europeans, one Muhammadan, and one Hindu, and they were unanimous in their decision. Preaching was resumed at once and is continued regularly. The Viceroy appears to have expressed strong disapproval of the course taken by the police.

Brahmans, and the Zenanas that were once closed against us are now open.

Mr. George Kerry of the Baptist Mission said, "There is, we shall find, a proportion between the result of Christian Missions and the amount of *work* expended on them. In Jamaica, which is one-fourth the size of the district of Barrisal, there has been a larger number of missionaries employed, and the result is consequently very different. The same amount of labour for the same number of years would probably have told equally in India as elsewhere."

The Rev. C. N. Banerjea, a converted Brahman, said, "There are two aspects of Mission work we need to consider, the *destructive* and the *constructive*. We have been dealing with the destructive side here in Calcutta, but Mr. H. S. Newman has shown us the constructive side to-night in the building up of native churches in South India. Until the natives give themselves to preaching the Gospel, India cannot be Christianized.

Mr. William Hastie, principal of the General Assembly's Institute in Calcutta, then observed, "I think we must be convinced that it is the *educational* phase of Mission-work that must, after all, break down the power of Brahmanism. We are too apt to apply the merely statistical test as to results. The young men from our colleges think that baptism is unnecessary, yet there are very many of them convinced of the truth of Christianity who have forsaken idolatry."

One thing that strikes me very much about this noble band of Calcutta missionaries is their *hopefulness*. They see tokens around them of great approaching change. The tens of thousands of young men who have been trained in the Calcutta colleges are becoming a recognized power, and the growth of sentiment among the educated natives in favour of Christianity is considerable. Thus while Brahmans are bewailing the diminishing support they receive, it is just the oldest missionaries in Calcutta who are the most hopeful, those who understand the change that has already taken place, and see that a further great movement forward is inevitable.

Early the next morning we called on Dr. Thoburn, at the Episcopal Methodist Parsonage. His chapel is a very large one, and frequented by hundreds of native gentlemen. Numbers of educated young Hindus and Muslims regularly attend his evening services. His influence for good in Calcutta is great. He is just the man to tell with power on the English-speaking part of the native population. We passed on to the London Mission Institution where there are 766 scholars. It was at this institute that Dr. J. Mullens laboured from 1844 to 1864, until invited by the directors of the London Missionary Society to assist in the secretariat in Blomfield Street. He returned to England by way of South India and China, visiting the Mission stations of the Society, and on the death of Dr. Tidman, in 1868, became foreign secretary of the Society, and energetically and conscientiously occupied that position, till his death at Mpwa-pwa in Africa in 1879, in the midst of a journey to Ujiji.

Mr. Baugh observed to me, "We want the *best* men from your home churches for the work in Bengal. Calcutta is the very heart of India, and needs picked and well-trained men."

Calcutta has received some of our best men. In the General Assembly's Institution we again had the pleasure of meeting Mr. Hastie. There are 400 young men in the College department, and 1200 scholars altogether. This was Dr. Duff's first effort.

Thence we passed to the Free Church Institution, where Mr. Robertson has charge of about 500 pupils. This was the second great effort in Dr. Duff's eventful life. After his appointment to India in 1829 he was twice shipwrecked before he arrived in Calcutta. After reaching India he had twice to return home to Scotland through failing health. Meanwhile he pleaded the cause of Missions in England and America, and whether at home or abroad was found industriously at his post labouring for Christ.

Running through the streets of Calcutta in the tramcars, we came to the large house appropriated by the Church of Scotland Ladies' Association. This is one of the centres of woman's work for women. It is under the care of Miss Pigot. We sat down to tiffin with Miss Pigot and Mrs. Ellis in the upper verandah, the merry music of hundreds of children's voices coming up to us from the court-yard below while they were at play. Zenana work has made rapid progress during the last ten years. "When I remember the cold way in which I was treated, and the insults I received when I first visited Zenanas in this city," remarked Miss Pigot, "and compare it with the open doors and the welcome that now greets me almost everywhere, I am astonished at the greatness of the change a few short years have made in the minds of the people." Including the twelve schools under the care of the Church Missionary Society, there are now fifty girls' schools in Calcutta in full operation, and the Zenana work in many ways runs parallel with these girls' schools. Mrs. Ellis makes a point of looking after the girls that come to school, seeing their parents at their homes, and visiting the pupils after they have left school. The girls' schools are the means of opening a multitude of Zenanas to the lady visitors as the children get married, and the ladies as they visit a Zenana find a valuable ally within its precincts in the old school-girl who can read, and sing Christian hymns, and who by her superior knowledge at once commends the Mission to others less favourably circumstanced. Mrs. Ellis delights in her work. She has twenty-five Zenanas under her care, and the other nineteen ladies who work in connection with the Scotch Mission have each from twelve to sixteen houses they regularly visit.

Miss Pigot's schools are divided into several distinct departments. First there are the low-caste girls grouped by themselves. On the other side of the court-yard we found ninety-five high-caste girls, the children of Brahmans. Every one of these high-caste children is destined in a few years to be secluded in the Zenana of some wealthy Babu. Their wrists and ankles are loaded with bracelets and bangles, their ears and noses with rings, and their necks with strings of beads and other ornaments. Young as they are, they will be married all too soon, and separated from the purifying influences that now surround them. In view of the isolation from Christian teaching that lies before many of them, and the temptations to forget God that will surround them, great care is taken to impress passages of Scripture distinctly upon their memory, that may never be forgotten. Swaying to and fro they sang to us in Bengali the well-known hymn—

> "Art thou weary, art thou languid, art thou sore distressed?
> 'Come to Me,' saith One, 'and coming, be at rest.'
> Hath He marks to lead me to Him, if He be my guide?
> In His feet and hands are wound-prints, and His side."

Part of the tenth chapter of John was then repeated, and they were questioned on it. They are taken away for the marriage ceremony when they

BABU OF NORTH INDIA.

are nine or ten years old, and the marriage is completed when they are thirteen or fourteen.

On the same premises is a school of a different character, for sixty children of missionaries. It is well there is such provision for the fair-faced children of the toiling witnesses for Christ.

Miss Hook, of the American Ladies' Union Mission, is also an active Zenana worker. In connection with this Union, thirteen ladies, irrespective of denomination, live together, and help one another with counsel and fellowship. Miss Hook informed me that they have twenty-four schools in active operation, with 900 scholars, and 120 to 130 Zenanas under their care.

Mr. Wenger acted as our guide to Serampore, a little to the north of Calcutta, where there is still the house hallowed by the memory of the prayers of Henry Martyn. We visited the tomb of William Carey who died in 1834. By direction of his will the words on his tombstone are,

> "A wretched, poor, and helpless worm,
> On Thy kind arms I fall."

When asked in the presence of the Governor General whether he was not at one time a shoemaker, he replied, "No, I was only a cobbler." Joshua Marshman, who died in 1837, and William Ward, who died in 1823, are buried in the same cemetery. These three men rest on the banks of the Hooghly, and their lives, with that of Mack who died in 1845, represent a whole epoch in the history of Indian Missions. Their intense struggle with the apathy of the churches at home, with the unrighteous edicts of the East India Company abroad, and with the crookedness and awkwardness of the men who surrounded them, are almost without parallel. The field was new and untried, and mistakes were made on all hands, yet in the infinite wisdom of an overruling Providence these men were hemmed in to the Dutch settlement of Serampore, that there they might do the very work God intended them to do, and just the work most needed, namely, the translation of the Holy Scriptures into the languages of India. The printing of the New Testament in Bengali was commenced in 1800, and finished in 1801. The first Bengali convert was baptized on the last sabbath in 1800.

The Baptist College at Serampore is an imposing building facing the Hooghly, but has at the present time only 172 scholars. The Rev. Albert Williams is the principal of the college. It is a pity there are not more students in such a large establishment, as the Rev. W. Urwick remarked, "The Mission has the air of decay." But we may soon hope for a revival of the work in this historic centre. The Rev. G. H. Rouse, has recently returned from England, to take up the presidency of the college, and act as Bible translator, to which he has been appointed in succession to the late Dr. Wenger. The old chairs of Carey, Marshman and Ward are still shown in their little committee-room, where they so often sat to discuss the difficult problem of ways and means.

Part of the first steam engine that ever landed in India, which did good service in the Serampore paper mills belonging to the Mission, is still exhibited. Here is also a fine piece of carved furniture, the work of the first native converts of Schwartz. The Serampore College library abounds in historic interest, containing about 13,000 volumes. Portraits of various members of the Danish royal family adorn the walls, patrons of the Mission in days when such patronage was scarce. In the library there is a copy of the *Tri-pitaka* in Pāli. Pāli was introduced into Ceylon by the Buddhists, and is now the sacred language of Burmah and Ceylon, in which all the Buddhist literature is written. It is closely connected with the celebrated rock inscriptions of Asoka which date from the second and third centuries B.C. The *Tri-pitaka*, or Three Baskets, form the sacred scriptures of the Buddhists, and consist of a collection of the sayings of the Buddha, formed at the first Buddhist council held after his death about 543 B.C. Another gem in the same library is the *Kāmmā-vākyā* from Burmah, written on palm leaves, the surface being gilded and the letters inscribed in Indian ink. There is also a beautiful coloured copy of the *Brahmanas* with a verse from the Vedas in the middle of each page and the Brahmanic exposition above and below. The *Brahmanas* stand in somewhat the same relation to the Vedas as the Talmud to the Mosaic code, only they are considered by the Hindu just as much a divine revelation as the Vedas. With regard to the laws of caste and the dominance of the Brahmans, the *Brahmanas* are even more important than the Vedic hymns. They consist of rambling prose compositions intended to serve as a ceremonial directory for the use of the Hindu priests. The oldest of them may have been written seven or eight centuries B.C. In the same library is Henry Martyn's translation of the New Testament in Hindustani, and the Serampore translations of the Scriptures in Bengali, Mârathi, Hindi, Sikh, Telugu, Pushto, and Assamese.

Bidding farewell to Serampore we crossed the Hooghly in a gondola with a little cabin erected at one end of the boat which entirely protected us from the sun, the dark figures of the Hindus in front being fully exposed to the heat as they toiled at the oars. At the other side of the river we seated ourselves on a flat wooden bearer with a man at each end to carry us over the mud to the landing-stage. It was in crossing the river at this spot that William Carey fell and broke his leg, and had recourse to the little crutches that we had just seen at the college.

At Barrackpur, is the pretty bungalow of the Wesleyan High School, on the banks of the river. Thence the railway in a few minutes brought us to Calcutta. One of the most flourishing efforts of the Baptists, at the present time, is their river Mission at Barrisal. They have there thirty Christian congregations, with nearly 5000 native members. Between twelve and one o'clock on Sunday, a drum sounds, and a multitude of little boats come to meeting with the large missionary boat in their midst. The low land of the Ganges delta, and the river life does not mar their Christianity. Dr. Mullens said of this Mission, "Its success is the result of quiet steady work on a favourable soil. The faithful preaching of evangelical truth, the personal conversation of the missionaries, the labours of consistent native catechists, and the steady maintenance of a kind but strict discipline, have been the instrumentalities in this interesting field of labour. It is with no satisfaction that their Hindu landlords have seen the people of fifty villages breaking from the thraldom of centuries, and refusing to pay illegal contributions to idolatrous festivals. Beatings, imprisonments, and money-fines have been frequent. On one occasion eleven persons were carried off and hidden for many days. On another occasion one of the native preachers was falsely accused and sentenced to two years imprisonment." Such oppression is now over, and the persecution has given backbone and depth to the Barrisal native church.

In Calcutta the Baptist Missionary Society has a Mission with some two hundred members in the native congregation, the native pastor supporting himself as a government clerk. Mr. George Kerry and his wife have charge of a Girls' Orphanage, and Mr. Kerry has 138 boys in his day school. The Baptists have also a vigorous printing press where the Scriptures are printed, and two chapels, in one of which Adoniram Judson was baptized, and in the other Dr. Wenger preached. Dr. Wenger was born in the canton of Berne, Switzerland, in 1811, and his name stands high on the roll of Bible translators. He prepared and revised an annotated edition of the Scriptures in Bengali, and translated the Bible into Sanskrit. He died at Calcutta in 1880.

The Free Schools of the Benevolent Institution were originated by William Carey and Dr. Penney. At these schools we found a number of young Jews and Jewesses with their clearly marked features and as clearly defined costume. Mingled with them in the same classes were Eurasians, Hindus and Chinese. These little Chinese, with their heads clean shaved in front, and their black pigtails hanging behind, are well able to hold their own, and it was beautiful to see all these nationalities thoroughly working alongside at the same lessons as East and West met together.

In passing through the Chinese quarter of the city we were struck with the cleanly, well-conducted, well-shaven population. The Chinese are the shoemakers and the carpenters of Calcutta, and as they sit busily at work in their little shops with their sewing machines, they are a class of colonists by no means to be contemned. By their plodding industry and their contentedness with a little, they may influence the labour market in a fashion that disturbs the equanimity of working men, but such immigrants in any country, with their evident aim to mind their own business and do their own work, deserve the protection of any Government whose heart is large enough to receive them.

A few streets further on we found the thoroughfare thronged with carts loaded with chests of Patna opium threading their way to the docks for China, each chest marked with the Government authorization, serving to enrich the revenue of a great empire at the sacrifice of Christian morality.

But in a multitude of ways good is being done. A Bengali convert in Calcutta overheard a group of men blaspheming the Lord Jesus Christ. He approached them and said, "My friends, will you listen to a story?" "Sit down," they said, "we will have a story from you, but none of your preaching." He then related the story of Christ's life, without mentioning His name, and when he dwelt upon His apprehension by His enemies and death, and the prayer He offered on the cross for His enemies, his hearers instinctively exclaimed, "Oh! He was a good man. His persecutors were wretches." The Christian then said, "My friends, this is the Man whom you have been daily abusing." They were ashamed, and ever after spoke of the Saviour with respect.

The Wesleyans were holding special services when we were in Calcutta, and invited me to occupy the pulpit. My text, on that last evening in Calcutta, was, "If thou hadst known, even thou, at least in this thy day, the things which belong unto thy peace, but now they are hid from thy eyes."

As our host, Mr. Baugh, bade farewell to us, he said, "You go in good company, the Lord travels with you." And with the missionary's blessing we proceeded on our way.

A SHADOW FROM THE HEAT.

CHAPTER XVIII.—THE BRAHMOS OF BENGAL.

"From poison thou may'st take the food of life,
From lumps of earth the purest gold,
Examples of good conduct from thy enemy,
Sweet speech and gentleness e'en from a child,
Something from all. From men of low degree
Lessons of wisdom, if thou truly humble be."

Statutes of Manu.

THIS remarkable movement was initiated by Rajah Râm Mohun Roy. He was a profound Sanskrit scholar and a true-hearted and earnest enquirer. In January, 1830, he formed a Brahmo Somāj, or Society of the Worshippers of the One Supreme Being. At first the movement professed to be a reformation of Hinduism, or return to the purer doctrine of the early Vedas. Finding that the Vedas were tainted with Pantheism, the Somāj ultimately became more eclectic, gathering from the Scriptures of all creeds whatsoever was considered best for instruction and worship. The two fundamental articles throughout have been the "Fatherhood of God," and the "Brotherhood of Man." The Brahmos have accepted many ideas from the New Testament, and not unfrequently adopt Christian phraseology. Râm Mohun Roy published a book which he called "The Precepts of Jesus, the Guide to Happiness." As a consequence of his views, he met with much personal abuse from his own countrymen. He was mobbed in the streets of Calcutta, and ultimately retired to England, and died in Bristol after a stormy life, having patiently endured much reproach for what he thought was the truth.

In 1840, the young and earnest Babu Debendro Nath Tagore consecrated his talents to the resuscitation of the expiring Somāj. He relinquished excellent business prospects to devote himself to what he regarded as a great cause. The rapid spread of high education naturally enlisted for him many supporters. He presented the Society with a printing press, and did much to place the organization on a more prosperous basis. Branch Societies were successfully established at Burdwan, Krishnaggar and Dacca.

Babu Keshub Chunder Sen has led the movement much further. He has insisted on the destruction of caste as utterly opposed to the brotherhood of man. Many of the Brahmos were unwilling to go so far. He therefore formed a new Society called the Progressive Somāj, while the others remained as the Adi, or original Somāj. All alike view idolatry with contempt. There are now three branches of the Brahmo Somāj in existence in Calcutta, the last separation being on the ground of early marriages. Babu Keshub Chunder Sen had declaimed eloquently for years against the child-marriages of India, but subsequently his own daughter was married at the age of sixteen to the wealthy Maharajah of Kuch Behar in 1878.

For this and other reasons some of his disciples formed an independent Somāj of their own. Many of the Brahmos have drifted off at tangents, some have become re-absorbed in Hinduism, a few have come out boldly as Christians. It is not enough to have holy aspirations, and until the Brahmo Somāj definitely accepts Christ as the Saviour, it can never obtain a firm foothold, or meet the needs of souls.

The covenant of the Brahmos is as follows :

1. I will live consecrated to the worship of the One Supreme (Brahma), who is the creator, preserver, and destroyer, the giver of present and eternal good, all-wise, all-pervading, full of joy, the good, and without form. I will worship him with love, and by doing those things that will give him pleasure.

2. I will worship no created thing as the supreme God.

3. Unless disabled by sickness or calamity, I will every day in faith and love, fix my thoughts in contemplation on the Supreme.

4. I will live earnestly in the practice of good deeds.

5. I will endeavour to live free from evil deeds.

6. If overcome by temptation, I perchance do anything evil, I will surely desire to be freed from it, and be more careful for the future.

7. Every year, and in all my worldly prosperity, I will offer gifts to the Brahmo Somāj. O God, grant unto me strength that I may entirely observe this excellent religion.

The Brahmos say in their writings, "Brahmism is a universal religion. It is the vital part of every religion under the sun. Christianity, Muhammadanism, Hinduism, or any other religion whatever, can be proved to be Brahmism alloyed with some other particular opinions and tenets which are the chief source of religious disagreement. No religion can safely attack Brahmism, it is wounding one's own legs. It is intended by our Heavenly Father to be the religion of the world."

Some of the practical duties of the Brahmos as stated by themselves are, "Be prayerful. Without prayer, religion is hypocrisy and man a beast. Thank God, and be content with what you have. A heart without thanksgiving is made of stone. Be grateful to Him for what you have. Murmur not against the Lord, but live contented as long as you live. You must pray Him, not that He should make you a sovereign, not that you should have the riches of Crœsus, the might of Alexander, or the beauty of king Edward, but that your heart may be fortified against vice, that it may be His beloved dwelling place, that it may be ennobled by His presence, that you may master your passions, that you may be strengthened in the cause of truth, and that you may stand aghast against every temptation of this treacherous world, against every persuasion of evil. The servant of God has the best Master in the world. He is the richest man who has God for his Friend. Take every man for your brother, and every woman for your sister. The world is a house, all men are brothers, and God the common Father. You must stretch your right hand to every brother in need. You must wipe the tears from the widow's eyes. You must be all sympathy. You must feel grieved at others' grief, delighted at others' delight, blest in others' blessings. You must support the poor, and dry the orphan's tear. You must cultivate friendship with all, and never be enemies. If your enemy be ever weighed down with distress, lighten his burden, and he, out of the impulse of his own heart, will become your best friend. He who forsakes his needy brother is forsaken by God. If you do evil you may expect evil. Be always at peace. He who does no ill has nothing to fear. Where peace is, there God must be. If you would have revenge, leave it with God."

"To believe in the fatherhood of God," says Babu Chunder Sen, "is to believe in the brotherhood of man, and whoever therefore in his own heart and in his own house worships the true God daily, must learn to recognise all his fellow-countrymen as brethren. Declare a crusade against idolatry, and the very sight of that will drive caste to desperation."

"If we pray in a humble spirit, if we kneel down and open up the depths of our hearts, our longings, our sorrows, our afflictions, unto the one living God, He who is plenteous in mercy will hear us and grant our prayers."

"True penitence humbles man in the dust and makes him put his entire trust in the Lord for the purpose of salvation. Such repentance is essential to faith, for not till man's proud heart is humbled under an overpowering sense of his own unworthiness will he cling to God's feet, not till he distrusts himself will he trust the redeeming and all-sufficient grace of God. Repentance begins the work of conversion. By opening the eyes of the sinner to his iniquities, it fosters a longing for deliverance."

The following is the voice of another of their teachers :—"Happy among us is he who feels the presence of his great loving Father. The knowledge of this is the entrance to real life. You are the sons of God. Know then your great Father. The knowledge of God is more than the soul can contain at once. The soul is dignified beyond measure by His presence, but it humbles itself. Pride and vanity fly away like the wind. The soul is enlarged, but self falls short. Knowledge that thus breaks in upon us like lightning bears the impress of its heavenly origin. It engenders hope, joy, and peace. God thus revealing Himself to us manifests Himself in His attributes. This is no figment of the imagination. Imagination lags behind, being earthly in its nature. The spirit knows God to be infinite, *knowable*, but not *comprehensible*. The divine spirit in man knows God as Spirit, Spirit ever active, ruling the universe. God appears to us as the overruling Providence, full of energy, perfect energy. Oh, solemn thought! He is working in us and without us. He appears to us as the living God. The soul sees that God is perfectly happy. This makes the soul happy. God is known to us as Love, perfect love. He is our loving Father, from Him is all love. Ye sons of God, what fear ye? Infinite Love looks down upon you."

One marked peculiarity in the Brahmo Somāj has been that they have held themselves open to continually receive new truth and fresh light, and they maintain that in the search for truth it is our duty to discard everything that any man can prove to us to be false. Thus, when the Somāj was accused of change, the Babu Chunder Sen replies in these words, "Doubtless it is very hard to repudiate long-standing usages. Associations of old institutions, however ridiculous or obnoxious, are oftentimes irresistible. Old laws, old customs and privileges, stick to us with unflinching tenacity; yet by the grace of God the Brahmo Somāj, as soon as it has arrived at the conviction that a particular opinion was not right, has immediately abjured it; that very moment the opinion was drowned with the cry, 'Away with it! away with it!'"

In another passage Babu Chunder Sen says, "Brahmism not only reveals God to me in the inmost depths of my heart, but assures me that He whom I worship is my Father and my Saviour; that He who gives us food and raiment will also open the gates of salvation to all who sincerely repent of their sins, and humbly pray to Him, and conscientiously discharge their duties to Him. He saveth those who hunger and thirst after salvation."

In a recent lecture Babu Chunder Sen says, "It is Christ that rules India. None but Jesus, none but Jesus, has deserved this bright, this precious diadem of India, and Christ shall have it."

While there is much in Chunder Sen's teaching which we cannot endorse, the courageous protest against caste and the advocacy of many social reforms have proved a great practical blessing to the native community. Chunder Sen would himself in all integrity adopt the words of St. Paul, "Not that I have already attained, or am already made perfect, but I press on if so be that I may apprehend," and he would probably sincerely enter into the spirit of the charge of pastor Robinson to the Pilgrim Fathers, "I charge you that you follow me no further than you have seen me follow the Lord Jesus Christ. *The Lord has more truth yet to break forth* out of His holy word. I cannot sufficiently bewail the condition of the reformed churches, which are come to a period in religion, and will go at present no further than the instruments of their reformation. Luther and Calvin were great and shining lights in their times, yet they penetrated not into the whole counsel of God. The Lutherans cannot be drawn to go beyond what Luther saw, and the Calvinists stick fast where they were left by that great man of God. I beseech you remember it, as an article of your church government, that you shall be *ready to receive whatever truth shall be made known to you* from the written word of God."

Chunder Sen resides at Lily Cottage, Calcutta. As we drove up under the portico we were informed by the servant that his master was at *puja*, that is, at prayer, and had given orders never to be disturbed at prayer. The fact is, there are meetings of the Brahmo missionaries at his house every morning and evening, and it is at these meetings that the missionaries receive strength and instruction ere they go forth to distant parts of India on their errand. The native drums, tambourines and stringed instruments resounded in the air as their morning song of praise and thanksgiving to the Divine Being ascended to heaven, and heartily respecting the instructions of Chunder Sen not to be disturbed at prayer, we concluded quietly to wait his leisure, and were introduced by one of his disciples into an upstairs sitting-room. On the table lay two volumes of the "Early years of the Prince Consort," handsomely bound, presented by Her Majesty the Queen, and signed with her own fine autograph at the beginning. Alongside these books was a large folio edition of "The Sermon on the Mount," beautifully illuminated, and another volume with an elaborate inscription, from the Shoreditch Total Abstinence Society, presented when Chunder Sen was in England. On the walls were a portrait of the Queen, presented by herself in September, 1870, and a fine picture of Jesus Christ breaking bread. The morning prayers usually occupy about an hour.

Over the doorway of the room in which the meeting was being held was the word "Sanctuary." It was full of devout natives sitting cross-legged on the floor. One gentleman, unable to get in, sat outside with his eyes closed in profound meditation. Chunder Sen gives no sermon at these daily gatherings, but his prayers are supposed to be inspired, and in them his disciples believe they receive divine intuitions. Consequently, the prayers form really the basis of daily instruction for the missionaries who are being trained for their work. Every day in these prayers the disciples find "new thoughts," and thereby grow wiser. Equally remarkable is that which follows the prayer. When the minister's voice ceased, a harp began to play gently and quietly, accompanied with the native drums as the rhapsody of the harmony kindled into enthusiasm. This harpist is named Troiluko Nath Sandle, in honour of the "Supporter of the Universe." This man extemporises a hymn of praise, or rather a chant, embodying the main lines of thought that have been evolved in Chunder Sen's long prayer. A reporter sits by him and takes down the inspired words of Nath Sandle as they

STREET IN CALCUTTA.

fall from his lips. As I watched this native poet, apparently utterly absorbed in contemplation, playing with his fingers on the strings of the harp and chanting, it carried the mind back to the schools of the prophets in the days of King Saul. The hymns are carefully revised by the poet, and the Brahmo Somāj has now more than one thousand of these original productions.

The Somāj has twenty-two missionaries in various parts of India. For the first year these missionaries stay in Calcutta under the training and instruction of their minister. During the year they support themselves by some worldly occupation. If they then "leave the world and forsake all," they are supported by the "Brahmo Mission Fund."

But the morning prayer meeting is now over, and Chunder Sen enters with a scarlet dress thrown gracefully over his shoulders. He looks much older than when I sat by him in meeting at Devonshire House, Bishopsgate, in 1870. I reminded him of the need we all have to come under the teaching of the Spirit of God. "Yes, we need to be led by the Spirit of God," he replied, "but missionaries made a mistake formerly in persuading their converts to wear trowsers and adopt European customs. We are Orientals. If you want the people of India to adopt Christianity, you must not paint Christ in European clothes. Be content to let Christianity come to us in her own Oriental dress. In the course of history the aspect of Christianity has been altered, though Christ is not altered. We in India are seeking Him as He was in Palestine, going about doing good, and giving the Water of everlasting Life freely."

I opened my Bible and referred to the word "satisfieth," in the 103rd Psalm, and endeavoured to point out that we are not to be drifting about on the waves of opinion, but to have real soul-satisfaction in Christ.

"We Hindus are satisfied," he responded, "we are happy. But these Psalms are in their Oriental garb. We do not come to a determination when we have found out one truth. We find there is yet a deeper truth beyond it. We cannot comprehend the Bible without the help of God's Spirit."

"True," I answered, "but God has given us a revelation of Himself in the person of Jesus Christ. He was sent from God. The Hindus bathe in the Ganges, and bring offerings to their gods to wash away their sins, but there is only One Offering for sin, the Lord Jesus Christ."

He answered at once, "*We* do not worship idols."

The Rev. G. Baugh then remarked, "You might become a great power for good, Mr. Sen, if you would only accept Jesus Christ fully as your Saviour."

Chunder Sen replied, "I do not know what lies before me. That must be left with God. I am not to-day what I was yesterday, and I know not to-day what I shall be to-morrow."

"I hope you will do your duty whatever you find it to be," answered Mr. Baugh.

"Respecting our duty," continued Chunder Sen, "we must be influenced by the power of God, and obey Christ as he obeyed God. He was lost in God, and became one with the Father—God was in Him, and He was in God. We must follow Christ and be like Him, and like Him cast all that is of self aside. We need to lose sight of self. The less we have of self, the more we have of God."

So we parted, shaking hands warmly, and feeling how near such a man is to the Kingdom of God, and wondering why he should stand outside.

In the Mission Colleges we find some of the most

clever teachers avow themselves Brahmos, and appear to be really thoughtful men. We visited one of the large Brahmo chapels in the city, and found it throughout intensely simple, like a dissenting Meeting-house in England, without any decoration or device. There were four long rows of forms, and in front a square erection instead of platform or pulpit. On this square pedestal the minister sits cross-legged to preach, and the book of Brahmo Sanskrit hymns lies upon it. All who have seen the rude, gaudy, Hindu temples full of unmentionable uncleanness, must recognise that such a place of worship as that of the Brahmos of Calcutta, with its Puritanic simplicity, is a great relief and an immense advantage.

Keshub Chunder Sen delivered a notable address in the Town Hall, Calcutta, on the 22nd January, 1881, entitled, "We Apostles of the New Dispensation," which shows pretty distinctly his present standpoint. A paragraph or two may illustrate his attitude towards Christ.

"Shall a sinner vie with Christ for honours? God forbid. Jesus was a born saint, and I a great sinner. Blessed Jesus, I am thine! I give myself body and soul to Thee. If India will revile and persecute me, and take my life-blood out of me drop by drop, still, Jesus, Thou shalt continue to have my homage. I have taken the vow of loyalty before Thee, and I will not swerve from it, God help me! These lips are Thine for praise, and these hands are Thine for service. Son of God, I love Thee truly, and though scorned and hated for Thy sake, I will love Thee always, and remain an humble servant at Thy feet. Yet I must tell you, gentlemen, that I am connected with Jesus' Gospel, and occupy a prominent place in it. I am the Prodigal Son of whom Christ spoke, and I am trying to re-

STUDENT.

turn to my Father in a penitent spirit." "If I honour Jesus and claim a place among His disciples, is there not another side of my life which is carnal, and worldly, and sinful? I am Judas-like so far as I love sin. Then tell me not I am trying to exalt myself. No, a prophet's crown sits not on my head. My place is at Jesus' feet. Fear not, then, my friends, that a man of conscious sin, one so vile in his own estimation, will covet high prophetic honours."

Turning to the English missionaries Chunder Sen in the same address said, "Ye ambassadors of Christ in India, what is it that has brought you to this distant and foreign country? Is it duty, or is it love, the same love that your Lord Jesus felt for the whole world? India's pitiable condition has excited in your hearts the deepest sympathy, and you have felt drawn towards us as only the true philanthropist can feel drawn. The more you have thought of the evils of the land, its ignorance and superstition, its moral and spiritual destitution, the tyranny of caste, the reign of grim idolatry; the more you have reflected on these and other evils, the more you have felt sympathy and compassion for the miseries of our people, and the more devoutly you have implored Divine blessing for the redemption of the country. India's sorrows you have made your own sorrows, and with the whole weight of our national sufferings pressing upon your hearts, you have approached God and said, "Lord of the weak and helpless, send unto this land copious showers of Thy grace, that its teeming millions may have eternal life."

There is much in Chunder Sen that is hard to understand. It may be that he does not quite understand himself. It may sometimes appear as though he aims to be an apostle of some new dispensation of the Spirit. He believes that he receives divine intuitions. Many of his expressions are such as an acute theologian would never use, and yet we may say of the movement he represents, as Norman MacLeod has said of it, "Its existence, in spite of all I have read and heard against it, brightens my hope of India's future."

The Church of the New Dispensation, as Chunder Sen now styles the Somāj to which he ministers, recognises the four principal Scriptures of the world, the Rig-Veda of the Brahman, the Tri-pitaka of the Buddhist, the Christian Bible, and the Ku-ran of the Muslim. The Unity of the Godhead is its fundamental doctrine. One of its strange peculiarities is the system of "pilgrimages," in order to realize more fully the "communion of saints." In these "pilgrimages," a room in Calcutta is transformed into an historical site in Palestine, Greece, or Arabia, and a supposed conversation is carried on with the saint invoked. A vivid imagination brings the historical personage invoked before the assembly, and the utterances of past centuries are applied, more or less skilfully, to the exigencies of the present time. "The human soul has an *absorbent* character. To the simple enquirer it may appear absurd to call a room in Calcutta the Mountain of Sinai, and there to converse with Moses as with a guest, but in all this there is no absurdity to the devout believer." *

The usual services of the Somāj are simple. They commence with a hymn, followed by an invocation, an address, silent communion and prayer. In January, 1881, the "Flag" of the New Dispensation was unfurled. Lights were swung in front of the flag and hymns chanted. Upon a small table covered with scarlet cloth were the four principal Scriptures

---

* *Contemporary Review*, October, 1881.

of the world. In front stood the banner on a tall silver-plated pole, and from the pole was suspended the Bugle of the Expeditionary army. Chunder Sen exclaimed, "Behold the flag of the New Dispensation! The silk flag is crimson with the blood of martyrs. It is the flag of the great King of Heaven and Earth, the one Supreme Lord. Behold the spirits of all the prophets and saints of heaven assembled overhead. Glory to God in the highest; unto the New Dispensation, victory." The disciples then marched past and kissed the flag.

A new sacramental ceremony has also been instituted which is thus described in their own periodical. "Jesus! is the sacramental rite meant only for those nations that are in the habit of taking bread and wine? Wilt Thou cut us off because we are rice-eaters and teetotalers? That cannot be. Therefore the Hindu shall eat Thy flesh in rice, and drink Thy blood in pure water. On Sunday, the 6th March, the ceremony was duly performed, the Hindu apostles of Christ gathered after prayer, in the dinner-hall, and sat upon the bare ground. Upon a silver plate was rice, and in a small goblet was water, and flowers and leaves around both. Prayer was offered, 'Touch this rice and this water, O Holy Spirit, and turn their material substance into sanctifying spiritual forces. Invigorate us with *Christ-force*, and nourish us with saintly life.' The rice and water were then served in small quantities, the men ate and drank reverently, and the women and children also ate and drank and blessed God."

The "Vow of Self-surrender" is another novelty of the New Dispensation, forming the order of *Grihastha Vairagi*, or ascetic householders. They are not missionaries, but work at their trades, and lay all their earnings at the feet of mother Church. This appears to be really a kind of community of goods, the aim being "that covetousness and worldliness may be impossible."

Another development is the singing of hymns in the streets of Calcutta. This was commenced on the Bengali New Year's Day in April, 1881. The disciples form themselves into groups of "Dispensation Minstrels," singing "God's sweet name" in the evening, before the houses of the wealthy and the huts of the poor.

On the 7th June, 1881, Chunder Sen introduced another novelty, in imitation of the ancient Hindu Fire Sacrifice. A large iron fire-pan was placed in the "Sanctuary," with bundles of sticks, and an earthen vessel containing *ghi*, or clarified butter. Chunder Sen lighted the fuel, poured over it the butter, and producing a brisk fire, thus addressed it, "O thou blazing *Agni*, thou art great among the forces of creation. Thou art not God, we do not adore thee. But in thee dwells the Lord, the Eternal Inextinguishable Flame. O thou brilliant *Agni* in thee we behold our Resplendent Lord. Our venerable forefathers, the ancient Aryan Rishis, performed the sacred *Hom* unto thy glory. O God of *Agni*, in thy holy fire we desire to burn to-day our sins and iniquities, our foul desires and the lusts of the flesh."

This is called the "Ceremony of overcoming temptation," and was followed the next week by a "New Baptismal Ceremony," in which Chunder Sen, after reading the third chapter of Matthew, went down into the water and bathed in it, immersing himself thrice. Immediately previous to this performance he thus addressed the water at the pond in his own garden, "O thou great *Varuna*, Water of Life, sacred water, mighty expanse of seas and oceans and rivers, we glorify thee. Thou art not God, but the Lord is in thee. Thou art full of the beauty and glory of heaven, a most helpful friend to us. * * To-day, as in days gone by, the Ganges, the Jumna, the Nerbudda, the Godavery, and all the sacred streams in the land, are greatly revered by the people. * * In the holy Jordan was the Son of God baptized. Why did Jesus plunge into the water ? Because He saw the water was full of God." After the immersion Chunder Sen prayed, "O Lord of Rivers and Seas, Lord of Water, cleanse Thy poor servant, and purify my body and my soul." A number of earthen and metallic vessels were then filled with *Santa-jal*, or Water of Peace, and many of the people joyfully carried home the vessels of water. The *New Dispensation* of June 23rd, says that "the rite was administered by John the Baptist himself who was present in spirit on the occasion," and thus Chunder Sen is aiming to make his New Dispensation "the wonderful solvent which fuses all dispensations into a new chemical compound."

It could not be expected that such a series of startling innovations would be endorsed by the majority of the Brahmos of India, and very many of them have vigorously protested against Chunder Sen's later developments. The Sadharan (or universal) Brahmo Somaj, whose Prayer Hall is in Cornwallis Street, Calcutta, has stood aloof from these eccentricities, and it would be a great mistake to conclude that Chunder Sen by any means represents the thought of the Somajes of India.

There are at the present time 140 Somajes, or Brahmo churches, scattered through India from Assam to Sindh and from Lahore to Madras, and many of them are purely Theistic in character.

The Sadharan Somaj thus sums up its aspirations in the enunciation of its principles, on the 22nd January, 1881. "The spirituality of our doctrine shall be carefully maintained. Flowers, spices, burnt-offerings, candles, and other material accompaniments of worship shall never be used, and care shall be taken to avoid everything tending to reduce religion to mere parade and lifeless forms. It shall be the object of all our preachings and discourses in this place to teach men and women to love God, to seek piety, to hate sin, to grow in devotion and spirituality, to promote purity amongst men and women, to uproot all social evils, and to encourage virtuous deeds." *

The practical benefits of the Brahmo movement in North India may be thus summarized. In the first place they advocate a complete abolition of all caste restrictions, and this alone is an immense gain to Hindu life. They repudiate the worship of deceased ancestors, the *Sraddha.* They have reformed the ceremonies of birth and cremation, and marriage customs. They promote female education and emancipation, they limit men to one wife, and they plead for the suppression of intemperance of all kinds. However much they seem in some respects to be groping in the dark or floundering into the daylight, we do well to recognise and rejoice in the practical good they are accomplishing; and while we regret many of their wild imaginations and intuitions, we cannot but sincerely sympathise with their aspiration after truth and holiness.

---

* See article by Sophia Dobson Collet in *Contemporary Review* for November, 1881.

NATIVES OF THE NORTH-WEST PROVINCES.

Chapter XIX.—North-West Provinces.

> "None can live by sitting still and doing nothing,
> It is by action that a man attains true rest;
> I am the Pattern for man to follow;
> This universe would perish if I did not work my work."
>
> *Voice of the god to Arjuna in the Bhagavad-Gita.*

We travelled through a wide tract of country in Bengal largely devoted to opium cultivation The white poppies looked beautiful in the fields, and there were plentiful marks of abundant prosperity among the cultivators. Here and there an opium den in the cities tells a different tale even in India itself. But the gigantic wrong of the opium traffic is kept out of sight. Villages and towns flourish on it, a great Government acquires an enormous revenue from it, and China is wronged and suffers. The entire revenue of the Government of India is about £45,000,000 annually. The opium revenue is about £8,400,000, or more than one-sixth of the whole. The area of opium cultivation is, firstly, in China, where increasing quantities are produced; secondly, in the Native States of India, where about one-third of the amount exported from India is cultivated, known as the Malwa opium, on which our Government levies an export due of £70 per chest; and thirdly, the Patna opium, produced under the direct monopoly of the English Government, forming the other two-thirds of the opium exported from India to China. The *Times* says, "Our Indian Government is the largest manufacturer in the world," but not only so, it is manufacturing a pernicious and insidious poison that demoralizes and degrades the Chinese. We have 550,000 acres of land at the present time under opium cultivation in India. Not a pound of opium must be produced in all Bengal without being delivered to the Government.

Sir William Muir says, "A few years ago the Government of Bengal was straining every nerve to extend the cultivation of the poppy."

Sir Cecil Beadon says, "They resolved to push the cultivation by every possible means."

The great opium merchant says, "The Chinese *will* have the poison, why should not we get the profit out of it as well as anybody else?"

But what do the Chinese themselves affirm and re-affirm? The words of Li Hung-Chang the Viceroy and Secretary of the Chinese empire, are as follows, "Opium is a subject in the discussion of which England and China never meet on common ground. China views the whole question from a moral standpoint, England from a fiscal. England would sustain a source of revenue in India, while China contends for the lives and prosperity of her people. The ruling motive with China is to repress opium by heavy taxation everywhere, whereas with England the manifest object is to make opium cheaper, and thus increase and stimulate the demand in China. My Government is impressed with the necessity of making strenuous efforts to control this flood of opium before it overwhelms the country, and I earnestly hope that you and all right-minded men of your country will support the efforts China is now making to escape from the thraldom of opium."

Thus writes the Chief Secretary of State for China in 1881, and it is a stain on our escutcheon that we give so little heed to such appeals. A practical solution of the question would appear to be, firstly, to permit China to interdict the import of opium entirely, if she chooses to do so, and to strengthen the hands of the Chinese Government by insisting that our merchants who trade with China shall respect her laws ; secondly, to continue the charge of £70 per chest on all Malwa opium grown in the Native States ; and thirdly, for our Indian Government to withdraw entirely from the trade monopoly, and, as suggested by Sir William Muir and Lord Lawrence, to charge a duty of say £70 per chest on all opium grown in our own territory, and continue the policy of restricting the use of the drug as much as possible throughout our own empire.

A magnificent bridge 3224 feet long carries the railway across the Jumna into Allahabad. The railway journey from Calcutta to Karâchi is 2123 miles in length, while the line from Calcutta to Bombay, *viâ* Allahabad, is 1409 miles. The population of the North-West Provinces is more than thirty-two millions, nearly as many as the whole of the United Kingdom. Such figures give some vague impression of the vastness of the area and responsibilities that we are grappling with in the East.

The Rev. Francis Heyl of the American Presbyterian Mission entertained us at the Mission bungalow on the banks of the Jumna, in the very house that was burnt out during the mutiny, and Mr. Owen, who was then resident missionary, saw his valuable library burning as he stood on the bulwarks of the fort where the Europeans fled for refuge. Mr. Heyl has charge of an important educational establishment, with an average attendance of 116 scholars, and has also the care of the Blind Asylum in Allahabad.

The Rev. W. F. Johnson is engaged in the publishing department of the Mission, and we spent a most interesting hour in their book and tract depôt. With the rapid spread of education, the value of an attractive Christian literature becomes of immense importance.

The Rev. John James Caleb has charge of the large printing office where we found Muslims busy at work at three presses printing the Holy Scriptures in their own language.

Allahabad is the seat of Government for the North West Provinces, and has a population of 143,000. Adjoining the city is a Christian village under the care of the Church Missionary Society, consisting mostly of the employés in the Government Press. We went through this Christian settlement with the native pastor, the Rev. David Mohun. Most of the men are in the receipt of good wages, and entirely independent of the Mission. The Home Committee has concluded to withdraw from all pecuniary support of the pastorate and schools, and the native members of the community are expected to uphold the work themselves. David Mohun has been forty-two years in Mission service, and feels the importance of the crisis. The Church Missionary Society expresses the earnest hope that the village may still "shine forth as a witness for Christ among the surrounding heathen;" but a quiet, self-contained community is not easily roused to an aggressive spirit. In the church we noticed a large baptistry for the immersion of converts as well as the usual font. David Mohun informed us that it is optional with converts to be either sprinkled or immersed, and this option must have an excellent effect on the native mind in teaching the converts not to depend on any outward rite for salvation.

At Cawnpore we visited the lovely monument

RIVER LIFE.

erected in the park, "Sacred to the memory of a great company of Christian people, chiefly women and children, who near this spot were cruelly massacred, and cast, the dead with the dying, into the well below, on the 15th day of July, 1857." The palm tree and the cypress now wave in peace where raged the hurricane of man's hatred.

A short railway ride took us to Lucknow, the capital of Oudh, a city containing 300,000 souls. The province of Oudh has a population of eleven millions. The mosques and ruined palaces of Lucknow tell of the glory of the past. Our carriage drove through the Kaiser Bagh, formerly the harem of Wajid Ali Shah. The palace is still scarred with the bullet-marks, though the chief historic interest of the mutiny rests in the Residency outside the city, where the English were closely besieged for months. The whole city was in the hands of the mutineers. For one hundred and fifty-six days the siege lasted. Sir Henry Lawrence had most prudently accumulated loads of corn at the Residency ready for the emergency, but fresh spring water was obtained at the risk of life, and we saw the cellars in which the women and children lived for months to protect them from the shells and musketry. Sir Henry Lawrence was himself struck by the fragment of a shell, and died, giving instructions to have no words on his tomb save, "Here lies Henry Lawrence, who tried to do his duty." Sir Henry Havelock, General Outram, and Sir Colin Campbell ultimately re-established order, and to-day we are engaged in the aim to do good. But we must not underrate the forces that are arrayed against Missionary progress. In Lucknow alone, as shown by the recent census, there are 730 different castes, and each of these castes is an opposing element to Christian enterprise. The Hindus make vigorous use of the printing press.

There is one Hindu press in Lucknow employing 740 men, under the direction of Munshi Nerval Kishore. This press has a branch establishment at Cawnpore, employing another 360 hands. They adopt the latest inventions of Photo-Lithography, and keep themselves abreast of the times, in the publication of a prolific heathen literature. This one house has published seven different editions of the Maha-bharata, and thirty-eight editions of the Kurān.

The Hindus of North India are shrewd, quick-witted men, belonging to the same Aryan race as ourselves, having had a civilization and voluminous literature of their own when England was peopled with savages. In the crowded streets we pass bands of Pilgrims with bamboos thrown across their shoulders swinging a round basket at each end containing bottles and other belongings. They are all going in one direction, and as they pass us they shout, "*Gunga ji Kijai*," Victory to the Ganges, "*Gunga ji Kijai*," Praise to the Ganges. These bottles are the precious property of many a devout Hindu, and are returned home again full of holy Ganges water.

The Rev. Thomas Craven of the American Episcopal Methodist Mission gave us a cordial welcome, and as we drove up to his bungalow, six bright rosy children climbed up and saluted us, and then proceeded to lay hold of our baggage and drag it into the house with tottering steps, merrily carrying packages ever so much bigger than themselves.

The missionaries had just been holding a genuine Methodist camp-meeting at Shahjehanpur. There were 843 native Christians present, and the village native churches were greatly cheered by it. One man met another on the road, saying, "It is good to be here. It is like the Mount of Transfiguration.

Let us kneel down and praise God." After the camp-meeting had been held three or four days, the question arose, "Shall we meet again next year?" The missionaries thought better not, as it occasioned considerable expense to the natives, but they replied, "It has cheered our hearts, and we will at once begin to put by a little, until we have saved enough to meet next year." Many of the villagers around Shahjehanpur have become Christians.

On Sunday morning we attended the Hindustani service in Lucknow, and listened to an earnest discourse from a native pastor of the Rohilcund district, named Janvier. His text was "God is love," and he concluded his sermon after this fashion: "God gives us breath. It comes to us from above. We cannot do without it. It enters into our body, and gives us life. Did I say life? Not exactly so. It requires something else to give us life. I must breathe out as well as breathe in, if I am to live. I must give forth the air I inhale, or I die. So it is with God's love. God loves all people of every race. But we have not all the new life. Why? Because while God loves us all, we do not all love Him. It is necessary for us to breathe out the love that God breathes into us. Then we live."

"When I first came to Lucknow," observed Mr. Craven, "there was no Sunday School in connection with the Mission. I had been in the midst of such work in America, and thought, 'Cannot I have one here?' I began, and presently our senior missionaries were shaking their heads and saying, 'We must stop young Craven or he will spoil our day-schools. The parents of the children will be afraid we are going to make Christians of them, and will take their children away.' Dr. Thoburn of Calcutta heard what was going on and said to them, 'You see the young man is fresh and enthusiastic. Let him go on.' The Sunday School was suffered to continue, and it spread until we have now thirteen Sunday Schools in Lucknow containing 1,000 scholars, and in the whole district we have from 9,000 to 10,000 Sunday scholars, for when the other missionaries found it was a success in Lucknow, they said, 'Why cannot we have a Sunday School too ?' Very few of the scholars are Christians as yet, but they willingly hear about Christ. At Christmas we had a festival for all the children, and a thousand of them marched in procession through the streets of Lucknow, with music and banners and elephants."

I attended the Sunday School for the English children which is held at the English church of the American Methodists in Lucknow. I talked to the children and told them English stories, and some of the children went home and told their mother that Santa Claus had appeared at school that morning.

We afterwards attended one of the large native Sunday Schools. A large flag was hanging over the door as we entered, and the walls within were decorated with pictures. Groups of heathen children were clustered round the different teachers. The long eyelashes, the black hair, and the brilliantly coloured head-dresses, make such gatherings singularly picturesque. They read from the "Saadut Gunj American Sunday School Berean Question Book." Under this long title were the words, "These were more noble than those in Thessalonica in that they received the word with all readiness of mind, and searched the Scriptures daily whether these things were so."

The older boys are under Mr. Craven's charge. He hit them so hard with his arguments, that they fairly laughed at him with delight. Then he questioned them, and they gave bright intelligent answers far more like Christian lads than heathen. One singular official was labelled "Recruiter of emigrants for Natal," but he appeared to have no direct connection with the school or Mission. "We learn something fresh at every place we go to," was the remark of my friend Samuel Baker to me as we passed on; and we learned a lesson at Lucknow as to the power of Sunday Schools in leavening the masses of India, and bringing them to Christ.

In company with Mr. Badley, we called on the Rev. James Mudge, the editor of the *Lucknow Witness*. The printing press is doing excellent work here under the energetic management of Mr. Craven, who compiles dictionaries, revises proofs, publishes tracts, and in 1880 issued four million pages of healthy literature. Mr. Henry Mansell of this Mission, was called to be a missionary at seven years of age by reading "Little Henry and his bearer," and thus the providences of God are dovetailing, to raise up a succession of workers for the great Christian enterprise of these last days.

We spent a very happy Sabbath evening at the large bungalow of the Women's Foreign Missionary Society of the American Methodists. The ladies of this Mission are actively engaged in day schools and Zenana work. One branch of the Ladies' Mission in this district is the Medical work of Mrs. Monelle Mansell, M.D., at Moradabad, supported by New England Christians. During 1880 there were no less than 11,470 patients at Mrs. Mansell's Dispensary, and 21,000 prescriptions were administered. Every dose of medicine that is carried out of the Dispensary is enclosed in an envelope containing some Scripture truth. In July, 1880, cholera of a virulent type broke out and carried off thousands, from thirty to one hundred dying daily. There was a panic among Europeans and natives. The Europeans fled to the mountains for safety. Natives ran to the jungle, or rushed to bathe in the Ganges, or sacrificed kids, goats and buffaloes, to the goddess Kali. In the midst of all this, Mrs. Mansell stood to her post unflinchingly. Many patients were treated for cholera at the Dispensary, and many were brought to her own house, and *not one died.* The treatment was very simple. Mrs. Mansell simply said to each one, " Open your mouth, and I will put the medicine in. You must *pray all the time*, and I will pray too." The patients seemed to gain faith and strength at the same instant, and thus the diligent use of means, accompanied with the " prayer of faith " was blessed to many.

As we left Lucknow, the morning sun rose behind the great Mosque, and the harvesters in the fields were gathering in the plentiful harvest that God had given them.

THE TAJ, AGRA.

CHAPTER XX.—AGRA.

To God belongeth the East and the West, therefore whithersoever ye turn yourselves to pray, there is the face of God, for God is omnipresent and omniscient."

Kurān.

As each race leaves its mark indelibly on the history of a country and on national character, so one race after another has left a reflex of its mind in the architecture of India. The Taj of Agra stands forth pre-eminently as a reminiscence of Muslim rule.

That the Muslims designed such an exquisitely beautiful work of art, speaks volumes as to the immense superiority of their civilization, as compared with the grotesque piles of gaudiness and unseemliness that constitute the Hindu temples.

The Taj was built by Shah Jehan as the tomb of his favourite wife Noor Jehan, "The Light of the World," a woman of extraordinary beauty. Commenced in 1630, it was completed in 1647, at a cost of three millions sterling. Twenty thousand workmen were employed in its erection. The whole mass is built of beautiful white marble, each stone being carefully polished.

The Taj, 964 feet wide, stands on a platform of red sandstone to which we ascend by a staircase. At each corner is a white marble kiosk. From the platform rises a terrace of white marble 313 feet square, in the centre of which stands the Taj itself with its lofty dome and minarets. The whole is in the most perfect preservation.

The first view of the tomb as we pass through

the gateway from the city, is at the end of a shady avenue of tall, dark, cypress trees, with a long sheet of water up the centre of the avenue. The whole enclosure is laid out with shrubs at the expense of Government. The white dome and minarets against the blue sky present a beautiful contrast with the mirror of quiet water and the cypress avenue in the foreground. The building itself assumes different colours according to the state of the weather, its white polished surface in early morning before the sun is up appearing a light blue, as the sun rises taking a roseate hue, later on a yellow tinge, and when a storm approaches acquiring a delicate violet colour. The white marble walls of the interior are exquisitely inlaid with coloured marbles, representing lilies and other flowers, and imbedded in this inlaid work are jasper, cornelian, turquoise, agate, onyx, chalcedony, amethyst, and sapphire. Above this the Kurān, chapter after chapter, is inlaid in coloured marble letters in the solid walls of polished white marble. Screens of open trelliswork carved in marble, with elaborate scrolls and floral designs encompass the interior of the mausoleum, wrought in patterns of marvellous richness and variety. Bishop Heber truly said of these people, "They designed like Titans and finished like jewellers." Great as the dimensions of the Taj are, it is executed as perfectly as the little caskets of ivory that come to us from China. The tomb itself, inlaid with jewels, is in the vault beneath. Shah Jehan's tomb is by the side of his wife. The sloping passage that conducts us to this vault is so arranged that the rays of light from the main entrance fall direct upon the queen's last resting-place. The interior of the dome contains a marvellous echo. As we spoke, the voice floated and soared away overhead in a long series of undulations such as we had never heard before, and thus as the Persian lament for the lovely Noor Jehan was sung by the choir of girls around her tomb, the echo of their song must have resembled the harmony of angels responding from the vault of heaven.

In vivid contrast with the splendour of the Taj is the grave of the daughter of the great Shah Jehan, who was faithful to him when he was imprisoned by his own son in the midst of his grandeur. A simple grass mound near Delhi marks the place of her burial, with a plain stone at the head of it inscribed in Arabic in her own words, "Let no rich canopy cover my grave. This grass is the best covering for the tomb of the poor in spirit."

We may well ask, What is there in Muhammadanism to produce such a pure work of art as the Taj? Why is it that Muslim architecture is so incomparably superior to the Hindu Temples? As there are forty-one millions of Muhammadans at the present time under English rule, far more than under any other Government on the face of the earth, we need to understand them.

"In my travels through India," observes Monier Williams, "I repeatedly passed from Hindu to Musalman places of worship, and my spirit, troubled by the hideous idolatry witnessed in the temples of Vishnu and Siva, was instantly tranquilized by the severe anti-symbolism in all the surroundings of Muhammadan mosques. Yet the attitude of a Muhammadan towards Christianity is far more hopelessly hostile than that of a Hindu. The teaching of the Kurān has a tendency to make them more intolerant. They are certainly more proud and bigoted, and are often left behind by the Hindus for the simple reason that they refuse to avail themselves in the same way of the educational advantages we offer."

The Old and New Testament, and the Kurān are all regarded by the Muhammadan as the Word of God, but the Kurān being the latest revelation is considered the most sacred and obligatory. The people whom we call Muhamadans, call themselves Muslims, that is, believers in the Unity of God, and in resignation to His will. They claim Abraham, Moses, and Christ to have all been good Muslims.

Muhammad admits that he himself was an imperfect man who needed every day to pray for the pardon of his own sins. Born at Mecca in 571 A.D., he early lost both father and mother, and became a shepherd boy under the care of his uncle Abu Taleh, acquiring as a lad the name of "The Trusty." He took charge of the caravans of a rich widow named Khadijah, who made him an offer of marriage, which he accepted. The Arabs were at that time sunk in gross idolatry and vice, and Muhammad's heart was stirred within him at the wickedness he saw around him. When forty years old, he announced that as he was meditating in a cave on Mount Hira he received a heavenly visit. A second revelation bid him arise and preach, and for the remaining twenty-three years of his life he professed to receive divine messages, which were afterwards collected in the Kurān, the "Book for all to read." His public denunciations of idolatry raised such a storm of persecution that in 622 A.D. he fled to Medina, and from this epoch dates the Muhammadan Hegira. From this time Muhammad sought to propagate his cause by the sword, and the remainder of his life was passed in almost constant fighting. "The earth is the Lord's. God claims it for himself, and man is His servant." This thought inspired the soldiery with the conviction they were fighting for God.

In 630 he marched on Mecca with 10,000 men,

MUSLIM CALL TO PRAYER.

and established the new faith by force of arms. Falsehood, treachery, cruelty, and bloodshed mark those later years, and the character of Muhammadanism became fixed. Polygamy, divorce and slavery are maintained and perpetuated. Freedom of thought and private judgment are crushed. Toleration is unknown. The sword of Muhammad and the Kurān are among the most stubborn enemies of progress, liberty and truth which the world has known. Islām is in its essence stationary. There is a saying current among Muhammadans that prayer carries a man half-way to heaven, that fasting brings him to the gate, and that almsgiving secures admission, that the charge to the angel at heaven's gate is " Look for the marks on his knees." The Muslim is consequently very devout. Whereever he is, and in whatever way engaged, he openly or privately is punctual in prayer. He maintains the outward tokens of morality, but the inner depth is stagnation. One or two devout Muhammadans entered the Taj as we passed out, but the hard white marble, with all its symmetry, is dead, and a people who will not acquire the fresh lessons of each age must stand aside while other races march on. We may admire the past as we admire the lovely form of a Grecian statue. We may see germs of truth sparkling amid the corruption of Muhammadanism, but it is without life, and error inevitably becomes its own mausoleum.

The Church Missionary Society and the Baptist Missionary Society are doing good work in this city of 149,000 souls, the former capital of the Mogul empire. Our quarters in Agra were with Miss Elizabeth R. Alexander. This lady came out thirteen years ago and has conducted an independent Mission unconnected with any society. It would be well if many ladies of good position in England followed her example. There is an abundant opening for workers of all kinds. Miss Alexander has erected a substantial bungalow, and lives almost entirely on the flat roof. Her day-school and her Sabbath School are on the house-top. The children of the East love fresh air, and when the roof is provided with proper protection from the sun, it forms a much more appropriate scene for slates and lesson-books than a small class-room where the cubic feet of air per child is a question of Government measurement. The children were questioned in Scripture and answered well, and the musical ring of their young voices as they sang to us was refreshing.

Miss Alexander is now an invalid, but has that attractive power of Christianity which draws people to her, and with that singular familiarity that exists between animals and mankind in India, the wild squirrels make their way to her along the ledges of the roof, perching themselves on her shoulder and eating out of her hand as she lies on her couch. The inner thought of such a missionary may best be told in Miss Alexander's own words :—

Christ is no mendicant,
Dependent on our aid for food or drink ;
The cattle on a thousand hills are His.
His word can reach the souls
He has created, and His Spirit teach
The ignorant, the rebel heart control.
He needs no human voice to make more plain
The message of His love to sinning men,
But He would have us sharers of His joys,
And graciously invites us now to share
His ministries of love, and seek with Him
In tender pity those who, orphan-like,
Traverse the earth unblest, His children all,
Howe'er by sin degraded and enthralled.
Thy work must prosper, though we faint and fail ;
Thy counsel stand, though ours frustrated be.

Accept us, then, in tender love O Lord,
As tools that powerless and useless lie
Till by the skilled hand grasped of Workman wise,
Thou take us for Thy own ; and for Thy use
Prepare and fashion us, that we may serve
Thy holy ends, and Thy behest fulfil.

On Sunday afternoon I drove over to the Secundra Orphanage. The public conveyances, or *shigrams*, along this road are unique. A camel with his odd tread, his long stride, and nautical gait, drags the conveyance along, and the *shigram* itself appears top heavy from having not only an upper storey, but that upper storey roofed in and capable of holding fourteen women, with room for another dozen people in the lower compartment. These conveyances are monopolized by the natives, and there are cabs for the more luxurious European. The cabman with his *Gari* answers to the call of *Koi-hy*, and having received the *Hookum* of Sahib, proceeds slowly, amid many ejaculations of "*Chalao! Juldee jao!*" to the house of the Padre Sahib at Secundra.

Hindu marriages are no respecters of the Sabbath, and I was met on the road by the noisy drums and music of two or three such processions. The friends of the happy couple are adorned with much finery, but the hero is stowed away in a palanquin. February is the great month of the year for weddings, and in consequence of the great scarcity two or three years ago, many cautious families postponed the nuptials, and with more prosperous times, have now to make up for arrears.

The Rev. J. Erhardt has charge of the Secundra Orphanage. He was born at Boennigheim in Wurtemberg, and was educated at Basle. Like so many Germans, he makes an excellent missionary. "How many have you under your care?" was one of my first questions. "I can easily tell you that," he replied, "for I have just made up the census paper, we have 660." "But have you as many orphans as that?" "No, we have 463 boys and girls at present in the orphanage. The remainder of the colony consists of the people and their families employed at Secundra." The Orphanage and Christian village were initiated by the Church Missionary Society after the terrible famine of 1838. When the Relief Committee broke up, two hundred children were left on their hands. One hundred of these died, and the surviving hundred formed the commencement of the present work. Government gave the Mission the tomb of Zamani, the supposed Christian wife of Akbar. She was probably a Portuguese woman.

The mausoleum of the great Akbar, the fourth descendant in a direct line from Tamarlane, is also in Secundra. The tomb of Akbar's wife has proved a valuable acquisition, as one hundred acres of land pertain to it. The Government has for many years, through the kind arrangement of Sir John Lawrence, given two rupees a month for each child Government officials choose to send, and this covers about half the cost. The Church Missionary Society has severed its connection with the institution, and Mr. Erhardt has to provide for the education of the children with the staff that he has around him. The institution is therefore partly supported by Government and partly by special subscription.

The pretty peal of village bells rings from the church on the compound, and obedient to the sound a long line of girls with white veils over their heads march along the paths in procession, wending their way under the trees to church. When they are seated, another bell sounds, and from another quarter comes a corresponding procession of boys.

MAUSOLEUM OF AKBAR, AT SECUNDRA.

Then follow the little groups of neatly dressed Christian villagers.

"I find every boy his first situation, and give him a fair start, and an opportunity of earning his own living. I do nothing for him after that," observed the Pastor. "As for the girls, we marry them all from here. I might supply the North of India with wives if I had enough, they are in such demand. I have no trouble whatever in disposing of them. Whatever may be the experience of other orphanages, we have no difficulty in getting them all married." With such converse we reach the church portal, and as I enter I find myself facing rows upon rows of neatly dressed clean-looking young women with no ugly nose rings, and as they sit on mats on the floor from one end of the church to the other without a break, I cease to wonder at the success of Father Erhardt in disposing of his girls. The other side of the church is equally well filled with the boys, all sitting cross-legged on the floor, and whoever else may have cause to bless the Secundra Orphanage for well-trained women, I imagine these boys commonly have first chance in making their selection.

The Germans have a faculty for making the ordinary Church of England service wonderfully adaptive to their requirements. Several good popular hymns were sung, some parts of the liturgy were omitted, and before long Pastor Erhardt, with gold spectacles and long grey beard, is leaning over the pulpit, getting as near to his children as church furniture will permit, and giving out his text. It is the 105th verse of the longest Psalm in the Bible, "Thy word is a lamp unto my feet and a light unto my path." But if Erhardt knows how to deal with the church service, he equally understands how to manipulate his sermon. It was almost entirely question and answer from beginning to end. He steadily put leading questions to his audience, and that church-full of people, numbering five to six hundred, just as naturally responded. It would rather non-plus an English congregation to be catechized after this fashion, though a Scotch one might stand it, but the Secundra people are evidently accustomed to the process, and the preacher carried his audience with him throughout.

But Pastor Erhardt also has a wife, and the wife is half the man. Her part in the church service is to play a large harmonium. She has thriven well at Secundra, and the musical instrument calls for no little exertion. Arms and feet, head and voice are called into full requisition, and her whole body sways to and fro with the effort. A Hindu lad stands by diligently fanning her the whole time that the volume of music proceeds. The arrangements for *Punkahs* in many of the Indian churches, especially those frequented by Europeans, is a great comfort to many of the congregations. The methodical *punkah wallahs* are industriously at work the whole time pulling the ropes in the verandahs outside. As the last strains of melody die away, Mrs. Erhardt flings open the window behind her, and leans back in her chair as if saying, "Now I have done." She pleasantly remarked to me afterwards, "You know I felt as though the whole weight of the church rested on me at the time." Her success appeared to me complete, but not so to the mind of Madame Erhardt, for as soon as the service was over, she gathered her choir together, and like a truly indefatigable organist commenced again. She had detected some flaw in the harmony, and was anxious, by means of a rehearsal, to teach her people how to improve upon it another time. Such men and women conquer, whether their sphere is in

England, or Germany, or India. These church services are essentially popular. Not only was the church crowded that warm afternoon, but four tiny little fingers were to be seen pressing through the woodwork that protects the congregation from the sunshine. Those fingers are the property of a little child who would very much like to attend church service, but is considered too young, and has therefore to represent the outside public.

We adjourned to the tomb of Miriam, the wife of the illustrious Akbar. It is now a printing office! Not only so, there is an active type foundry in it, and a bookbinding establishment. There is also a smith's forge, a carpenter's shop, and a tailoring department. Doubtless two hundred boys can keep a tailor's shop going all the year round. Father Erhardt says that the Industries of Secundra all clear their own expenses. If no other situation turns up for the boys, they are apprenticed for four or five years to one of these trades on the compound.

The Government press was formerly at Secundra, but is now removed to Allahabad, and the rooms that were originally the type foundry are now the boys' dormitories. As we passed through the girls' apartments we met a number of children who came here during the famine of 1878. They have not yet recovered from the privation they then endured. The children clustered round Mr. Erhardt and called out "father, father," to win a smile from the good man as he laid his hands upon their heads, and truly the Christian cheerfulness of the Secundra Orphanage is something far brighter and better than all the palaces and tombs of the Moguls.

INDIAN MAIL CART.

Chapter XXI.—The Punjab.

"Thou thinkest, O good friend, thou art alone,
But there resides within thee
A Being who inspects thy every act,
Knows all thy goodness and thy wickedness;
Grieve thou not the great internal Witness,
The omniscient Spirit within thy breast."

Statutes of Manu.

Perhaps no city in the world has known more frequent change of rulers than Delhi. Six times has the city been rebuilt and its site changed, and the ruins of the ancient cities now cover twenty miles round Delhi. Here King Bharata, the hero of the Indian epic of the Maha-Bharata, held sway as the renowned monarch of the Lunar Dynasty centuries before Christ, and the Hindus flourished here for thirty-one generations. The Rajput sovereigns followed, and were in their turn deposed by the Muhammadan conquerors. The Afghans secured possession in 1288, and Tamarlane the Tartar, conquered Delhi in 1398. The Lodhi Dynasty dispossessed the Tartars in 1450. Baber established the kingdom of the Moguls here in 1526, and the present city with its twelve gates, was built by the Emperor Shah Jehan in 1631. Its wealth and splendour became the prey of Nadir Shah, the Persian conqueror, in 1739, who removed the Peacock Throne of Shah Jehan, with its jewellery, valued at six millions sterling. The Marâthas plundered Delhi in 1759, and lastly it fell into the hands of the English. The English lost it again during the Mutiny, but recovered it on the 18th September, 1857, and finally Queen Victoria was proclaimed

Empress in Delhi in the last days of the Earl of Beaconsfield.

We visited the Fort enclosing the sumptuous palace of the Emperor Shah Jehan, where the beautiful Royal Bath Rooms of white marble are still exhibited. We also examined the exquisite Pearl Mosque or *Moti Musjid*, where the ladies of the Harem assembled for worship.

But it was the Mission work in the city that principally engaged our attention. This is for the most part in the hands of the Society for the Propagation of the Gospel, and of the Baptist Missionary Society. I had a note of introduction to the Rev. R. R. Winter from Mr. R. N. Cust, and went with Mr. Winter to the Memorial Church. This church was erected in memory of the native and European Christians who suffered during the Mutiny in Delhi. The Rev. A. R. Hubbard, and three assistant missionaries were put to death by the rebels. Over the porch are inscribed the words, "Be thou faithful unto death, and I will give thee a crown of life." In the church there is a baptistry as well as font, and Mr. Winter leaves it optional with converts either to be sprinkled or immersed. The men sit on one side of the church and the women on the other, in accordance with oriental custom. In front of the church facing the street is a large portico, that passers by may step in during service. By this simple arrangement numbers come and listen to the Gospel message. Mrs. Winter superintends the schools and the Zenana work, and has her hands full. The "Cambridge Mission" is working in connection with Mr. Winter, and is carried on by the Rev. E. Bickersteth and five associates.

Through the kindness of the Rev. James Smith, at whose residence we stayed in Delhi, we obtained much valuable information respecting the working of the Baptist Missionary Society. His residence formerly belonged to the Nawab of Patoudi, and from the roof near by Mrs. Smith showed us the wonderful Kutub Minar, 238 feet high, the highest pillar in the world, commenced by the Hindus and completed by the Muslims.

These missionaries in India are no mere copyists. While they rightly learn much from each other, different men have fearlessly struck out for themselves fresh lines of service and are blessed in it. The harp has but few strings, yet on those strings may be played ten thousand harmonies. The early work of the Baptists was conspicuously in Bible translation. It was the right work at the right time. But the main work of the Baptists in North India now is the direct preaching of the Gospel and the building up of native churches. The main success of Mr. Smith has been among the Chamars, or leather-worker caste.

After the storm-cloud of the Mutiny, Mr. Smith found only one native member of their church left. Now the Baptist Mission has 400 native members in the neighbourhood of Delhi, and 2000 people attending their services every week. Their plan of working is a simple one. Every Saturday morning about thirty of the European and native Christian helpers, meet together for prayer and counsel. One of the workers prepares a sermon, which is criticised freely by the rest, and its weak parts pointed out. This helps to train the native evangelists in clear exposition and exegesis. A time of devotion follows, and appointments are made for the various services of the coming week. Some idea of the energy and zeal of this band of workers may be gathered from the fact that they have seven recognized services in various places on the Sabbath, three on Monday, four on Tuesday, three on Thursday, one on Friday, and an open-air meeting in front of their book-shop on Saturday.

The native church contributes thirty-five rupees a month to one man as their own evangelist, but with this exception none of these workers are paid for preaching. All the Mission agents are schoolmasters, and as schoolmasters earn their own living. The school teaching lasts till twelve o'clock. The master then has three hours' rest, and afterwards engages in house to house visiting, and has a cottage meeting in the evening. One or two of the schoolmasters who have not "the gift," do not preach. They have divided Delhi into eight districts, each district has a school, and each school forms a centre for a meeting. There are six other districts for work in the suburbs, making fourteen centres in all.

Mr. Smith has been forty years in India, and is so well known in Delhi as "a friend of the people" that he easily secures attention in the open air. His plan is, to preach the Gospel and not attack the heathen gods by name. If a man interrupts, Mr. Smith calls him up and gives him an opportunity to speak. In about two minutes the man has said all he can think of, and Mr. Smith proceeds. If some one disturbs the meeting, he observes, "I am sure that is not a Delhi man, Delhi men are always polite," and the whole mob acquiesces, and the disturber is glad to back out as quickly as he can.

In forming a native church organization, Mr. Smith has laid hold of the national system of *Panchâyats*. The word is derived from *panch*, five, because five men of old times formed the quorum of judgment in the different native fraternities. The *panchâyat* among the Hindus is a very ancient mode of settling disputes by arbitration. Now that the laws of arbitration are becoming more understood in Europe, it is interesting to find the system has been at work for a thousand years among the natives of India. This Hindu native court of arbitration, commonly inflicts some slight punishment on the offending party, such as beating with a shoe, or inflicting a fine, or "*hookah páni bund,*" which is a kind of minor excommunication. The natives intuitively submit to its judgment as to the voice of public opinion, and recognize it as their own system of popular government. Each of the districts under Mr. Smith's care has therefore a *pancháyat* for regulating the discipline of the infant church, and there is a central one as a Court of Appeal respecting all the decrees of the district *pancháyats.* One of the duties devolving on these Christian *pancháyats* is with relation to marriages. The marriage of native Christians with Hindus involves great difficulty, and yet the area of selection among the Christian community is at present small. Then again, the church has to set its face firmly against the loose Hindu ideas respecting divorce.

Mr. Smith tried to persuade one of the young men to marry a certain young Christian woman. "No," said the young man, "I would rather go to Secundra for a wife." "What do you want to go to Secundra for?" enquired Mr. Smith. "Because there the girls grind their own corn, and I shall want a wife who can grind corn for me," was the practical reply, and he was allowed to make his own selection.

In the evening we attended one of the native Christian gatherings among the Chamars. It was held in the very heart of the native quarter. The natives gathered slowly in the court facing us, and sat on the ground. Hymns were sung to native tunes until there was a goodly muster of people. They evidently recognize Mr. Smith as their warm friend and helper. His address was a clear Gospel statement, enforcing the truth by the simple exposition of Scripture. The meeting closed with a solemn prayer, to which the audience heartily responded. The aim is to make Christianity indigenous, and to present it in a form that is attractive to the Oriental mind. It is by coming right down to the people, and sitting down among them, and talking to them in their own phraseology, that the Baptist missionaries are steadily winning their way. The tendency of these people is to move in bodies, as in Madagascar, and Mr. Smith has "no doubt that the whole Chamar tribe is on the move towards Christianity."

Another line of thought which the Baptist Missionary Society is striving to work out, is the employment of native evangelists who shall not require any foreign support. "Christian Fakirs," lay hold of the native mind in a way that no European can. Such a man was Seetul Das. He wore a black coarse blanket, not unlike a garment of camel's hair, and was usually called John the Baptist. He travelled extensively in the distant villages, and many heard the glad tidings of a Saviour's love from his lips. He depended entirely on the people for his food, literally carrying out the injunction of Christ to His disciples, to carry neither purse nor scrip, nor two garments; and the people readily supplied him with all his wants.

Romanath Chowdhry is another Baptist Evangelist whose personal experiences give a lively portraiture of aggressive Mission-work in North India. He says, "The self-denial of Jesus has to face the asceticism of Siva and Krishnu. The ascetics of India are captain-generals of Hinduism. Christian Evangelists ought to go like them, without purse, from province to province, and proclaim Jesus and Him crucified. The same Hindus who honour and feed Muhammadan Fakirs will honour and feed the evangelists. I adopted this mode of preaching more than two years ago. Though strongly persuaded by my wife to give it up, I still held fast to it. In the district of Bhagulpur a Kabīrpanthī took care of me.* When I entered into his house I said, 'Peace be to this house.' The man treated me with veneration as long as I remained with him. It was the Spirit of our Lord which produced such sympathy in him. I often heard him say, 'Whoever offends God-fearing men, will bring a curse upon himself.' One night he said to me, 'There was nothing but the Word before the creation of the world, and we must return to Him one after another.' I asked him where he learnt this? He said, 'Kabīr said this in his book.' I read to him the first chapter of the Gospel of John. He exclaimed, 'Kabīr unconsciously preached Jesus, and prepared the way for His acceptance in this country.'

"While I was thus preaching from place to place, the Lord fed and clothed me by those to whom I preached. The people listened with such interest that love was produced, and they took me to their homes. One day when I was starving, a Brahman came to see me in the evening. After a short conversation, he asked me whether I had eaten anything that day? I told him 'No.' He instantly left me, saying, 'God will surely curse the place if one of His servants starves.' At the end of a full hour he brought me what the rich and respectable Hindus eat, and asked forgiveness for not taking notice of me before. At another time I was sent

---

* The Kabír-panthis are one of the many Hindu religious sects. They believe in one God, and do not observe all the Hindu ceremonies. Kabīr was the most celebrated disciple of Rāmananda, whose life is related in their favourite book, the *Bhaktu-mala*. He lived about the end of the fourteenth century, and is said to have been a Muslim by birth. *Bhakta* means "The Devoted One." The Sâdhs are another religious sect, who neither worship idols, *nor bow before men*.

for by a Mussulman. He listened to me without refutation and remarked, 'As a preacher you can touch the heart, because it appears that in speaking you do not speak, but He who is within you speaketh.' At the end of one of our addresses we asked those whose hearts God had touched to stand. A Hindu Brahmo stood up. Jealousy then commenced to work, and he was forcibly detained from attending our meetings. One morning we had an especial prayer-meeting for him. While we were in earnest prayer with one accord, the young man suddenly appeared in the midst of us, kneeled down, and prayed with us. He told me he was determined to be baptized, and he was baptized by Brother Anderson. The opposition from the Brahmos was most fierce. They are our friendly foes. It is more difficult to deal with friendly foes than with open enemies." Such experiences as these show that the instructions Christ gave to the twelve, and to the seventy, as He sent them forth, are exactly adapted to Mission-work among Orientals, and that men who go forth after that pattern will certainly make their way among the masses of India.

The Rev. E. M. Wherry of the American Presbyterian Mission, met us at the railway station on our arrival at Loodiana, and we spent a very pleasant evening with his children and his itinerating teapot. The work of the printing press is largely done by lithography, as it is better suited than type for the Arabic and Persian characters. The Holy Scriptures and the weekly newspaper, *Nur Afshan*, or Light-Giver, are worked on stones, and well executed. The presses that were burned during the Mutiny have been re-fitted, and are still giving light around them, blessing those who cursed them. The *Zabur Aur Git* which cheers and comforts so many a Christian congregation in India, is published here.

It is the work of the Rev. Julius Frederick Ullman who came from Berlin in connection with Gossner's missionary enterprise in 1839, and 313 of the hymns in the book were his own composition. It was from Loodiana that the request went forth for the Week of Prayer for Christians of all nations.

In the quiet graveyard rest the remains of the missionary Janvier, who was killed by a fanatic in 1864. We slept in the very room where Janvier, Potter, and other missionaries were wont to meet for prayer and counsel. There are now 534 church members in the district, and 1,000 adherents, besides 5,000 school children. A large number of Muhammadans and Afghans live in the city, the followers of the exiled royal family of Cabul who are pensioners of Government.

Years ago the citizens built a huge wall to keep back the encroachments of the Sutlej. Now there is no river within seven miles. The river struck out a fresh channel for itself miles away, and gladly would the inhabitants welcome back the waters that once made inroads on them.

Adjoining the spacious American Mission compound, is the bungalow of the London Society for the Promotion of Female Education in the East. The light and brightness of Christian love pervade the whole establishment. It is under the charge of Miss West. The rooms are on the ground floor, and excellently adapted for their purpose. About seventy girls are educated here, including thirty-two boarders. We watched them at play, and can bear witness to the activity and animation of the children of the Punjab. Such an institution of course must grow. Ladies who go in for such harvesting, must pull down their barns and build greater. This is no barn, but it will soon need two wings if it goes on prospering as at present.

One of the important adjuncts of the Presbyterian Mission is the Leper Asylum, and Dispensary for out-patients at Sabáthú, under the care of the devoted Dr. John Newton and his wife. This Asylum is largely supported by the Mission to Lepers in India, of which Mr. W. C. Bailey is Indian secretary. Mr. Newton himself is out of health. His strength declines year by year; and it is only on the hills he can work at all. Most of the members of the little Christian congregation at Sabáthú are inmates of the Leper Asylum. The extreme dullness of mind that pertains to the leper, the ignorance, the domestic isolation, and the shortness of their lives, all tend to surround the work with difficulty. For instance, Mr. Newton finds a leper on the road going up to Simla. He has travelled a long distance, but has no money, and is without food, and very ill. Mr. Newton provides him with food at a neighbouring village, receives him into the Asylum, takes every possible care of him, and in two days the man dies. Hundreds of lepers have lived and died in peace in this Asylum, and thousands of out-patients receive medicine at the Dispensary. There have been 108 leper inmates during the past year, and 75 were resident at the end of the year, of whom 27 were Christians, the remainder Hindus.

A leper's life is very monotonous. Almost their only occupation is the cultivation of the fields. Small plots of land are allotted to all who are able and willing to cultivate them, and in this they take great interest. They sow a crop of Indian corn, and plant it out, weed and reap it.

They have also small vegetable gardens, and they can tend the fruit trees. The chief causes of suffering in leprosy are from the frequent ulcers. Preparations of cinchona and iron, the application of solid nitrate of silver, and carbolic dressings to the ulcerated surfaces, are the usual alleviations. Morphia injected under the skin with a syringe also allays the pain, but the alleviation is only temporary. Those lepers suffer least who have a nourishing diet and plenty of clothing.

The morning prayer meeting and the distribution of medicine and clothing are the great events of each day. A passage of Holy Scripture is read and explained. They sing a *bhujan* or native hymn, and conclude with the solemn repetition of the Lord's prayer. These lepers are weary and heavy laden, and Jesus alone can give them rest. Surely such work is true charity. He that went about healing all manner of sickness and disease, cares for these lepers, and year by year souls are being saved.

HIMALAYANS.

CHAPTER XXII.—THE PUNJAB *(continued.)*

> "Bear with me, as a father with a son,
> Or as a lover with a cherished one.
> Now that I see thee as thou really art,
> I thrill with fear! once more display to me
> Thy human form, thou habitation of the universe."
>
> *Prayer of Arjuna.*

GENERAL BIDDULPH had said to me while we were crossing the Indian Ocean, "Be sure and visit the Punjâb. If you want to see the really fine races of India, you must go to the Punjâb." It is so. There is more manly vigour, more independence of spirit, and a larger admixture of Aryan blood in the North than anywhere else in India. About one-third of the population is Hindu and one-half Muhammadan. A glance at the Language Map will show that the Punjâb, or land of the five rivers, from lying in the midst of so many nationalities, has an immense variety of languages spoken within its compass. Afghan and Persian, Sindhi and Kashmiri abound, as well as the ordinary Hindi and Urdu. The area of the Punjâb is equal to Great Britain, with about one-half the population. It is through the Punjâb that one race of invaders after another has poured in upon India.

During the days of English rule, the Punjâb has been blessed with good Governors. Under the wise and able administration of Sir Henry and Sir John Lawrence, the turbulent population became as quiet and loyal as any in India. During the mutiny of 1857, Sir John Lawrence was able to send every soldier in the Province to the siege of Delhi, without risk of disturbing its tranquility, and it was providentially the Punjâb that at that time saved British rule in North India. The successful administration of the Punjâb was certainly not due to any cautious religious neutrality on the part of the Lawrences. Breaking through the old traditions of the East India Company, they both fearlessly avowed their faith in Christ, and their desire to infuse that faith among the people they governed. "We may rest assured," exclaimed Sir Herbert Edwardes, Commissioner in the Punjâb in 1853, "that the East has been given to our country for a Mission to the souls of men. To the Hindus we have to preach one God, and to the Muhammadans one Mediator. Our Mission in India is to do for other nations what we have done for our own. We have no fear that the establishment of a Christian Mission will disturb the peace. In the crowded city we may hear the Brahman in his temple sound his *shunkh* and gong, while the Muezzin on his lofty minaret may fill the air with the *azân*; and the civil Government, which protects them both, will also protect the Christian missionary who goes forth to preach the Gospel."

As we ran along the railway we had a magnificent view of the Himalayas with their snowy tops and deep ravines. The clouds, like a girdle, rested on them, leaving the base and the summits clear. At one of the railway stations for Simla, we found twenty-one elephants waiting for transit northwards.

Amritsar derives its name from the Sacred Tank that surrounds the golden temple of the Sikhs, and signifies "The fountain of immortality." It is the great commercial capital of the Punjab, a walled city with thirteen gates, with a population of 143,000, and standing to Lahore something in the relation

TRAVELLING IN THE NORTH.

of Glasgow to Edinburgh. The providence of God that watched over us all through our journey was with us as we entered the city. Contrary to our usual practice, we quartered ourselves at the hotel, where our accounts were handed to us in Persian. As we sat down to table d'hôte we found ourselves in a little company of Christians. The gentleman who sat by my side was Mr. G. S. Lewis, Extra Assistant Commissioner, an active magistrate in Amritsar, and formerly a pupil in the Presbyterian Mission at Lahore. He offered to take us the same night to the Temple of the Sikhs (pronounced Seeks) and I gladly availed myself of the opportunity so kindly presented. The Sikhs who fought so fiercely against the English at Moodkee and Ferozepur, became, through the able influence of the Lawrences, our firm friends, and proved themselves our most faithful allies during the Mutiny. The Sikh Reformation is about contemporary with the Protestant Reformation in England, and was a vigorous protest against the denomination of Brahminical priestcraft.

Nānak, the founder of their religion, was born in the village of Talwandi, on the banks of the Ravi, in 1469. As a boy he gave himself to meditation, and at the age of seven began to learn Sanskrit. As he increased in wisdom and stature he associated himself with Hindu and Muslim ascetics, and professed to renounce the world. "In his spirit he was occupied with the Lord." His thrifty father was distressed to find his boy so disinclined for mercantile pursuits, and called in the family physician, under the impression that the boy's mind was affected. Nanak, however, discoursed on religion with the physician and got the better of the argument.

"There is no Hindu and no Mussulman," he exclaimed, "A pure body is the true Veda, the mind is the right sacrificial garment, meditation on God the proper vessel for worship." "Compassion is the true Mosque, modesty is the true circumcision, holiness is the true fasting, right conduct is equivalent to a pilgrimage to Mecca, speaking the truth is the best mystic formula, excellent behaviour is the true praise of God." Such are his maxims, and though there is comparatively little originality in his system, his mission was professedly to call men away from all sects.

Nānak was one day struck by a Muhammadan priest for lying on the ground with his feet toward the holy city of Mecca. "How darest thou, infidel, turn thy feet towards the dwelling-place of God?" exclaimed the Muslim. "Turn them if you can," replied Nānak, "in a direction where God does not dwell." He spoke much of "the inward Governor," who expands and works in the heart of man. His last words were words of prayer, "Have mercy upon me, the lowest sinner! Blessed be the Lord."

The Bible of the Sikhs is the "Grunth," which is preserved with the greatest care in the Golden Temple at Amritsar. This book is supposed to contain the inspired teachings of Nānak, and was written under the direction of the *Gurus* who succeeded him. There appear to be some thirteen contributors or more to this volume, or twelve and a half as the Sikhs express it, one of the contributors having apparently been a woman, who is counted as half. Some of the fine parts of the *Grunth* are quotations from the poet Kabīr. It also contains extracts from the writings of the Marâthi poet Namdev, of the fourteenth century. The volume was first compiled by Urjoon or Arjan, the fifth *Guru*, who, in consequence, was put to death by the Muhammadan authorities in 1606. There

THE GOLDEN TEMPLE AT AMRITSAR.

have been ten leading *Gurus* who gradually formed the Sikhs into a *Khâlsa,* or Commonwealth, *Khâlsa* meaning Pure. The last of the *Gurus* was Govind Singh, who died in 1708. His injunctions to his followers were, "No material resemblance of God is to be made. The eye of faith alone can see Him. Caste is to be forgotten. Hinduism is to be abandoned, and all its superstitions. All men are to be one in the *Khālsa* or brotherhood. Wherever five Sikhs shall be assembled, there will I also be present among them in Spirit."

The Sikhs at first aimed at being a distinctly religious community. Govind Singh, however, taught them that an active secular life was no less acceptable to God than retirement from the world. He also prohibited the use of tobacco. "Hitherto you have been Sikhs (disciples), henceforth you shall be Singhs (lions)." He was assassinated by an Afghan, and being requested in his last hours to nominate a *Guru* as his successor, replied, "Nay, I entrust my people to the bosom of the Timeless One."

Dinner being ended, and night having set in, Mr. Lewis drove me through Amritsar to the Sacred Tank. There are fine buildings on both sides the streets, the houses of wealthy merchants, emporiums for Kashmir shawls and *Chadars* of all kinds, and to our left hand a large co-operative store, under the management and for the benefit of the native Christians. But we have soon to dismount, and as we walk the pavement a policeman notifies us to proceed no further in our barbarian boots. We sit down on a form in the street, take off our boots, and committing them to the police, receive in exchange red Morocco slippers. We then descend a flight of steps to the Sacred Tank. The pavement on which we tread is solid marble. The houses that surround the Tank are the dwellings of princes.

Each Sikh Rajah esteems it an honour to have a mansion in sight of the holy waters. A Sikh kisses the very gates of the city as he enters, and falls down in adoration with his forehead on the white marble pavement, ere he enters the sacred temple. The palace of the *Akális*, or priests, is at the head of the quadrangle in front of the temple. The baptistry is here, where those who join the *Khalsa*, and the children of Sikhs, receive their initiation. The initiatory rite is called the *Pahal*, at which time the new disciple undertakes not to cut his hair, and promises to wear a knife and a sword, and to repeat a portion of the *Grunth* morning and evening when he commences work, and when he partakes of his meals. In the quadrangle are two enormous flagstaffs with banners flying. Some may ask, Why is the water supposed to be so holy? The legend runs thus, "A beautiful woman, poor in worldly wealth but rich in devotion, desiring some means whereby she might glorify God, took compassion on a crippled leper who had lost his fingers and toes, and consented to be his wife. Begging her daily bread, she shared it with her spouse, carrying him tenderly in a basket on her shoulders. She wandered to the banks of this stagnant lake, footsore and weary, and left her burden on the bank while she searched for food. The leper in the basket saw, it is said, a black crow fly down and bathe itself in the water, and rise again white as a dove. Crawling out of the basket he plunged his hand into the water and it was instantly made whole. He then bathed his whole body, and the leprosy was gone; his skin had become fair as that of a child. On the return of the faithful wife, she could no longer find her husband. To her horror this handsome young man claimed to be her husband, but she refused his attentions with disdain.

Just then, Rām Das the Sikh *Guru*, appeared, and interposed in the domestic quarrel, reassuring the wife, and making peace. Henceforth the Tank was styled the Fountain of Immortality."

The Sikh Temple, with its golden cupolas, stands in the very centre of the lake. We approach it by a beautiful marble causeway across the water. The magnificence of the temple grows upon us step by step as we proceed. Many lamps are burning in the interior, and the light shines brightly across the dark water. Numbers of priests solemnly sit cross-legged on the floor, forming a sort of open square or semi-circle. Between 500 and 600 priests are connected with the temple. Behind these grey-headed old men with their long white beards and turbans, stand groups of young men. A gorgeous canopy of silk drapery overhangs the centre. The wealth of many a rajah has been freely expended in decoration. In front of the chief priest is the one object of veneration. What is it? It is a book, the Grunth. Not that the book is read or even visible. It is scrupulously hid under silken coverlets. In front of it is a large square sheet on which the people cast their offerings. A band of musicians are chanting wild songs, with the accompaniment of *sitár*, and *sarangi*, and *tom-tom*, but the whole process appears to be 'the worship of the Book.' As we stand erect in the midst of all this adoration, the priest sends us a wreath of flowers, by the hands of a young man, in token of welcome. Gazing into the fine thoughtful countenances of the grey-headed worshippers, I longed that they might learn of Jesus, and receive the message of Eternal Life.

We rejoice to turn from such a spectacle to the energetic work of the Church Missionary Society in Amritsar. There is probably no station in North

India where the Church Missionary Society has a more complete organization. The native congregation consists of about 268 members, and there are three flourishing boarding schools. There is also a Christian settlement at Klárkábád, with 130 members, and a farm of some 2000 acres. The land is rented in small holdings to the Christians, thus they earn their own livelihood, and eventually may own the land they till. The Rev. Robert Clark is the senior missionary in the city. He has been twenty years in India, and is a successful pioneer.

The meetings of the Punjab Native Church Council are held here, consisting of the pastors and lay delegates, and a healthy, liberal, and independent spirit has been developed.

We called on the Rev. William Keene from Minety, in Gloucestershire, and he recommended us to visit the Alexandra High School, representing as it does an element in the Amritsar work which is unique. It is a large and handsome building, designed by Mr. Clark. He says, "I felt that in building it, I was building for posterity." The object is to train the higher classes of young women for teachers and Zenana missionaries, and fit them to become the wives of native pastors. Alongside the Colleges for young men, it is important there should be seminaries for ladies who may become real help-meets to the native pastorate. The students are the daughters of Christians, who have themselves given evidence of true conversion of heart. Miss Henderson was the lady in charge, and kindly showed us through the Institution. There are from forty to fifty boarders. Many of the parents pay five to ten rupees per month toward the education of their children. The morning we arrived two little sisters had just come from Karâchi. They were standing side by side, like two seedlings recently transplanted. Yet the bright rooms and the clean comfort of their beds were reassuring. Miss Henderson was leaving for England, and in the schoolroom the elder girls had prepared a large

farewell banner, on which were inscribed the words, "My presence shall go with thee."

A cold wind was blowing when we reached Lahore, and we found fires in the grates as though we were in England. In the hotel a special notice in English arrested our attention, a notice which ought to be entirely unnecessary. "Visitors are earnestly requested not to illtreat the hotel servants." The need for such notices is, we trust, rapidly ceasing to exist in India.

The American Presbyterian Mission was established at Lahore in 1849, almost as soon as the country was opened out by the English. The Rev. John Newton and his sons have long worked here. The old man had four sons and two daughters. He made two requests to God on their behalf, first, "Let all my children be the Lord's people; secondly, let them all be missionaries." The four sons have all become missionaries, and the two daughters have both married missionaries, and thus the good man's prayer is answered. The Rev. Charles W. Forman had charge of the American Mission when we were in Lahore, and we went with him through their large Mission-schools. We found 700 children present, and Mr. Forman informed us that there were some 900 children in their other schools in the city, making 1600 children in Lahore under direct religious instruction. In one large class of boys we found four Muhammadans, three Brahmans, one Sikh, and the rest Hindus. In another Class consisting of about 150 boys, we found three Muhammadans, six Brahmans, and the rest Hindus, although the Muhammadans are nearly one-half of the population of Lahore. This shows conclusively how much more ready the Hindus are to avail themselves of the privileges of a good education in Mission-schools than the Muhammadans. The consequence is that the latter are steadily sinking in the social scale while the Hindus advance, and another generation will tell terribly against them.

Professor Monier Williams observes, "Missionary schools in India are in my opinion doing the best work. The education they impart is openly and professedly founded on a Christian basis. They teach the Bible without enforcing ecclesiastical dogmas on their pupils. Indeed, my second tour has impressed me more than ever with the benefits which India derives from the active efforts of missionaries of all denominations. The European missionary is daily becoming a more important link between the Government and the people. He is confided in by natives of all ranks, and he is often able to do what the Government, with its wise professions of neutrality, cannot effect. Missionary schools attract the children of parents of all creeds, though they openly aim at permeating their minds with a spirit hostile to those creeds."

The American Presbyterian Mission has four chapels in four different centres in the city, with about eighty members altogether. The services are all in Hindustani. The students in the Divinity School, under the care of Bishop French of the Church Missionary Society, frequently assist in the services at these chapels of the Presbyterian Mission, and the two societies work together in true harmony and Christian friendship.

"What is the great hindrance," I enquired, "to more converts in this population of 110,000 people?" Mr. Forman replied, "*The sense of sin is so utterly deficient.* To break caste is a great sin in their minds, but to lie or steal is of small account." Mr. Forman kindly undertook to direct us to the great mosque. In driving through the streets we saw nothing of the English. The crowds of people in the narrow thoroughfares are orderly and well-conducted, and busy with their own affairs. The houses and the shops look just as they may have done centuries ago. The inhabitants of Kashmir and Afghanistan come here freely to trade. The Persian merchants once a-year come through Afghanistan with a strong military escort of some two hundred soldiers. They leave all their military defence behind them as they cross the frontier into British territory. They travel through the North of India for months, trade, and return again under the ægis of British protection to the frontier, with their well-earned riches, and once more take up a strong military escort immediately they cease to be under our protection. The Sikh, the Jew, the Pathan, and the gipsy, all find their busy mart in Lahore. Costumes of all hues, and beards of many colours greet the eye, for it seems to be the fashion in Lahore to dye the beard red or with ochre.

The Jama Mosque was built in 1674 for the Emperor Aurungzebe. The quadrangle of the mosque contains the mausoleum of Ranjit Singh, the great Sikh monarch who ruled Lahore from 1799 to 1839. In the centre of this mausoleum is a large marble lotus flower covering the ashes of the king. It is surrounded by eleven smaller lotus flowers, covering the eleven women who perished as suttees on his funeral pyre. Muslims were at prayer in the large open quadrangle, and there was a lame man sitting at the beautiful gate asking an alms. The man in charge of the mosque brought us a present of fruit, which we accepted, and we found that Mr. Forman was highly respected. Ascending one of the towers we had a magnificent view of the great city, looking on the busy traffic of passengers in the streets below, and far beyond the city walls. The kites were wheeling round and round below us seeking for food, as we looked on the multitude of flat roofs. Mr. Forman's own children have sometimes called out to him, "Father, the kites have taken the bread and butter out of my hand," much as the birds in the dream of Pharaoh's baker stole the meat out of his basket. Two mottoes are inscribed in Arabic upon the mosque, "God is sufficient," and "God is to be praised."

A curious religious movement has been initiated near Lahore by Chet Rām, a Fakir. He lives with his disciples in the village of Bhuchoke. They have built a small house of worship, and preach the Gospel, as far as they understand it, to Hindus and Mussulmāns. Chet Rām, pointing to the Christian teachers, says, "These Christians are so holy that we should wash their feet." One Sabbath morning Chet Rām and some of his followers came to Mr. Forman in concern because one of their number had been wounded and injured for saying that Christ was the Lord. They seem to be enthusiasts, and are under the impression that Chet Rām is inspired of the Spirit. These Quixotic movements around Christianity show how Orientals adopt part-truths and work them out in their own fashion. The Church of Christ in India can hardly clothe itself in the garb of European ecclesiasticism, and we may see much more of Oriental character evolved in the native church than has hitherto been the case. Yet it would seem as though the influence of the cultivated, sober mind of the West, is pre-eminently needed to assist in building up a firm and permanent church in the East.

CHAPTER XXIII.—SUMMING UP.

> "A combination of e'en feeble things
> Is often potent to effect a purpose."
>
> *Hitopadésa.*

AND now, in reviewing our position, there are certain landmarks of thought which stand conspicuously on the horizon.* On entering India at its great Western Gate, the Towers of Silence rose before us with the devout thought of the Parsi that mother earth is sacred; and the Caves of Elephanta, with their grim architecture, told of the Buddhist who would retire from all passion and unhallowed desire, with some comprehension of the vanity of vanities of earth, and the frailty of humanity, and would hide away in the nothingness of self. The Cave of Elephanta also recorded in stone how the Brahmanical faith again overcame the Buddhist Ritual and supplanted it. Crossing the broad steppes of Marâtha chieftains, we turned southwards, and found the Hindu temples of Madura towering to heaven with the gaudiness and laboured tinsel of idolatry. Still onward we entered the chaste churches of Christian communities

* The present population of our Indian Empire, as shown by the Census of 1881, is 252,000,000, being an increase of about 13 millions (nearly half the population of Great Britain) in ten years! The Bombay Presidency contains 14 millions, or three Swedens. The Madras Presidency, 30 millions, or more than Italy and Greece. Bengal, with Assam, numbers 73½ millions, or double France. Oudh, 11½ millions, or three-quarters of Spain. The Punjab, 23 millions, or nearly the population of Great Britain. The North-West Provinces, 32 milllons, nearly as many as the whole United Kingdom.

and found whole populations worshipping the true Christ. Turning northwards, past the forest fortresses of Gondwana, we reached the thousand idol-temples of Benares, abounding in bigoted Brahmans defiling the earth with their idolatrous abominations. In Calcutta a purer faith grew brighter in the native mind, reflecting somewhat of the light of Christianity in the Brahmo Somaj of Bengal. In Agra we beheld the perfection of Architecture in the Taj of the Muslim, and marvelled how such despots could conceive such beauty. In the Mosques of Lahore and the Durbar of the Sikhs at Amritsar, we met the medley of nationalities which marks a district subject for ages to the incursions of conquerors, and thus in the very architecture of India is chronicled the ebb and flow of human thought, as the strata of geological formations record the epochs in the creation of a world.

But behind this bulwark of masonry, and *chunam*, and gilded marble, we found written records of the past, the Zend Avesta of the Parsi, with its inclination to fire-worship; the Tripitaka of the Buddhist, aspiring for Nirvana; the Kurān of the Muslim, asserting One God, and claiming the world for God and His prophet; the Grunth of the Sikh, with its attempted abolition of caste; and the Vedas, the Ramayān, and the Mahâbhârata of the Hindu, with their lofty aspirations after heaven, yet grovelling in earth. Each of these Scriptures are of binding obligation to their respective communities. The Brahmans say that one of the villages of India was peopled with the blind, and that a discussion arose among them as to the appearance of an elephant, when one day an elephant passed down the street, and the blind villagers had an opportunity of gratifying their curiosity. One man held the trunk and declared an elephant was like a plantain tree bending to the wind; another caught hold of an ear and said an elephant was like a fan that the women use to winnow the wheat; a third felt one of his legs and pronounced an elephant to be a pillar standing firm and strong; a fourth laid hold of the tail and found an elephant to be a kind of snake. They all brought their reports to the wise man of the village, who declared there must be some truth in all, and that if all their testimonies were heeded some right understanding might prevail. So in the Scriptures of India; some truth may be discovered, but it is encompassed with a superabundance of perversion and misunderstanding.

Muhammad's declaration that there is One God and that the world is His, embodies a truth that cannot be too often proclaimed in a land full of idols. The thought of the Brahman that none but the man who is 'twice born' can hold communion with the Divine, is true in itself. The thought of the Buddhist respecting the vanity of setting the heart on earthly things, and the need for self-renunciation and patience, is good as far as it goes. The thought of the last of the Sikh Gurus, that a man may serve the Lord in the midst of the busy traffic of life, is a contribution to the truth. And yet as all these waves of thought flow in, they ebb again as though judgment had gone forth against them; they are weighed in the balances and found wanting. Add another thought, the necessity for a divine incarnation if the world is ever to be reclaimed from evil, as we find it in the words of the beautiful Ramayān, 500 years before Christ, and we must confess that man has made some strange guesses at truth, whether or no we call such thoughts intuitions from One divine universal Spirit. In the Ramayān the cry ascends to the Eternal respecting the Evil one, in these words :—

"Mad with Thy boon, he vexes in his rage
The angel, seraph, Brahman, saint and sage.
O Father, lend us Thine avenging aid
And slay this Fiend."
They ceased. Then pondering in His secret mind,
"*One way*," He said, "to stay this scourge I find
Man, only man, this hideous pest may slay,
None else can take his charmed life away."

Again the voice of prayer ascends—

"*O Lord divine*, Thine aid we crave,
Friend of the worlds, the ruined worlds to save,
And for the sake of gods and men
Man's nature on Thee take.
We with the sages, Lord, to Thee draw nigh,
And crave Thy succour, that the Fiend may die;
Angel and chorister before Thee bow,
Our surest hope, O conquering Lord, art Thou,
Arise, O King, regard the world below,
And slay in fight the gods' tremendous foe."
To the suppliants the Lord in answer spake—
"Fear not, ye sons of heaven, but comfort take,
The Fiend, your terror, by this hand shall fall,
His friends and counsellors, his kith and kin
Shall share his ruin as they share his sin.
Thus will I triumph o'er the foe, and then
Dwelling as man among the sons of men
The while ten thousand seasons roll away
Will guard the earth with mine imperial sway."
Then nymph, and angel, and the minstrel throng,
With heavenly voice replied in choral song,
"Go forth and fight, avenging Lord,
Slay him and all his race abhorred,
Then turn triumphant to Thine home on high,
And reign for ever in the ransomed sky."

But these lines are gleanings from among many, and are mixed with an immensity of extravagance. When Christ came among men, he came not as a conquering hero, but as a lowly Sufferer, the Sacrifice for sins, and no conception of human poet, priest, or heathen sage, can compare with that Atonement offered once for all on Calvary.

The missionary, with the divine revelation in his hand, stands among the 252 millions of India, and an answer is given to the aspiration of ages, to the deep yearning of sin-conscious hearts, and to the vague dreaming of philosophers and poets.*

An experiment has been initiated in India, which in magnitude baffles every other experiment in human history. India is the arena, Christ Himself the hero, angels the watchers. The light of Buddha has faded away, the power of the Brahman is collapsing, the traditional Muslim resigns himself to an iron fate, and tens of thousands of blind souls have their eyes opened, and are rejoicing in the dawn of Christ's Kingdom.

As we journeyed homewards from North India, the magnificent harvest-fields of the Central Provinces shone in the sun-light and waved in the breeze. Thousands of harvest-men were reaping the golden grain, while the wives and children gathered the sheaves into the garner. At the railway stations, one after another, the wheat lay in heaps, waiting for the merchant to convey it to the crowded city, or to export it as a thank-offering to England. Again, the track passed into the vast jungle and tangled forests of the Nerbudda, and the locomotive swept among trees hanging with scarlet blossoms, and tall palms and mango groves.

In Bombay the multitude kept holiday, for it was the midst of the Holî Festival, a feast of unmen-

---

* There are 34 Missionary Societies and 10 private or independent Missions now at work in India. Of these 34 societies, 13 belong to Great Britain, 13 to America, and 8 to the Continent of Europe. The number of missionaries at work in India in 1871 was 622 ; in 1880, it was 689, a gain of 67 men. Of these 689 missionaries, 329 have been in India more than ten years, 345 were born in Great Britain, 168 on the Continent of Europe, 117 in the United States, and 30 are the sons of missionaries, born in India. The Church Missionary Society has 103 missionaries in India, the Basle Society 75, of whom 61 are Germans. The native Christian adherents were 224,258 in 1871, and 340,623 in 1880, showing a gain of 116,365. The native communicants in 1871 were 52,816 ; in 1880 there were 102,444, an increase of 49,628, that is, the number of communicants has nearly *doubled* in nine years. Can the churches at home show such signs of progress ? For further information see *Badley's Indian Missionary Directory*.

tionable follies. Groups of excited people perambulated the streets in gay dresses, and the *gula*, a solution of red powder, was syringed promiscuously on passers by. Numbers of young men had their faces and clothes disfigured from head to foot with this vile crimson dye. Lewd songs and vulgarity abounded, and at night bonfires were lighted, and wild antics and dancing and screaming prevailed.

As I embarked on board the "Rohilla" for home, I could not but contrast the magnificent harvest of a bountiful Creator in the Nerbudda Valley, with the puerile folly of the great city where the heathen kept holiday.

The devout aspiration of the idolater WITHOUT GOD collapses into profanity, the trite saying and shrewd philosophy of the Hindu, fails to save him from the quagmire of his own pollution. None but Christ can redeem India ; and the missionary's motto, and the devout prayer of every heart must be, "India for Christ."

But if India is to be won for Christ, it can only be by true cross-bearing, in the spirit of the Master. It is soul-surrender and life-surrender that is blest to the winning of souls. It is not by hoping and wishing at home, but by working and witnessing abroad. The constraining love of Him who yearns for India's millions must impel workers. India needs the best men and women of our home churches. Each age has its own special work and opportunities, and the special work and opportunity of this age is the evangelization of the nations. These are truly days of grace in India.

INDEX.

ADAMS, General, 46.
Adi Somaj, 242.
Afghan War, 36.
Agra, 272.
Agriculture, 42.
Ahmadnagar, 100, 108.
Ahmadnagar Converts, 16.
Ahriman, 30.
Aikya, The, 101.
Akbar, 281.
Alexander, E. R., 278, 279.
Alfred, King, 139.
Allahabad, 263.
American Baptist Telugu Mission, 124, 125, 127.
American Episcopal Methodists, 12, 81, 114, 116, 267.
American Ladies' Union Mission, 234.
American Methodist Women's Mission, 270.
American Mission Board, 15, 21, 23, 100, 107, 169, 173, 176.
American Presbyterian Mission, 263, 264, 294, 310.
Amritsar, 300, 308.
Anderson, Dr., 150.
Anglo-Indians, 114.
Anglo-Indian Evangelization Society, 115.
Animal Life, 38.
Anstey, Miss, 133, 134, 135.
Ant Hills, 166.
Apostles of the New Dispensation, 252.
Apprentices' Home, 20.
Arbuthnot, Sir Alexander, 114.
Architecture, 170.
Arcot, 198.
Arden, Rev. A. H., 157.
Armenians, 23.
Aryans, 55, 109, 110, 299.
Asceticism, 26, 256, 292.
Asoka, 24, 27, 236.
Aspirations of Hindus, 318.
Assam, 82.
Astronomy, Hindu, 205.
Atonement, Need of, 317.
Audience, Hindu, 92.
Aurangabad, 98, 99.
Aurungzebe, 203, 312.
Ayenar, 166.

BABAI, 65.
Backsliders, 105.
Bacon, Rev. J. R., 121.
Badaghir Falls, 96.
Badley, Mr., 270, 319.
Bagra, 65.
Bailey, W. C., 296.
Baitool, 93.
Baker, Samuel, 40, 49, 87, 92, 97, 100, 116, 270.
Bakhsh, Ali, 66.
Balagunj School, 50.
Bâl Mukand, 66, 67, 83, 86.
Bamboos, 175.
Bananas, 43.
Banerjea, Rev. C. N., 229.
Baniyas, 81, 88.
Bangalore, 129.
Baptism of Converts, 106.
Baptist Missionary Society, 133, 211, 213, 234, 236, 237, 238, 278, 289.
Baptist Telugu Mission, 125, 128.
Barrackpur, 237.
Barrissal, 229, 237.
Basle Missionary Society, 141, 143, 144, 146, 148.
Bathing, Sacred, 53, 85, 204.
Baugh, Rev. G., 227, 230.
Bazaar Preaching, 10, 16, 33, 49, 66, 71, 81, 92, 142, 182, 194, 195, 213, 214, 227.
Beadon, Sir Cecil, 262.
Beard, Elkanah and Irena, 94, 95, 203.
Bees, 95,
Begum of Bhopal, 45.
Belgaum, 119, 120.
Bellary, 121.
Benares, 203, 205, 208.
Benevolent Institution, 238.
Bengal, 225, 237, 240.
Beni-Israel, 112.

Bernard, Miss, 112, 116, 133.
Betel, 69.
Beypoor, 139.
Bhagavad-Gita, 261.
Bhagulpur, 222.
Bhîls, 55.
Bhopal, 45, 85, 86.
Bhûts, 87.
Bible Classes, 182.
Bible in Schools, 99, 118, 153, 162, 184, 311.
Bible, Power of the, 121, 158, 174.
Bible Read in Mosque, 14.
Bible Society, 21, 81, 86, 121, 128, 132, 158, 161.
Bible Women, 101, 116, 174.
Bickersteth, Rev. E., 288.
Biddulph, General, 299.
Birds, 96.
Birmân, 90.
Birth of Children, 89.
Bishop Caldwell, 186, 188.
„ of Bombay, 98.
„ of Lahore, 311.
„ of Madras, 166, 167.
„ Sargent, 181, 183, 185.
Bissell, Dr., 100, 101, 107.
Bissell, Mrs., 107.
Black Town, Bombay, 21.
Blind Asylum, 263.
Blind Villagers, 316.
Boating, 89, 95, 141, 236.
Boerresen, 222.
Bombay as it is, 3, 8.
Bombay Education Society, 19.
Bombay Harbour, 1, 23, 34.
Bombay Review, 17.
Bongas, 217, 221.
Bookapatnam, 121.
Book Store, 49.
Born, Twice, 53.
Bose, Rām Chandra, 162.
Bowen, Rev. George, 12.
Bradlaugh, 156.
Brahma, 24, 110.
Brahman Converts, 66, 67, 83, 142, 158, 229.
Brahman Lady, 184.
Brahman Priests, 53, 182.
Brahmanas, 236.
Brahmanism, 9, 24, 53, 59, 61, 62, 71, 73, 74, 76, 80, 84, 85, 94, 110, 111, 164, 171, 173, 180, 184, 185, 229, 316, 317.
Brahmos, 163, 164, 228, 242, 250, 256, 294.
Bread, Native, 80.
British Rule in India, 2.
Brooke, Major, 46.
Brown, Mr. Wm. D., 81.
Buddhism, 4, 24, 201, 235, 236, 315. 317.
Bullocks, 40, 44, 82, 195.
Bunderabund, 58.
Bungalows, 41.
Burden of Sin, 10.
Burdwan, 225.
Burmah, 227.
Burning the Dead, 44.
Byculla, Bombay, 19.

CALCUTTA, 225, 239.
Caldwell, Bishop, 186, 187, 188.
Caleb, John James, 264.
Calicut, 141, 144.
Camballa Hill, 13.
Cambridge Mission, 288.
Campbell, Sir Colin, 266.
Camp Meeting, 267.
Canadian Presbyterian Mission, 93.
Canal, Buckingham, 126.
Canarese, 119, 129.
Cannamore, 142.
Capron, Mrs. 174, 175.
Carey, William, 234.
Carpenters, 84.
Carpenter's Work, 147.
Carss, Rev. Thomas, 5, 98.
Caste, 41, 150, 156, 193.
Caste Marks, 8.
Catechists, 66, 158.
Catholics, Roman, 139, 167, 194, 195.
Cave of Elephanta, 23.
Cawnpore, 264.
Census, 216.
Central Provinces, 40, 46, 79, 85, 96.
Ceylon, 160, 198.
Chabutra, 77, 84.
Chack Tree, 148.
Chadars, 68.
Chamars, 50, 289.
Chamberlain, Dr., 161.
Champion, Rev. Elias, 55.
Chandler, Dr., 169.
Chang, Li Hung, 262.
Chapâtis, 80.
Charles II., Dowry of, 4.
Chester, Dr., 168.
Chet Rām, 213.
Child Marriages, 48, 51.
Children at School, 84.
Children's Hospital, 135.

Children's Service, 136, 283.
China, 227.
Chindwara Mission, 92.
Chinese Emigrants, 238, 239.
Chinese Opinion on Opium, 262.
Cholera, 270.
Chota Najpore, 222.
Choultry, Christian, 188.
Chout, 97.
Chowdhry, Romanath, 292.
Christ, India as in times of (Title page)
Christ's coming, 78.
Christ's constraining love, 103.
Christ, the only Saviour, 59, 86, 318.
Christian College, 150.
Christianity *versus* Heathenism, 60, 62.
Christians, Syrians, 139.
Christian Vernacular Education Society 108, 160.
Christian Villages, 97.
Christlieb, Professor, 109.
Churches, Native, 157, 179, 189, 190, 268, 290.
Church Missionary Atlas (Preface)
Church Missionary Society, 5, 17, 55, 93, 94, 97, 99, 157, 179, 180, 185, 189, 203, 206, 222, 264, 278, 283, 307, 308, 319.
Church of Scotland Missionary Society, 149, 155, 230, 231.
Church of the future in India, 161.
Church Unions, Native, 101, 290, 291.
Cinchona, 140.
Clark, Dr., of Boston, 169.
Clark, Rev. Robert, 308.
Cleveland, Mr., 222.
Clough, Rev. J. E., 125.
Coalfields. 96, 219.
Cocoa Cultivation, 148.
Cocoa Nuts, 144.
Coffee Estates, 161, 190, 192.
Colar, Mission at, 133.
Coleman, Miss, 135.
Coles, Rev. Joseph, 121.
Colleges, 31, 117, 150, 156, 210, 229, 230, 231, 235.
Collet, Sophia D., 259.
Colportage, 80, 81, 158.
Comorin, Cape, 192.
Compounds, European, 42.
Conder, Mr., 14.
Conference, Missionary, Allahabad, 94.
„ Bangalore, 129, 154, 191.
„ Calcutta, 227, 229.
„ Cuddapah, 119.
„ Mildmay, 142.
„ Nasik, 98.
Congregations, Native, 46, 47, 179, 190, 268, 283, 290, 291.
Consecration to Mission Work, 21, 50, 310.
Contact, Points of, 9.
Contemporary Review, 255.
Contributions of Converts, 101, 181, 182, 185, 190.
Controversialist, 213.
Controversy, 16, 93.
Conversation, Power of, 10.
Conversions in College, 12.
Converts, 6, 7, 22, 29, 32, 55, 66, 102, 103, 127, 130, 134, 142, 147, 173, 183, 189, 190, 199.
Converts, Total Abstainers, 127.
Coolies, 35.
Coonoor, 199.
Co-operative Store, 305.
Cosmus, 139.
Cottayam, 189.
Cotton, 42, 68, 70.
Cotton, Bishop, 133.
Councils, Church, 157, 179, 308.
Cow, Golden, 171.
Cowley Fathers, 34.
Craven, Rev. Thomas, 267.
Cremation, 44.
Crime, Statistics of, 57.
Crocodiles, 96.
Cuddapah, 121, 123.
Cullis, Dr., 133.
Cultivation of the Betel, 69.
Cust, Mr. R. N., 288.
Customs, Eastern, 58.

DAK Bungalow, 90.
Dancing Girls, 180.
Danish Mission, 167.
Darius, 30.
Dasasamedh, 204.
Das, Seetul, 292.
David, the Colporteur, 80, 81.
Deaconesses, 222.
Deccan, 37.
Deimler, Rev. J. G., 99.
Deism, 157.
Delhi, 287.
Devasagayam, 190.
Devi Dyal, 50.
Dhûr, 125.
Diminution of Crime, 57.
Dindigul, 168.
Discipline among Converts, 105.
Dispensary, Medical, 155, 177, 188, 270.

Dispensation, New, 252.
Disturbances in Santâlistan, 217.
Divining, 77.
Doctrine of the Buddhists, 25, 27.
Dodabetta, 140.
Dost Muhammad, 46.
Dravidians, 55.
Dress of Parsis, 31.
Duff, Dr., 231.
Durbar, 117, 316.
Dutch, 139.
Duthie, Rev. J., 189, 190.
Dyeing, 68.
Dyer, Dr., 220.

EAST India Company, 5.
Eastern Customs, 58.
Ebenezer, 222.
Eclipse, 84.
Eden, Sir Ashley, 114.
Edeyengudy, 186.
Edinburgh Home Mission, 155.
Education, Higher, 151.
Educated Natives, 227, 228.
Edwards, Sir Herbert, 154, 300.
Elder, Dr. W., 155.
Elephanta, Cave of, 23, 315.
Elephants, 85, 142, 171, 300.
Ellis, Mrs., 231.
Ellis, Rev. Percy, 108.
Ellora, Caves of, 24, 100.
Emigration, 39.
Empress of India, 287.
English Influence for good, 38, 312.
English Opinion, 62.
Enquirer, 67.
Episcopal Methodists, 12, 81, 114, 116, 230, 267.
Erhardt, J., 280.
Etarsi, 40, 79.
Eunuchs, 64.
Eurasians, 21, 114, 115, 133, 238.
European Bungalow, 41.
European Residents, 5, 19, 114.
Evangelists, American, 34.
Evangelists, Native, 292.
Evil Spirits, 87, 166, 180.
Examinations, School, 152.

FAIRBANK, Dr., 101, 102.
Faith Work, 133, 137.
Fakir, 85, 86, 216.
Fakirs, Christian, 292.
Falls of the Nerbudda, 96.
Famine, 120, 126, 131, 133, 145, 281.
Family Missionary Zeal, 2.
Farms, Mission, 308.
Farmers, 39.
Farm Work for Orphans, 134.
Farrar, Canon, 97.
Farrar, Rev. C. P., 97.
Female Education, 17, 31, 50, 66, 143, 147, 177.
Female Education, London Society, 295.
Ferns, Tree, 140.
Fertility of Soil, 38.
Festivals, 44, 51, 58, 62, 63, 142.
Feuchter, Mr., 147.
Fever, 57.
Finney, President, 102.
Fireworship, 30.
Floods in India, 54.
Forest Life, 73, 74.
Forman, Rev. Chas. W., 310.
Fort of Delhi, 288.
Fortune-telling, 77.
Fountain of Immortality, 300.
Francke of Halle, 167.
Free Church Missions, 14, 23, 111, 116, 149, 150, 152, 155, 156, 218, 221, 231.
French, Bishop, 311.
French Territory, 147.
Friends' Foreign Mission Association, 46, 47, 66, 85.
Frontal Marks on Foreheads, 9.
Fryer, Rev. George, 158.
Funeral Ceremonies, 29, 44.
Funds, Native, 181.
Future Life Questions, 31.

GAOLS, Mission-work in, 13.
Ganesa, 170.
Ganges, 203, 267.
Gathas, 30.
Gautama, 24.
Gayatri, 110.
Gayford, Charles, 66.
General Assembly's (Scotch) Mission, 149, 155, 230.
German Missions, 141, 143, 144, 148, 211, 222, 280.
Ghari Kings, 45.
Ghâts, 37, 53, 100, 203.
Gillan, Rev. G.,227.
Girgaum, 17.
Girls' Schools, 17, 31, 50, 66, 143, 147, 177, 182, 185, 188, 206, 210, 231, 232, 308.

Giridhi, 215.
Gits and Lyrics, Native, 107, 174.
Goa, 139.
Godavery, 100.
Gods, Heathen, 24, 59.
Golden Temple, 304, 306.
Goldsmith, 11.
Gônds, 55, 65, 68, 70, 77, 92.
Gônd Missions, 55.
Gônd Rajahs, 45.
Gôndwana, 316.
Gooty, 124.
Gopal-rao, 173.
Gopâ, The Princess, 24.
Gopuras, 169.
Gosain, Dubé, 216.
Gosavi, 107.
Gossner, Pastor, 211, 213.
Gossner's Missions, 211, 222.
Government Census, 216.
" Colleges, 210.
" Inspection, 150.
" Officials, 98.
" of India, 2, 38, 39, 173.
" Schools, 99, 184.
Govind Rām, 83.
Govind Singh, 305.
Græter, Rev. B., 144.
Grants, Government, 23, 134.
Great Indian Peninsular Railway, 36.
Greeks, Their Worship, 59.
Grieve, Alexander C., 10.
Grihastha Vairagi, 256.
Grunth, 303, 306, 316.
Guinness, Rev. H. Grattan, 33.
Gujerâti Newspapers, 33.
Gulliford, Rev. Henry, 129.
Gumastahs, 126.
Gunghery Ghât, 87.
Gula, 320.
Gurus, 58, 86, 303, 305.

HADJIS, 89.
Haegh, Rev. H., 129.
Haig, Mr. James S., 108.
Hall and Notts' Arrival, 5.
Harda, 81.
Hardy, the Catechist, 93.
Harley House, 33.
Harvest, 57.
Hasan and Husain, 62.
Hassan, Mysore, 131.
Hastie, Mr. William, 229, 230.
Havelock, Sir Henry, 266.
Haynes, Miss, 135.
Hazaribagh, 216, 222.
Healing by Faith, 133, 135.
Health, 57.
Heber, Bishop, 274.
Hebich, 142.
Hebich's Own, 142.
Heinig, Pastor, 211.
Hegira, 276.
Henderson, Miss, 308.
Hermits, 74.
Heyl, Francis, 263.
High School, 308.
Himalayas, 300.
Himalayans, 298.
Hindi, 47.
Hindu City Life, 3.
Hindu Funeral, 44.
Hinduism 9, 59, 61, 100.
Hipsley, Henry, 167.
Hitopadésa. 203, 315.
Hodson, Captain, 184.
Hœrnle, Miss, 206.
Holi Festival, 319, 320.
Hooghley, 225.
Hook, Miss, 234.
Hooper, Mrs. 206.
Horse Sacrifice, 166.
Hoshangabad, 44, 62, 79.
Hoshang's Fort, 45.
Hoshang Shah, 45, 46.
Hospitals, 135.
Hotel Life, 310.
Houses, Native, 50, 75.
Howrah, 225.
Household, Native, 75.
Hubbard, A. R., 288.
Hudson, Rev. J., 130.
Hume, Mr. and Mrs., 21.
Hunter, Dr., 68.
Hyder Ali, 168.
Hymns, 107, 174.

IDOL Worship, 77, 87, 170.
Idolatry, 59, 163, 170.
Idols, 86, 170, 124.
Igatpuri, 36.
Ignorance of India in England, 62.
Immorality, 60.
Indifference, 156, 173.
Indore, 93.
Industrial Mission Work, 126, 134, 144, 145, 147, 285.
Industrial Work in Jails, 56.
Infidel, English Literature, 156.
Inquisition in India, 139.

Inskip, 34.
Inspiration, 77.
Intuition, 83, 78.
Invasions, Effect of, 55.
Iron Ore, 96.
Itineracy, 129, 182.

JABALPUR, 94, 95, 96.
Jacobs, Major, 98.
Jagarnâth, 59.
Jails, 56.
Jains, 4, 28, 219.
James, Mr. W. R., 227.
Jamtara, 215.
Janvier, American, 295.
Janvier, Native, 268.
Japan, 227.
Jeffrey, Russell, 167.
Jehan, Noor, 272.
Jehan, Shah, 272.
Jerrapur, 85.
Jewelry, 8, 75, 78.
Jewett, Dr., 124, 127.
Jewish Synagogue, 21.
Jewish Converts, 22, 112.
Jews, 138, 139, 238.
Johnson, J. J., Rev., 204.
Johnson, W. A., 264.
Jones, Rev. T. P., 173.
Joshua, Pastor, 191.
Judson, Adoniram, 238.
Jumna, 263.
Jungles, 38, 65.
Justice, Temple of, 205.

KABIR-PANTHIS, 293.
Kali, 225, 271.
Kalugu-Mali, 158.
Kanarese, 119, 129, 135.
Kamma-vakya, 236.
Kanhu, 221.
Kapula Vastu, 24.
Karâchi, 263.
Kareli, 90.
Karens, 153, 227.
Keene, Rev. William, 308.
Kenidah Hills, 140.
Kerry, Rev. George, 229, 238.
Kho, Game of, 50.
Khadijah, 276.
Kherwerism, 216.
Khalsa, 305.
Kinder Garten, 147.
Kindness to Animals, 43.
King, Mr., 108, 111.
Kiratarjuniya, 119.
Kirk, Mr., 135.
Kishore, Jugal, 67, 93.
Kishore, Nerval, 267.
Kirttan, 107, 155.
Klarkabad, 308.
Knoblosh, Rev. J., 142.
Kôls, 219.
Konkan, 37.
Kotar, 194.
Krishnarow, 107.
Kshirsagar, 101, 106.
Kuran, 22, 255, 267, 272, 276.
Kurhurballee Mines, 219.
Kutub Minar, 289.

LACE Workers, 187, 190.
Ladies, Native, 75, 184.
Ladies' Zenana Missions, 231.
Lahore, 309, 312.
Lalita-Vistara, 201.
Land Question in India, 39.
Lange, Norman de, 57, 71.
Language Map (Frontispiece)
Languages of India, 119, 120, 299.
Lawrence, Sir Henry, 266, 299.
Lawrence, Sir John, 281, 299.
Lazarus, Dr., 210.
Leases, 40, 41.
Legend, Native, 306.
Lepers, 10.
Leper Asylum, 296.
Lepers, Mission to, 296.
Leupolt, Rev. C., B., 206.
Levitical Law, 57.
Lewis, Rev. Edwin, 121, 133.
Lewis, Mr. G. S., 302.
Life Work, Missionary, 13.
Linga, The, 100.
Livingstone, Dr., 97.
Liberality of Converts, 181, 182, 185, 190.
Literature, Christian, 132, 156, 160, 161, 174, 264, 270.
Literature, Infidel, 156, 267.
Library at Serampore, 235.
Lodhi Dynasty, 287.
Lohardugga, 222.
London Missionary Society, 119, 120, 121, 123, 131, 176, 189, 207, 210, 230.
"Lone Star," The, 125.
Loodiana, 294, 295.
Lucknow, 266.

Lucknow Witness, 270.
Lunar Dynasty, 287.
Lundborg, Rev. N. E., 93.
Lyrics, Native, 107, 174, 220.

MACAULAY, Lord, 9, 60.
McCumby, 213.
Macdonald, Dr., 14.
Macdonald, Rev., 225.
MacIvor, Mr. 140.
Mack, Mr., 234.
MacLeod, Norman, 38, 60, 71, 109, 163, 255.
Mado Rām, 94.
Mádigas, 126.
Madras, 149, 158, 161.
Madras Bible Society, 158, 161.
Madura, 163.
Magic Lantern, 68.
Maha-bharata, 65, 74, 79, 109, 189, 215, 267, 287, 316.
Mahadeo, 59.
Mâhars, 97, 107.
Maidan, The, 64.
Mail Runners, 223.
Malabar, 139.
Malabar Hill, 28.
Mâlas, 124.
Malaria, 65.
Malays, 141.
Malcolm, Sir John, 81.
Malwa Opium, 261.
Mango Grove, 71, 143.
Mângs, Mission to the, 14, 97.
Man-Mandil Observatory, 204.
Mansell, Henry, 270.
Mansell, Mrs. Dr., 270.
Mansion House Relief Fund, 133.
Manu, Code of, 97, 149, 242, 287.
Manuel, Rev. D., 130.
Manuscripts, 139.
Marâthi, 12.
Marâthas, 17, 73, 97, 101, 116.
Marble Rocks, 95.
Market, Native, 74.
Marriage Ceremonies, 47, 280.
Marsden, Rev. E., 133.
Marshman, Joshua, 234.
Martyn, Henry, 234.
Mason, Pastor, 123.
Mault, Rev. Charles, 189.
Max Müller, 71.
Mecca, 89.
Medical Dispensaries, 155, 177, 198.
Medical Mission Work, 13, 155, 199, 223, 270, 296.
Meeting, A Strange, 75, 76.
Meeting, Baptist, 292.
Melás, 58, 90, 91, 142.
Membership in Churches, 103.
Memorial Church, 288.
Memorial Hall, Madras, 158.
Mendes, Dr., 94.
Mercantile Mission, 147.
Merchants, 68, 148, 172, 224.
Messiah, Jews praying for, 139.
Metcalfe, Rachel, 50, 60, 66, 206.
Methodist Missions, 12, 81, 114, 116, 129, 130, 133, 228, 230, 267.
Mildmay Conference, 142.
Military, Work among the, 130, 142, 160.
Miller, Dr., 133, 150, 152.
Mill, Stuart, 162.
Minâkshi, 170, 172.
Mirage, 70.
Mission Bungalows, 41.
Missions, What they have achieved, 181.
Missionary, a Patriarch, 48.
Missionary Atlas, Preface.
Missionary Directory, 319.
Missionary Success, 319.
Mission Work, 47.
Mitchell, Dr. Murray, 227.
Modak Krishna, 102.
Mody, Mr., 10, 29, 32.
Mohun, Rev. David, 264.
Money-lenders, 71.
Money, Robert, 5.
Money Schools, 5.
Monkey God, 59.
Monkey Temple, 205.
Monthly Meeting, Friends', 85.
Moradabad, 270.
Mosque, 288, 312.
Mothers' Influence, 106.
Motto, American, 22.
Mourning for the dead, 167.
Muddapur, 215.
Mudge, James, 270.
Muezzin, 276.
Muhammad, 276, 317.
Muhammadans, 14, 16, 22, 62, 63, 64, 89, 99, 177, 204, 272, 275, 310.
Muhammadan State, 45.
Muharram Festival, 62, 63.
Muir, Dr., 201.
Muir, Sir William, 262, 263.
Mukand, Bâl, 66, 67.
Mullapah, 122.

Mullens, Dr. J., 230, 237.
Mundlha, 55.
Munshi, 183.
Murdoch, Dr., 132, 133, 160.
Muslims, 89.
Muslim Rule, 272.
Mutiny, 108, 207, 266, 289.
Mysore, 129.
Mysore, Maharajah of 136.
Mythology, 9, 59, 60.

NAGERCOIL, 189.
Nagpur, 93.
Nanak, 302.
Nanjenaud, 192.
Narsingpur, 93.
Nasik, 97.
Native Character, 90.
Native Churches, 157.
Native Church Councils, 157, 179, 308.
Native Home-life, 75.
Native Servants, 41.
Nazul Land, 41.
Newspapers, 3, 17, 108.
Nepean, Sir Evan, 5.
Nerbudda River, 44.
Nerbudda Valley, 38, 40, 58, 94, 96.
Nineteenth Century, 91.
Nedawathun, 140.
Neil, Colonel, 207.
Nellore, 125.
New Dispensation, 252.
Newton, Dr. John, 296.
Newton Rev. John, 310.
Neyoor, 193.
Nilgiris, 140.
Nirvana, 26.
North Arcot Mission, 198, 199, 200.
North-West Provinces, 261, 263.
Nullahs, 40.
Nundial, 124.
Nur Afshan, 294.

OBSERVATORY, 204, 205.
Officers Mess, 142.
Oil, 146.
Oldham, Major, 17, 94.
O'Neil, Father, 34.
Open-air Preaching, 10, 92, 94, 142, 182, 194, 227, 290.
Opium Den, 49.
Opium Eater, 70.
Opium Export, 239.
Opium, Government Monopoly, 263.
Opium, Injustice to China, 262.
Opium, How to deal with it, 263.
Ongole, 124, 125, 126.
Ootacamund, 140.
Ormuzd, 30.
Ornaments, Native, 75.
Orphanages, 19, 97, 99, 112, 116, 131, 133, 135, 145, 183, 281.
Oudh, 266.
Outram, Sir James, 20, 56, 266.
Owen, Mr., 263.

PACHAMBA, 217, 219.
Pachmari, 45.
Pagodas, 169.
Pahal, 306.
Paharis, 222, 223.
Pahlad Ghât, 203.
Paikava Falls, 140.
Palaces, Native, 117.
Palamcotta, 181.
Palms, 140, 141.
Palmyra Climbers, 180.
Pali, 235.
Pân, 69, 70.
Pani, 179.
Panchâyats, 291.
Pandit, 83.
Pantheism, 110.
Parasnath, Mount, 219.
Pariahs, 150, 193.
Park, Rev. Charles W., 15, 23.
Parker, 227.
Parsis, 4, 10, 28, 52.
Parsi Converts, 32, 99.
Parsi Spy, 33.
Partridge, Surgeon-Major, 13.
Pastors, Native, 16, 94, 122, 123, 126, 127, 131, 132, 181, 292, 293.
Pastorate, Fund for, 181.
Pastorate, Native, 182.
Pasumalai, 173, 174.
Patels, 70.
Patience, 90.
Patna, 225.
Patna Opium, 261.
Patteson, Bishop, 121.
Paul, Rev. Job, 132.
Pava-nasam, 182.
Payne, Rev. J. E., 228.
Peasants, 104.
Penney, Dr. 238.
Persecution, 184, 193, 237.
Perumaul, Seramen, 143.

Phadke, 117.
Philosophy, love of, 151.
Pigot, Miss, 231.
Pilgrimages, 89, 267.
Pindharis, 46, 105.
Pipal Tree, 70.
Plutschau, Henry, 167.
Poets, Native, 107, 109, 155.
Points of Contact, 9.
Police, 227.
Police, Native, 56, 57, 141.
Pondicherry, 167.
Poona, 111.
Pope, Dr., 133.
Population, 4, 34, 225, 315.
Porter, Rev. Edward, 123.
Postman, 11, 286.
Potham, 139.
Prakashah, 108.
Prayer Meetings, 60, 94, 107, 136, 160.
Prayer, Power of, 271.
Prayers, Parsi, 30.
Preach, How to, 10.
Preachers, Native, 268, 292, 293.
Presbyterian Missions, 10, 14, 23, 93, 111, 117, 149, 155, 156, 219, 221, 227, 230, 263, 294, 310.
Priest, Brahman, 53, 94.
Prince of Wales, 23.
Printing Press, 19, 113, 238, 264, 267, 270, 294.
Prisoners, 56.
Prosperity, 57.
Processions, 63.
Progress made, 319.
Publications, Christian, 108.
Pulney, 169.
Puja, 89.
Punjab, 287, 294, 299, 308.
Purana, 53, 163.
Purda, 116.
Puxley, Mr. E. L., 222.

QUEEN Victoria, 85.
Quilon, 139.
Quinine, 140.

RAGGED Schools, 155.
Ragland, 179.
Railways, 35, 36, 37, 38, 90.
Rainfall, 58.
Raipur, 82, 84.
Rajahgopal, Rev. P., 155, 157.
Rajahs, 171.
Rajmahal Hills, 223.
Rajputs, 287.
Rām, 84, 166.
Ramayan, 109, 316, 317, 318.
Ramapatam, 126.
Ranchi, 222.
Rangoon, 227.
Ranjit Singh, 312.
Recreations, A Missionary's, 187.
Reformers of Bengal, 259.
Reformers, Sikh, 303.
Reformed Church Missions of America, 198, 199, 200.
Religion, Hindu, 9.
Religions of the World (Note), 24.
Religious Teaching in Schools, 7.
Religious Tract Society, 161.
Rendell, Rev. J., 169.
Repartee, 10, 11, 183.
Revivals, 102, 127, 193.
Rhasalpur, 88.
Rice Fields, 192.
Rice, Rev. Benjamin, 121.
Riddett, Rev. A. T., 131.
Rig-Veda, 109.
Riots, Cloth, 193.
Ripon, Lord, 1.
Ripon, Marchioness of, 1.
Rivers, 54, 57, 226.
Rivers, Worship of, 44.
Roads in India, 40.
Robbins, Rev. W. E., 32, 115, 116.
Roberts, Rev. W. A., 98.
Robertson. Mr., 231.
Robson, Rev. John, 59, 60.
Rocks, Marble, 95,
Rohilla, 320.
Rohilcund, 268.
Roman Catholics, 139, 167, 194, 195.
Rouse, Rev. G. H., 235.
Roy, Rām Mohun, 241.
Ruttonji-nowraji, 99.

SABATHU, 296.
Sabbath Christian, 47, 51.
Sacrifices, Idolatrous, 166, 204, 214, 225.
Sadharan, Somaj, 258.
Sadhs, 293.
Sagrīs, 28, 32.
Saise, Dr. Walter, 219.
Saivas, 8.
Sakuntala, 109.
Sakya Muni, 24.

Samuels, Wesley, 131.
Sandle, Troiluko Nath, 248.
Sangor, 92, 93.
Sanitariums, 45, 140, 169.
Sanskrit, 23, 61, 83, 109, 110.
Santâls, 215, 217, 220.
Sanwalkhera, 71.
Saola, 222.
Sapha Hor, 216.
Sargent, Bishop, 181, 183, 185.
Sargent, Mrs., 182.
Sastri, Babu Deva, 205.
Satthianadhan, Rev. W. T., 157.
Sathia Vedam, 161.
Satpuras, 45, 55.
Scepticism, 162.
Schools, Money, 5.
Schools, 5, 17, 20, 22, 23, 50, 66, 84, 107, 108, 117, 120, 129, 130, 132, 142, 147, 155, 157, 174, 185, 210, 237, 238, 308, 310, 311.
Schoolmasters, 50, 102, 108, 158, 174, 184, 290.
Schrenk, Rev. E., 142.
Schott, Secretary, 147.
Schwartz, 167, 168.
Scinde War, 20.
Scotch Missions, 10, 14, 23, 93, 111, 117, 149, 155, 160, 219, 221.
Scottish Education Society, 23.
Scrupulous Natives, 4.
Scriptures in Schools, 6, 153, 154.
Scriptures, Parsi, 30.
Scriptures, use of, 174.
Scudder Family, 198.
Scudder, Dr. Jared, 199.
Seasons in Central India, 57.
Sectarianism to be avoided, 155.
Secundra, 281.
Seeta Rām, 121.
Semree, 65.
Sen, Keshub Chunder, 228, 242, 247, 256.
Seoni, 79, 80.
Serai, 67, 80.
Serampore, 234.
Sermon, Native, 268.
Serpent Charmers, 70, 128.
Servants, Native, 41.
Service on Sabbath, 46, 112, 130, 181, 283.
Shaffter, Rev. H. J., 179, 184, 185.
Shahjehanpur, 267.
Shahurao, 16.
Shanárs, 180, 193.
Shâranpur, 97.
Shastras, 213.
Sherring, Rev. M. A., 207.
Sherring, Mrs., 207.
Shigrams, 280.
Sigra, 206.
Sikhs, 300, 302, 306, 317.
Silk Weaving, 68.
Simla, 300.
Sinclair, Rev. D., 149.
Sin, Conviction for, 102, 311.
Siva, 24, 170, 180.
Sivavákayar, 179.
Skrefsrud, 222.
Slater's Tracts, 160.
Small, Rev. John, 111.
Smith, Dr., 227.
Smith, Mrs. Amanda, 15.
Smith, Rev. James, 119, 288.
Snakes, 82.
Sobhapur, 65, 70.
Society for Promotion of Female Education in the East, 295.
Society for the Propagation of the Gospel, 101, 108, 183, 186, 187, 188, 222, 288.
Sohagpur, 65, 67.
Soil of Central India, 40.
Somajes, Brahmo, 228, 241, 250, 256, 258.
Sonasawari, 80.
Souls, Hindu Thoughts about, 7.
South India, 159.
Sportsmen, 36, 81, 95.
Spirit of God, 78, 83.
Spencer, Herbert, 164.
Squires, Rev. H. C., 98.
Standard of Membership, 103.
Start, William 211.
Statistics, 39, 57, 120, 183, 188, 319.
Stevenson, Mr. W. H., 218, 221.
Street Preaching, 16, 33, 227, 290.
Subadar, Beni Singh, 45.
Sunday Schools, 47, 112, 182, 268, 269.
Support of Missionaries, 160.
Sustentation Fund, 182.
Sutlej, 295.
Sutras, 225.
Suttee, 312.
Swedish Missionaries, 37.
Swedish Missionary Society, 93.
Swiss Missions, 141, 144.
Syrian Christians, 139, 193.

TAGORE, Debendro Nath, 242.
Tahsildars, 79.
Tahsils, 79.

Taj, 272, 273, 275.
Taljhari, 222.
Tamasha, 63.
Tambiravarni, 182.
Tamils, 130, 155, 169, 179, 181, 185, 192.
Tanjore, 167.
Tank, Sacred, 305.
Tawa, 57.
Taylor, Rev. William, 31, 32, 114.
Taziyas, 63.
Teetotalers, 98, 127, 169, 199.
Telugus, 120, 124, 126.
Temple, Sir Richard, 2, 38, 39, 92.
Temples, Hindu, 53, 59, 92, 169, 170, 171, 204, 206, 304.
Theological Seminary, 130.
Thoburn, Dr., 114, 116, 228, 230.
Thomas, St., 139.
Tigers, 54, 55, 82.
Tile Works, 144.
Tinnevelly, 155, 179, 180, 185.
Tirumalai, 171, 172.
Tittuvilei, 192.
Tonga Driving, 46, 130.
Topis, 89.
Torr, Miss Isette Teresa, 33
Total Abstinence among Converts, 127, 169, 199, 200.
Totonath, 16.
Towers of Silence, 28.
Tracts, Use of, 14, 132, 160.
Tracy, Mr. J. E., 173.
Tranquebar, 167, 168.
Translation of Bible, 128, 235, 236, 238.
Transmigration of Souls, 44.
Travancore, 139, 155, 189, 191, 197.
Travelling, Mode of, 35, 195, 280.
Trees, Flowering, 38.
Treusch, Mr., 206.
Trichinopoly, 167.
Tri-pitaka, 235, 236, 255, 316.
Tropical Vegetation, 139, 140, 192.
Tukeruma, 19.
Tulsi Plant, 75.
Turtles, 45.

ULLMAN, J. F., 295.
Umbrellas, Native, 141.
Unions, Native Church, 101.
Unity in Work, 98.
Unity of God, 30, 83, 110.
Upa-ni-shad, 163.
Urdu, 47.
Urjoon, 303.
Urwick, Rev. W., 235.

VAISHNAVAS, 8.
Vanes, Rev. Jas. A., 129.
Vedantism, 156, 157.
Vedas, 35, 109, 110, 129, 139, 214, 241, 255, 316.
Veeranakavoo, 193.
Vegetation, Tropical, 28, 139, 140, 197, 203.
Velavely, 124.
Vellore, 198.
Vernacular Education Society, 108, 160, 161.
Vesparad, 30.
Vethanayagam, Rev. V., 180.
Viceroy at Bombay, 1.
Vice, 9, 60.
Village Life, 71, 73, 101, 105, 219.
Village Missions, 97, 106, 120, 122, 191, 194, 221, 292, 293.
Villages, Christian, 97, 264.
Vindhya Hills, 45.
Vishnu, 24, 59, 170.
Vizianagram, Maharajah of, 210.
Vultures, 30.

WADALE, 101.
Walters, Mr. R. E., 19.
Ward, William, 227, 234.
Warora Colliery, 96.
Washburn, Dr., 174.
Wasps, 50.
Watch-night Service, 107.
Water Carrier, 118.
Waterfalls, 96, 140.
Water, Holy, 267, 258.
Wat-wud, 15.
Wazir Muhammad, 46.
Weather, 57.
Weaving Establishment, 148.
Week of Prayer, 160.
Welcome in India, 41.
Wenger, Dr., 238.
Wesleyan Missionary Society, 129, 158, 227, 237.
West, Miss, 295.
Wheat Crops, 40, 319.

Wherry, E. M., 294.
Whitehouse, Mr., 189.
Widows, 59.
Widows' Fund, 181.
Wild Beasts, 82.
Wilkie, Rev. John, 93.
Williams, Effie, 66.
Williams, John H., 2, 66, 76.
Williams, Monier, (Preface), 170, 210, 275, 310.
Williams, Moses, 124.
Williams, Rev. A., 235.
Williams, Rev. T., 108.
Wilson, Dr., 10, 31.
Winter, Rev. R. R., 288.
Winds, 57.
Wise Men of the East, 31.
Wolves, 82.
Women, Native, 51, 72.
Women's American Methodist Mission, 270.
Worship, Hindu, 59, 60, 77.
Worship of Rivers, 44, 100.
Wurtemberg, 99.
Wynds of Glasgow, 218.

XAVIER, Francis, 194, 195.

YASNA, 31.
Young Men of India, 151, 162, 227.
Young Men's Christian Association, 190.

ZABUR Aur Git, 294.
Zabbardast, 90.
Zamini, 281.
Zamorin of Malabar, 143.
Zenana Work, 33, 112, 116, 158, 174, 176, 177, 231, 232, 234, 270, 288.
Zend Avesta, 30, 316.
Ziegenbalg, 167.
Zoroaster, 30.
Zoroastrianism, 32.

Orphans' Printing Press, Leominster.